ON THEIR OWN:

The Poor in Modern America

Edited by
DAVID J. ROTHMAN
Columbia University
SHEILA M. ROTHMAN

ADDISON-WESLEY PUBLISHING COMPANY
Reading, Massachusetts
Menlo Park, California • London • Don Mills, Ontario

THEMES AND SOCIAL FORCES IN AMERICAN HISTORY SERIES
Under the Editorship of Robin W. Winks

Contents

INTRODUCTION

THE EXPERIENCE OF POVERTY IN AMERICA

From the opening decades of the nineteenth century to our own day, Americans' persistent efforts to understand the causes and conditions of poverty have fixed on the word "paradox." Writing in 1822, the managers of one energetic Jacksonian reform organization, the Society for the Prevention of Pauperism, puzzled over the presence of poverty in the new republic. "Our territory is so expansive, its soil so prolific," they exclaimed, our institutions "free and equal," and our citizens blessed with "ample scope for industry and enterprise," that surely "pauperism would be foreign to our country." Instead, to their dismay and wonderment, we confronted the "strange paradox that pauperism, as a practical evil, should be known among us." One hundred fifty years later, a presidential commission appointed to study the advisability of federal income maintenance programs, posed this same question with equal wonderment. Their report, aptly entitled *Poverty amid Plenty: The American Paradox,* tried to explain why in a nation as prosperous as ours, twenty-five million people had to "eke out a bare existence under deplorable conditions." For most of our national history, a mood of genuine perplexity has marked our stance toward poverty. And not surprisingly, this perspective has almost always led commentators to mix charges and countercharges, to censure some and exonerate others for this problem. From the Jacksonian period to the present, a number of critics have faulted the poor themselves, citing their supposed immorality and recklessness. Others have blamed the economy, pointing to its failure to sustain high wages and full employment. Still others have focused on the charities and state programs that attempt to alleviate need, insisting that they have so amply rewarded the poor as to trap them in their poverty. But despite the variety of responses, all these observers share the premise that poverty amidst plenty ought not to exist, that the paradox must be solved.

In fact, this notion is a comparatively modern one. Americans in the colonial period adopted a very different stance toward dependency. They were calm and complacent, not prone to allocate blame for poverty or design programs to eradicate it. From their perspective, need was in the order of things, a natural and inevitable part of social organization. This was the lesson that they learned in their churches. According to eighteenth-century Protestant clergymen, poverty was not a necessary evil but a blessing. The poor were always to be with us, in America as elsewhere; but instead of lamenting a tragic fact of human existence, they celebrated it as a God-given opportunity for men to do good. Relieving the needy, explained one Boston clergyman, was the highest Christian virtue. "It ennobles our nature, Charity conforms us to the Son of God himself." Benevolence justified the pursuit of wealth, for without it, men would grow "sensual, profane, and insolent, unjust, and unrighteous." It was therefore pointless to fear or suspect the poor, who were, rather, pawns in a divine game. It was also senseless to expect that poverty would disappear, given its essential place in God's order. Most clerics, it is true, conceded that a few unworthy beggars might be scattered here and there among the needy. But they advised parishioners not to devote much energy to this distinction. It would be foolhardy to let the "idle and even intemperate . . . suffer before our eyes. . . . [For] what if God were to refuse his mercy to those of us who do not deserve it?" In brief, the ministerial perspective made the poor impotent but safe, necessary and not dangerous, part of the social order, not an anomaly.

The secular definitions of society also encouraged a broad acceptance of the poor. Eighteenth-century Americans conceived of a well-ordered society as hierarchical, with a series of ranks moving from upper to lower. Each level enjoyed its special privileges and obligations; some men would be rich and powerful, others low, mean, and in subjection. This interpretation made the poor a permanent fixture, integral to the community. They were to respect those above them, show all due deference, and in return, receive assistance in time of need. Social theory as well as theology gave them a standing in the community. If townsmen made no effort to eliminate poverty, at least they did not ignore, harshly punish, or isolate the poor.

Another crucial element that encouraged the colonists' tolerance for poverty and yet marked the limits of this sentiment was a sharp and rigid differentiation between the town resident and nonresident, between the insider and the outsider. Townsmen relieved a neighbor's need without suspicion but showed little compassion for the plight of a stranger. Whether the outsider was an honest and poor man or a petty thief, the response was to move him beyond the town limits as quickly as possible. In part, the insularity of eighteenth-century settlements reflected English traditions; Elizabethan poor laws, for example, made relief the exclusive responsibility of each parish. But more important, localism fit well with New World conditions. Colonists, especially along the eastern seaboard, were bound together by strong ties. They depended on one another to accomplish vital economic tasks, such as establishing water- and waste-disposal systems, lighting the streets, building harbors and bridges, and protecting themselves against fire. They also relied on one another to safeguard the community. In an era when policemen were unknown (the few constables that paraded the streets at night were old men, incapable of apprehending a criminal), insularity was a major element in keeping order. A townsman who committed an offense could be whipped or fined or, even more typically, shamed before his neighbors by being displayed in the stocks. But outsiders were much less easy to control, especially when they were penniless and unembarrassed before strangers. Accordingly, the community was reluctant to admit propertyless strangers into its midst. They not only would increase poor-relief expenditures but threaten public security.

The day-to-day treatment of the poor fit well with these attitudes. Officials relieved neighbors quickly and without elaborate investigations, supporting them at home if possible or, when their disabilities were too great, in relatives' or friends' households. The dependent townsman remained within the community, not forced to enter such an institution as the almshouse. In fact, few towns bothered to construct poorhouses, and those that did used them only as a last resort, to treat the resident too decrepit to be boarded elsewhere or the stranger so ill that he would perish if sent on his way. To counter the danger of outsiders, communities enforced stringent settlement laws, establishing property requirements for those who would enter and reside in the town and harsh punishments for those who might violate them. Upon detecting a stranger in their midst, officials "warned him out," that is, told him to leave immediately under the penalty of thirty to forty lashes. In this way, they rid the town of vagrants, of poor but healthy strangers, of nonresident widows with children, and of unwed mothers with bastards. They guarded the boundaries with all the care that sentries give an international frontier. Those inside received sympathy and aid; those outside had no call on its tolerance or resources.

Americans' understanding and response to poverty underwent a revolution in the Jacksonian period. Beginning in the 1820's and increasingly thereafter, observers defined poverty as both unnatural in the New World and capable of being eradicated. Colonial complacency gave way to a reform movement in which a heightened suspicion of the poor went hand in hand with the promise of improvement.

The spread of Enlightenment ideology through the nation encouraged this change. The prospect of boundless progress wore away the grim determinism of Calvinist doctrines, so that men no longer believed that misery or want were permanent to society. As popular thinking became increasingly secular, God's will or the inherent depravity of man no longer seemed a satisfactory explanation for the differences in social conditions. Republican enthusiasm also enhanced the prospect of progress. In the aftermath of the Revolution, Americans believed that their republic would accomplish goals unreached by corrupt European monarchies. One obvious target for action was poverty, an evil which had to exist in lands where aristocrats oppressed peasants but not where men were equal, resources were abundant, and labor was scarce.

It was also impossible in Jacksonian America to maintain colonial localism and insularity. Men were now moving all the time, westward to the virgin territories or into the burgeoning cities of New York, Boston, and Philadelphia. A system of poor relief that attempted to distinguish between the neighbor and the stranger was no longer feasible when men picked up stakes on hearing rumors of more fertile land ahead or of new opportunities in growing urban centers. At the same time, citizens' close identification with their particular community was giving way to a wider view. Now one belonged not exclusively to the town but to the state and nation as well. This expanded perspective made eighteenth-century localism appear parochial and provincial.

Although such considerations increased Americans' willingness to eradicate poverty, they also encouraged a harsh and suspicious view of the poor. Observers invariably concluded that because of New World wealth, no one ought to be poor, and therefore those actually in need had to some degree themselves to blame. After an extensive tour of eastern cities, a Philadelphia investigatory committee unhesitantly reported: "The poor in consequence of vice constitute, here and everywhere, by far the greater part of the poor." The answer to the paradox of poverty reached by New York's Society for the Prevention of Pauperism was that "the paupers of this city are, for the most part . . . depraved and vicious, and require support because they are so." The poor had become objects, not neighbors, people to be acted upon, to be improved, manipulated, elevated, and reformed.

These new ideas and social conditions prompted the almshouse movement. In the Jacksonian period, cities and towns eagerly and rapidly constructed special institutions to confine all of the needy, devoting the bulk of public relief funds to this enterprise. The proponents of the program were a mixed lot. In Boston, for example, they included the city's mayor, Josiah Quincy, and its most prominent doctor, Walter Channing, as well as its noted Unitarian clergyman, Joseph Tuckerman. But all agreed on certain essentials. Certainly the poor were partly to blame for their own misery, having succumbed to the vice of idleness or intemperance. Yet their degradation was not entirely their own fault, these critics vigorously insisted. The poor were not inherently depraved; rather, they were the victims of a myriad of temptations set out before them. "Society has caused—and who can doubt whether it has caused —a great amount of poverty," contended Tuckerman. Who else but the towns licensed the grog shops and allowed gambling halls and dens of iniquity to flourish? And who else but the town supported the poor at home, giving them the wherewithal to subsist without working, the opportunity to languish in vice? Of all methods for supporting the needy, proclaimed Mayor Quincy, "the most wasteful, the most expensive, and most injurious to their morals, and destructive of their industrious habits, is that of supply in their own families." Therefore, reformers concluded, if poverty was to be eliminated, the poor had to be isolated from temptation and forced to acquire habits of industry and labor. This grandiose task they assigned to the almshouse.

The hopes for the program appeared in the designs for relief systems in New York and Boston. Outdoor relief, the mainstay of eighteenth-century policy, was to be abolished or severely curtailed; the poor, regardless of their moral standing or work history or residence, would instead receive aid only within an almshouse. Once inside such an institution, they would learn order, discipline, regularity, and habits of work, the very traits that the community had neglected to teach. The routine was to be precise and rigorous. An early morning bell would awaken the inmates, another would signal the time for breakfast. They would go to their assigned seats at long mess tables, eat their meals, and then head for the workshop. One bell would call them for lunch, another would send them back to work again until dinner. There would be no drinking, loafing, or gambling, only honest living and steady labor. As Walter Channing told a group of Boston philanthropists, the almshouse was "a place where the tempted are removed from the means of their sin, and where the indolent, while he is usefully and industriously employed . . . by a regular course of life . . . is prepared for a better career when restored to liberty again." After completing this regimen, the poor would return to society girded as in an armor against temptation, ready to earn their keep.

The almshouse, however, never fulfilled its founders' expectations. One reason was that the managers, generally recruited from the ranks of petty shopkeepers and small farmers, were ill-trained to run institutions. Another, was that the inmates almost without exception were not sturdy, able-bodied, corrupted, and lazy loafers, but the very old and decrepit and the very young. The routine that reformers had devised had little applicability to them. They were in no condition to march to meals, let alone perform steady labor. In short order, therefore, the almshouse degenerated into a custodial institution, characteristically overcrowded, in sad disrepair, lacking all internal discipline and order, and cruel and punitive in its methods. One observer's verdict on conditions at the New York City almshouse was typical. "One can hardly conceive of a more neglected place," he noted on the eve of the Civil War. "Dirt and vermin had been allowed to accumulate to such a degree as to almost discourage me." A statewide survey in New York returned a similar report. "The great mass of poor houses," the committee concluded, "are most disgraceful memorials of the public charity. Common domestic animals are usually more humanely provided for than the paupers in some of these institutions."

Yet, despite the incredible gap between reformers' ideology and institutional reality, almshouses not only persisted but proliferated in the last half of the nineteenth century. Everywhere, in coastal cities and in towns on the plains, their shadow fell over the lives of the poor. Part of the reason for their near monopoly over public assistance was the belief that institutional support was cheaper than home relief—and since the poor, by their immorality and lack of initiative, were responsible for their misery, officials did not have to be generous with provisions or accommodations. Indeed, should the almshouse become too comfortable—that is, less dreadful than the conditions in which the lowest-paid workers subsisted—the poor might flock to it. But even more vital to its popularity was the particular character of the inmates: in 1850 immigrants began to fill almshouse wards, and after 1870 they made up the bulk of the institutional population. The poorhouse became the preserve of the broken immigrant, first the Irish, later the Italians, the Poles, and the Slavs. In Michigan and Illinois, as well as in Massachusetts and New York, aliens crowded into institutions, prompting native Americans to turn their backs on the entire enterprise. Feeling little kinship with the poor in general and the immigrant in particular, they happily shifted the burden of care to the almshouse. If there had to be poor in America, then at least they ought to remain hidden behind sturdy brick walls.

The Progressive era marked a major shift in public attitudes and policies toward the poor. Beginning in the 1890's and culminating in the administrations of Theodore Roosevelt and Woodrow Wilson, a new and more complex understanding of the origins of dependency, together with a host of fresh alternatives to institutionalization, spread through the nation. These departures were never unopposed. A good deal of suspicion and hostility and a fair amount of reliance on the almshouse remained. Nevertheless, the Progressive period supplied the first impetus to the concepts and programs that we live with today.

The innovations were the work of clergymen like Washington Gladden and Walter Rauschenbusch, who preached a new social gospel; of social workers like Robert Hunter, Jane Addams, and Robert Woods, who practiced community work in their settlement houses; of sociologists like Margaret Byington and Crystal Eastman, who provided the first sophisticated and detailed studies of the causes and conditions of poverty; and of popularizers like Jacob Riis, who wrote newspaper articles and books to arouse the American conscience. Taken together, these groups influenced the thinking and responses of ordinary citizens and political leaders.

The new view toward poverty rested first on an understanding of the shortcomings of the economy, the periodic unemployment that forced many laborers below the subsistence line, the prevalent low wages that did not allow even the thrifty among them to accumulate savings. ("Many, many thousand families," wrote Robert Hunter in *Poverty,* "receive wages so inadequate that no care in spending, however wise it may be, will make them suffice for the family needs.") The new approach also was sensitive to the debilitating effects of slum conditions, the crowded and unsanitary tenements through which disease rapidly spread, particularly tuberculosis, robbing households of their main providers. ("Penury and poverty," declared Jacob Riis in *How the Other Half Lives,* "are wedded everywhere to dirt and disease.") The innovators emphasized the dangers inherent in work itself—the inevitable accidents that occurred when managers neglected to install safety devices, when employees were crowded into sweatshops that were firetraps, when laborers, after ten or twelve hours on the job, grew fatigued and careless. (We must do something, pleaded Crystal Eastman in *Work Accidents and the Law,* to ensure that modern industry is conducted "without the present wholesale destruction of the workers.") Critics recognized, too, the general misery of life for those at the bottom of society, a misery which understandably drove them to the tavern to gain a temporary respite from their troubles. There was a recognition that generation after generation would remain trapped in poverty; families, hard pressed to make ends meet, put young children out to work, depriving them of the education necessary to take skilled jobs. In brief, these reformers taught Americans to think of the needy as the laboring poor, the ones who "live miserably . . . [and] know not why. They work sore, and yet gain nothing."

To some degree, these conclusions almost forced themselves on social observers. Forays into the urban slums, whether to bring the gospel to the unchurched or to ameliorate their need, taught ministers and charity workers that the poor were victims not of immorality but of forces beyond their control. The deeper the sociologists explored, the more apparent it became that the moralism traditionally characterizing American attitudes toward poverty explained only a fraction of the problem. Ten million Americans, estimated Robert Hunter in 1906, earned less than subsistence incomes, and clearly the great majority of them were feeling the effects of social and economic dislocations. When newly graduated college students went into the ghettos to learn about the poor and to offer their help, whether at Chicago's Hull-House or New York's Henry Street Settlement, they too immediately recognized the many disadvantages that the poor could not escape. To all these commentators it was obvious that America had become, once and for all, an urban and industrial nation, with a frontier that was now practically settled and, given successive waves of immigrants, had a surplus of labor. The emphasis of Jacksonian reformers on personal reformation and rehabilitation now seemed largely irrelevant, and their willingness to isolate the poor in the almshouse seemed clearly an inadequate response.

The Progressives' novel outlook on poverty also reflected very special fears and hopes for American society. Most of the urban poor—and it was the city's needs that monopolized attention—were also immigrants. To reformers, the newcomers represented both a major threat to the national well-being and an unusual opportunity to do good. Two intimately related problems demanded resolution: the immigrant had to be assimilated to American life and his standard of living improved. The prospect of failure was haunting, for Progressives were deeply suspicious of the aliens, disturbed by many of their idiosyncratic customs (from their strange modes of dress to worshipping in Roman Catholic churches), and frightened that they might act on foreign principles (be it a slavish obedience to Rome or a dedicated allegiance to European socialism). And yet these critics were also confident that American society had the resources to counter such threats. They pinned their hopes on the opportunities for social mobility, for all men to climb the ladder of success, and for property mobility, for all families to enjoy an unprecedented material well-being. They expected to co-opt the newcomer into the system by having him share its benefits. Once the several barriers that penned the immigrant in his ghetto poverty were removed, once ambitious and energetic foreigners enjoyed the full chance to succeed, the nation's stability and security would be ensured.

Yet, despite the intensity and diligence of the investigations, the reformers themselves and, still more, their countrymen could not completely escape a moralistic view of poverty. The equating of the immigrant with the poor kept alive the notion that vice contributed to generating dependency. After all, one had only to walk through an ethnic ghetto to discover the omnipresence of taverns, beer halls, dance halls, and houses of prostitution. Even Robert Hunter, as sympathetic an observer as one can find in this period, maintained the older distinction between the worthy and the unworthy poor. "There is unquestionably," he conceded, "a poverty which men deserve, and by such poverty men are perhaps taught needful lessons. It would be unwise to legislate out of existence . . . that poverty which penalizes the voluntarily idle and vicious." And Progressives, like others before and after them, could not altogether reconcile the presence of poverty with their deep sense of the munificence of American life. A tone of condescension entered their rhetoric, reflecting a certain disdain not only for the "wretched refuse" of European shores but for those who had not been clever or ambitious enough to profit in the land of opportunity. This ambivalence operated as a brake when reformers moved to alleviate poverty.

They did put an end to the almshouse monopoly, establishing new procedures that kept at least some of the poor within the community.

The persons who benefited immediately were widows with small children —the group least suspect among the needy. In 1909, Theodore Roosevelt convened a White House Conference on the Care of Dependent Children and then happily publicized its major finding. "Poverty alone should not disrupt the home," he announced. "Parents of good character, suffering from temporary misfortune, and above all deserving mothers . . . deprived of the support of the normal breadwinner, should be given such aid as may be necessary to enable them to maintain suitable homes for the rearing of their children." To this end, Illinois in 1911 passed a widow's pension bill, and by the close of World War I, nearly every industrial state had emulated its example. The worthy widow and her children would no longer suffer separate incarceration in almshouses and orphan asylums. One major bloc of poor were now spared this miserable fate.

Reformers also moved to protect the lower classes both on the job and in the community, to extend the advantages of industrialism. They enacted accident insurance to compensate injured laborers, and they regulated the number of hours women and children could work. They passed stringent building and fire codes to offset the most glaring dangers of slum living. They also tried to rescue the children of the poor from their parents' fate by enacting compulsory school laws and establishing a minimum age (ranging from twelve to sixteen) for factory work.

There was an enormous amount that Progressives did not do. They paid little attention to the plight of the black, his economic or social disabilities, and almost completely ignored the rural poverty of tenant farmers, sharecroppers, and migrant laborers. They failed to enact health-care programs or extend government pension provisions to the general work force. Although proposals for unemployment compensation and retirement benefits circulated throughout this period, and although indeed several European countries were already administering programs for those purposes, no such advances were made here. Even the innovations that did occur were carefully circumscribed. Widows' pensions were limited to only the most deserving, so that mothers whose husbands had deserted them were not eligible, nor were those with illegitimate children. As a result, the majority of the poor still had to rely on the limited funds of private charities or turn to public relief for some coal or wood or suffer a stint in the almshouse. Nevertheless, the Progressives did signal a new departure. In attitude and in practice, they were the first to break with tradition.

Although documents that view the experience of poverty through the eyes of the poor are not plentiful, some historical materials do illuminate events from the bottom up. The needy do not, as a rule, keep or preserve diaries and letters, and they do not write articles and books—that literature belongs mostly to the upper and middle classes. But many verbatim interviews with the poor survive, recounted by settlement-house workers, taken down as part of a congressional investigation, reported in newspapers, or included as part of a sociologist's monograph. Taken together, they break through the traditional silence that envelops the annals of the poor.

These records demonstrate immediately that one cannot speak simply of a homogeneous and identical class of poor. This group is as diverse as any other, a composite of very different backgrounds and experiences. The situation confronting the eastern European immigrant and his perception of it often differed markedly from the situation facing the rural tenant farmer, black or white, and in turn the farmer's condition was not the same as that of the native white industrial laborer, the newly urbanized black, or the floating, transient poor. The members of each group interpreted their fate in dissimilar terms. Indeed, their particular definitions of the world about them frequently isolated them, minimizing their ability and inclination to unite to protest their plight or to ameliorate it.

To most immigrants, the poverty they faced in the New World was nonetheless a dramatic improvement over the wretchedness of their lot in the Old. Rather than bemoan their insufficiencies, they eagerly and energetically toiled at the machines, worked very long hours without complaint, and then stayed on to collect overtime, all in an incredible effort to make a decent living, to enjoy some of the benefits of industrial America. Their diligence and compliance at once puzzled some observers and infuriated others—especially native white laborers and union organizers, who denounced immigrant competition and were frustrated by their passivity. But down through the Progressive era, the newcomers' expectations were still bound in by their European background. They accepted the American ethos of consumption rather quickly, but sharp memories of the deprivations they had just escaped tempered their present disappointments. It was the future opportunity and not the current misery that seemed most vital to them. And immigrants did find some success stories around them. The man who made good stood as an example of the dream of the New World—and if statistically the number of those who rose from rags to riches was minute, their symbolic importance was great. Finally, immigrants also found solace from their poverty in the network of community associations. They banded together for social and economic purposes. Their clubs and self-help insurance societies and the daily comradeship that pervaded their ghettos made their lives more tolerable. Celebrations of religious holidays and family events offered not only a respite from arduous work but ultimately a justification for it.

On the other hand, sharecroppers and tenant farmers living in rural poverty were isolated from one another. Those who were up from slavery knew that they would have to fend for themselves. "The cow can't give much," one tenant farmer told black sociologist Franklin Frazier. "Times is hard and you have to scuffle yourself. White folks ain't gwine to give you nothing, jes' have to do the best you can." The whites around them had a similar sense of insularity, each family self-encapsulated. They lacked the modern means of communication, from the telephone to the automobile, to link them with the outside world; and they were also too suspicious and hard-working to join together one with another in meaningful community relationships. They accepted their fate, almost unaware of the prospect of improvement.

Southern Negroes migrating to northern cities perceived their experiences largely as the immigrants did. Interviewers in Chicago regularly heard blacks declare how much better their lives were in the city than on the farm. Almost all of them were writing home to tell friends and relatives to move north. To be sure, the tenements were dangerous, the discrimination rank, and the work hard for low pay. But these newcomers saw a new freedom and independence in Chicago. They preferred the city's jobs, parks, schools, and amusement places; they welcomed the chance to vote, the general feeling of good fellowship, the opportunity to breathe without fear of mobs or lynchings. They too found their present poverty so much more tolerable because of their past misery.

White, native-born factory workers, like those at Homestead, Pennsylvania, who were also locked into their poverty, were more bitter than many others among the poor but no more able to define an alternative. They often vented their anger at the immigrants, blaming them for their low pay and bad working conditions. But they could not see beyond the mill towns in which they lived. Parents expected children to take their places in the factory, joining father and brothers there, to lead the same life that they had led. There was no sense of escape, either through individual exertion or joint action. As for the transients, the hobos who began to dot the countryside after 1880, they were of course the most marginal to American society. They were the least able to imagine improving their existence or alleviating their wretchedness.

Some among the poor, it is true, did break out of their poverty—but for most it was a temporary escape. Generational, life-cycle changes affected their economic fortunes. Thus, if both husband and wife worked right after marriage and did not succumb to serious accidents or illnesses, they could make ends meet. However, the arrival of the first child, an event that usually occurred very soon after marriage, presented a crisis —not just in adding another mouth to feed, but in taking the wife out of the job market. The years from age 25 to age 40 were hard for the couple; there were more children to feed and clothe, and the wife was still tied to household duties. When the first child turned 12 or 14, circumstances began to improve. The youngster worked, and his siblings helped around the house, perhaps freeing the mother for part-time labor. As each youngster matured and joined the labor force, the family income increased. But eventually it declined again when the children married and set up their own households. By the age of 55 the couple were once more in trouble. They had never really earned enough to save substantial sums, and with health and energy beginning to fail, they became increasingly dependent. The children might give some bits of help, but they had their own families to support on equally low wages. (Having been forced into the labor market at such early ages, they had not acquired special skills and hence were also trapped in manual labor.) It was hard times all over again.

In the last resort, therefore, the poor were on their own. The assistance that neighbors could give was too uncertain and limited to count for much; and few among the poor could be confident of satisfying the requirements of private charities and fulfilling the expectations of home visitors. Public programs—in essence the almshouse—only reminded the poor of the wretchedness that would accompany an economic catastrophe. To avoid it, one had to sacrifice the careers of children, the welfare of mothers, the health of fathers.

Few advances in policy or thought occurred during the 1920's. It is in fact noteworthy, given the incredible tensions that pervaded the nation, that the moderate advances of the Progressives were not altogether eradicated. That was the decade when the K.K.K. and the temperance movement and immigration restriction reached the zenith of their power and appeal; feeding on a popular disillusionment which followed the end of World War I and a popular fear that immigrants would not assimilate, prejudice and bigotry generated vigilante raids and a closing of our borders to newcomers. Anti-alien, anti-urban sentiments also led to a resurgence of harsh and critical judgments on the poor, especially on those who were first- or second-generation Americans. If only they would stop drinking, gambling, and paying obeisance to Rome, the argument went, if only they would become full-fledged Americans, then poverty would disappear. To be sure, a few social critics, who did not succumb to this hysteria, continued to circulate among themselves analytic studies of the poor in the best Progressive tradition. Some explored the most efficient methods for organizing a national old-age assistance and pension program; others undertook the first investigations of conditions in black ghettos and among tenant farmers. And an occasional state legislature did manage to widen the eligibility requirements for widows' pensions. But in all, the 1920's were not auspicious years for innovation, and the record of public achievements remained thin.

In this period, the one significant change affecting the poor was the organization and professionalization of social work. The good-hearted but casual home visitor to the needy, who dispensed a little cash and a lot of homilies, gave way to the full-time social worker, trained in college and graduate school. The founding ideology of the discipline looked both to helping the needy adjust to society and to encouraging the society to better service the poor. But not surprisingly, in the 1920's it was the poor that had to do all the accommodating. Case work lost sight of social reform, focusing instead on teaching the lower class to cope with their situation, to budget more carefully, to be more industrious, to emulate those above them. Part of the narrowness of this vision reflected the inhospitable climate of public opinion. It also reflected the impact of Freudian theory and the eagerness of social workers to become professionals. Using psychological therapy as a way to establish and exert their expertise, social workers insisted that many of the difficulties confronting the poor resulted from their emotional problems. The needy were the victims not of vice but of maladjustment, and careful and sympathetic counseling would teach them to achieve. However, the net result of this new doctrine was to couch in modern terminology some very traditional ideas. The poor remained essentially responsible for their difficulties. Reformation and rehabilitation returned to the center of the stage, now rationalized in updated language. The unworthy poor had become the emotionally deprived poor. Hence, by the close of the 1920's, public programs and attitudes had rigidified. The nation was not well equipped to confront that incredible phenomenon, the Great Depression.

Suddenly we were all poor—or almost all of us were. The Crash of '29 sparked the most massive economic dislocation in our history, at its peak leaving 25 percent of the work force unemployed. Poverty was no longer the exclusive fate of the ghetto immigrant or the migrant farmer; they were now joined by blue-collar workers laid off the assembly line and white-collar workers dismissed from brokerage houses. The problem of poverty had unexpectedly become national.

At first, both powerful and ordinary Americans denied the magnitude of the crisis, insisting that recovery would be prompt. Herbert Hoover, wedded to an older American credo and fearful of undermining the country's moral fiber, refused to involve the federal government in relief. "I am opposed," he declared, "to any direct or indirect government dole. . . . Our people are providing against distress from unemployment in true American fashion." But true American fashion meant that local governments and private charities had to carry the entire burden, and by 1932, they were without the resources. Cities lacked funds and the taxing power to raise them. The Red Cross distributed bags of flour and the Community Chest, armfuls of coal. Distress was everywhere apparent: migrants pitched camps at one water spot and then another, their life's possessions piled on the back of a broken-down truck. The urban poor pasted together shacks in shantytowns in the parks and along the river banks. Those with some savings cut corners, trying to stave off a bank's foreclosure on an overdue mortgage or a landlord's eviction for unpaid rent. Often unable to clothe their families decently, they kept their children out of school and shunned their neighbors.

New Deal legislation alleviated some of the misery. Less bound by tradition than his predecessor, Franklin Roosevelt plunged the national government into the business of relief. By 1936, with the passage of the Social Security Act and the establishment of the Works Progress Administration, Washington was providing the states with relief funds and the unemployed with jobs. New Deal legislation permanently altered the character of public programs. To meet immediate problems, the unemployable (the aged, blind, and very young), after passing a means test, received direct relief at home; at the same time, federally sponsored projects made jobs available for destitute able-bodied workers. Unemployment compensation, funded by a tax on employers, provided incomes for the temporarily unemployed; and retirement pensions, paid for by employee contributions, gave the aged a new measure of security. The almshouse became a thing of the past, abolished through the combined effects of these innovations.

Still, the New Deal investment in relief fell considerably short of the nation's need. Afraid to violate the sanctity of the balanced budget or the prerogatives of the states and committed first and foremost to work relief, Roosevelt in his responses was all too often inadequate to the crisis at hand. He insisted on funding relief through the states, but he would not set national standards. (For example, the poor in Mississippi received about one-third the support of those in Massachusetts.) The sums allotted to the aged were far below subsistence, $19 a month when $40 would have been barely enough. WPA regulations required men to leave the rolls after 18 months, no matter how grim their economic condition. Social Security was not to take effect until 1942—and even then the pensions were too small to support recipients. The states were no more generous. For example, California packed migrant workers and the young unmarried unemployed off to work camps that were hardly better than penal colonies. They also tried to seal their borders, reviving stringent residency laws. In all, a great amount of hunger and deprivation pervaded the nation.

Despite the magnitude of the problem and the government response, a very traditional attitude toward poverty persisted through the Depression. The new leadership continued to preach many ancient axioms, and the average citizen retained old beliefs. FDR himself denigrated outright relief, keeping alive the term "dole." To some degree this approach was a conscious strategy to swell public support for the millions expended on WPA. But it also reflected his inner conviction that relief corrupted and weakened the recipient. "Continued dependence on relief," insisted Roosevelt, "induces a spiritual and moral disintegration fundamentally destructive to the national fiber." Those on relief or tottering on the brink felt an acute sense of dread and guilt, a painful reluctance to take what they still defined as charity. Hence, just when one might have anticipated a public furor over real suffering, when widespread turmoil and vicious riots might have broken out, the nation remained overwhelmingly quiescent. Some reliefers, to be sure, sat in at welfare offices or marched on city halls; and some farmers dumped their milk and prevented others from making deliveries. But most Americans remained silent, suffering alone, passive before these events.

In essence, poverty demoralized rather than activated the country.

The unemployed insisted on blaming themselves for their misery, defining their problems as internal, not external. If one looked harder or put up a better front, he would find a job. Instead of joining with others in faulting the system, the unemployed became immobilized and isolated. One after another, they passionately and honestly told interviewers that before taking relief they would "rather be dead and buried," or they would "hide their faces in the ground and pound the earth." Years later, when good times had returned, they still vividly recalled those feelings. "I didn't want to go on relief," one small businessman remembered. "Believe me, when I was forced to go to the office of relief, the tears were running out of my eyes. I couldn't bear myself to take money from anybody for nothing. If it wasn't for those kids—I tell you the truth— many a time it came to my mind to go commit suicide than go ask for relief." Their actions did not belie their words. Among a group of nearly one thousand unemployed in New Haven, Connecticut, less than one-quarter had asked for relief after being without a job for over a year! Only the most acute sense of shame can account for such reluctance.

Photographs of reliefers waiting on line in the 1930's reveal how widespread the feeling was. Each individual stands by himself, encapsulated in his own world, not talking with any of his fellow unemployed. There is no mutuality of comradeship among them, only self-embarrassment. People waiting at employment bureaus were much the same. "We sit looking at the floor," reported one of them. "Hunger makes a human being lapse into a state of lethargy. No one dares think of the coming winter. Everyone is anxious to get work to lay up something for the long siege of bitter cold. But there is no work. That is why we don't talk much. We look at the floor dreading to see that knowledge in each other's eyes. There is a kind of humiliation in it. We look away from each other. We look at the floor." One expectant mother told of that awful summer of 1933, when her husband had just lost his job and they were penniless. He "kept looking feverishly for work when there was no work, and blaming himself because he was unable to find it." Their relief application "was the last act of our desperation."

Desperation also took more comic or pathetic turns in the Depression. The board game "Monopoly" swept the country. If one could not eke out a living in the real world, one could accumulate a paper fortune in a fantasy one. Dale Carnegie's *How to Win Friends and Influence People* became a best seller, with an overt message of doubtful relevance: confidence, grace, personal style, and sensitive shrewdness would bring success. Its latent message was also obvious: a failure had only his own personality to blame. Soap operas—daytime serials—which fastened themselves on the radio public in the 1930's, provided a catalogue of troubles for the listener to compare with his own, but they always blamed failure on personal and emotional inadequacy, never on external and social events.

Public-opinion polls during the Depression accurately gauged the degree of persistence and change in American attitudes toward poverty and the poor. There can be no doubt of the popularity of the federal involvement in relief among all the sectors of society. The rich and the poor, the city and the country agreed that aid to the needy was a proper and vital government function. In March 1939, three-quarters of the American public, according to a Roper poll, affirmed the government's obligation to relieve all persons who had no other means of subsistence. They supported wholeheartedly the Social Security program. Yet at the very same time, a majority of the public continued to think of the poor in hostile and pejorative terms. Reliefers could get jobs, ran the common belief, if only they would try. In other words, the New Deal did institute new and important and widely supported relief programs, but the welfare recipient remained a target of suspicion, denigrated by himself and by others. Even the Great Depression could not wipe away the stigma of poverty.

This fundamental ambivalence has persisted and, in fact, intensified in our own times. A curious bifurcation remains as public programs expand and public hostility continues. The polls are again instructive. In November 1964, only a bare 20 percent of the country believed that the government should decrease expenditures on relief. Yet almost 70 percent insisted that some or most of those actually on relief were there for dishonest reasons. Only a slim minority defined poverty as exclusively the result of circumstances beyond the control of the poor; most Americans were convinced that "welfare and relief make people lazy." In short, we today retain two nearly contradictory views: yes, the government must assume responsibility for poverty—but welfare corrupts and the poor are corrupted. There is a paradox here, but not the one that observers usually note. The odd fact is not that there are needy among us but that we should simultaneously hold such conflicting views.

In the 1960's, Americans once again discovered poverty in their midst, and they seemed as startled by its presence as Jacksonians had been 130 years before. Now it was Michael Harrington's turn to prod the nation's conscience, demonstrating that the New Deal had not eradicated poverty; that even though everyone dressed more or less alike, this was not an egalitarian society; that the fact that commuter highways did not offer a view of the slums was no reason to believe that they had disappeared. Congressional investigations also helped to make the poor more visible. Hunger in Mississippi, congressmen and their constituents learned, was a real problem. Starvation existed in this country—impossible as that circumstance might seem to comfortable, suburban householders. Robert Coles, a Boston psychiatrist, listed for one Senate committee the evidence he had uncovered among Mississippi's poor of vitamin and mineral deficiencies; untreated skin infections; eye and ear diseases; bone diseases; chronic anemia; undiagnosed heart, kidney, and lung infections; neglected injuries; and bodily deformities. It was a shocking catalogue, but one that his colleagues extended to several other southern states as well. Claude Brown, author of the popular and sensitive novel *Manchild in the Promised Land,* told another Senate committee about the realities of existence in the urban ghetto—in this case New York's Harlem—how hunger, dirt, and disease demoralized the poor and brought them to despair.

These views did manage to affect public policy and stimulate new programs. Two Columbia University professors of social work, Richard Cloward and Francis Piven, outlined a new and daring strategy. They wanted to provoke a welfare crisis by enrolling *all* the needy eligible for relief. Many deserving candidates, they explained, were either ignorant of their rights or too embarrassed to claim them. If they were to receive the assistance they were entitled to, the present welfare system would be bankrupted; the federal government would then have to expand its responsibilities through some form of a guaranteed minimum income plan. Although the Cloward and Piven proposal did not in itself create such a situation, events in the 1960's actually followed along that line. The poor did clamor to get their rights, urban relief rolls did swell—and Congress was considering enactment of the first minimum income program in the nation's history.

Despite these signs of progress, however, a darker side still persists. There is no shortage of public officials ready to berate the poor for their poverty, to locate the origin of dependency in vice, crime, and immorality, to define the problem of dependency as getting rid of the loafers who will not work. As one opponent of the guaranteed minimum income legislation put it, "The recipients . . . as I understand it, could continue to get this guaranteed income not only if they resolutely refused to seek or take a job, but if they gambled the money away at bingo or at the races, or spent it on prostitutes, pornography, whiskey, gin, marijuana, heroin, or whatnot." A not dissimilar attitude marked the thinking in the well-publicized Moynihan report. The poor, in this instance the black poor, argued sociologist and presidential advisor Daniel Moynihan, are kept in their poverty not so much by external forces (a closed job market or white racism) as by their own pathology. Illegitimacy, desertion, and immorality create mother-headed households, and this deviant form of family organization inevitably produces and perpetuates poverty and crime. Once again, the poor emerge as guilty for their own troubles.

One new development, however, does raise the prospect of change, a way out of the paradox of expanding public programs and continuingly bitter and condemnatory public rhetoric. For the first time, the poor themselves are actively and vocally defending themselves, insisting that they are not culpable, faulting the system and not themselves, throwing off the stigma of poverty. They are insisting that they control their own communities and take responsibility for their own welfare. These sentiments are clearly expressed by the leaders of the Harlem Youth Program (HARYOU), organized under Presidents Kennedy and Johnson. "The core of the HARYOU programs," they declared, "and the basis upon which any claim for innovation must be judged, is in the persistent emphasis and insistence upon social action rather than dependence upon mere social services." Social action, they explained, "means and demands the stimulation of concern among individuals who share a common predicament." Self-determination, neighborhood responsibility, individual initiative, not a passive acceptance of a social worker's handout, are the bywords of this fresh effort.

A similar perspective is affecting other groups among the poor. At a recent Puerto Rican community conference, a spokesman for New York's newest ethnic group announced that the "central question is inevitably one of participation in decision-making by government. . . . Poverty in all its ugliness still stalks the Puerto Rican day and night." Existing anti-poverty programs seemed altogether inadequate. Most of them were "still directed toward traditional social welfare paternalism rather than a genuine war on poverty." The people, these leaders contended, must be reached directly, "not through professional social brokers." In essence, Puerto Ricans had to help themselves. There could be no substitute for "involvement and experience."

As the poor demand and achieve self-respect and some measure of political power and self-determination, Americans may finally learn the lessons so relevant to a history of poverty. The disparities between our language and our practices may decrease. We have in fact moved far from the days when the poor were shut up in the almshouse, but we have not yet shed the vestiges of nineteenth-century thought, its moralistic condemnations of the poor as guilty, its exalted and unqualified sense of New World opportunities. Perhaps we will soon make our peace with this issue, bringing inherited rhetoric into accord with present-day realities. Then we will be able to correct the discrepancies in our economic and social organization without berating ourselves or the recipients.

Part One

INDUSTRIAL POVERTY
IN AN AGRARIAN SOCIETY

1865–1890

Uplifting the Pauper:
Josephine Shaw Lowell describes
the friendly visitor

*One of the most representative statements of post-Civil War attitudes
toward poverty and its relief was made by Josephine Shaw Lowell, a
leading charity worker of the period. Born to a prosperous and well-
established family, Lowell was raised in New York, and many of her
welfare activities later centered there. She was a member of the State
Board of Charities, the supervisory committee overseeing charitable institutions (the first woman to hold the position), and was also a founder
of the Charity Organization Society, dedicated to bringing a new efficiency to private relief efforts. Her* Public Relief and Private Charity
*summed up the guiding principles of the COS and reflected accurately
its curious combination of solicitude for the poor and stark suspicion of
their moral condition.*

Charity, as I define it, must be a voluntary, free, beneficent action performed toward those who are in more destitute circumstances and inferior in worldly position.

By this definition, of course, all official and public relief is put
outside the pale of charity, since it lacks the voluntary element.

By this definition, moreover, I contend, that all indiscriminate almsgiving and all systematic dolegiving is proved not to be charitable.

Charity must be a good—a good forever, to him who receives it—
but however benevolent may be the motive, if the action be not beneficent, there is no charity. Almsgiving and dolegiving are hurtful—therefore they are not charitable.

Josephine Shaw Lowell, *Public Relief and Private Charity* (New York, 1884),
excerpts from pp. 89-111.

Almsgiving and dolegiving are hurtful even to those who do not receive them, because they help to keep down wages by enabling those who do receive them to work for less than fair pay. No greater wrong can be done, not only to those who receive the miserable pittance, but to all working people. Wages at the best are low enough, without being reduced by the action of the benevolent.

Almsgiving and dolegiving are hurtful to those who receive them because they lead men to remit their own exertions and depend on others, upon whom they have no real claim, for the necessaries of life, *which they do not receive after all.*

In this last fact lies one secret of the injury done—false hopes are excited, the unhappy recipients of alms become dependent, lose their energy, are rendered incapable of self-support, and what they receive in return for their lost character is quite inadequate to supply their needs; thus they are kept on the verge almost of death by the very persons who think they are relieving them, by the kindly souls who are benevolent, but who will not take the trouble to be beneficent, too.

The nature of doles is to be insufficient and to be uncertain. They would cease to be doles and would become pensions were they to assume a regular character and to be sufficient to meet the ascertained wants of the recipient, and in certain cases pensions are an excellent manner of bestowing charity. Indeed, where it is possible for charitable societies to support entirely such people as they decide to help, the effect on the latter individuals may not be any worse than if they had fallen heir to an adequate income in any other way, although it is of course a fact that sudden inheritances often do destroy good habits both among the rich and the poor; but even under these circumstances, the effect on others would have to be considered. The terrifying decay of industry, temperance, providence and natural affection not only among what are technically called "the poor" in England during the fifty years preceding 1835 but also among a large proportion of all the men and women who labored for their daily bread, is a warning that must not be overlooked.

The great point to be considered is what is possible. Could all men be made comfortable and happy by a charity so extended that it would amount to an equal division of the wealth of any given community, I should welcome the measure with my whole heart; but it has been proved, and surely it scarcely needed proving, that no amount of money scattered among people who are without character and virtue, will insure even physical comfort.

It is for this reason that nothing should be done under the guise of charity, which tends to break down character. It is the greatest wrong that can be done to him to undermine the character of a poor man—for it is his all. The struggle is hard, he needs all his determination and strength of will to fight his way, and nothing that deprives him of these qualities can be "charitable."

The proof that dolegiving and almsgiving do break down independence, do destroy energy, do undermine character, may be found in the growing ranks of pauperism in every city, in the fact that the larger the funds given in relief in any community, the more pressing is the demand for them, and in the experience and testimony of all practical workers among the poor.

Before entering on any explanation of how the poor may be raised and helped, we must form some idea of who the poor are. There is a mistaken and dangerous, but I fear not uncommon, impression, that in every community there exists a given and constant number of individuals who may be classed under that name, who are absolutely helpless, and whom it is *somebody's* duty to feed, clothe, and generally care for.

The line of division between this mass of suffering people and everybody else is supposed to be clearly defined, and the former are to be treated on quite different principles from the rest of the world. Thus, while it is thought to be a good thing to drive a hard bargain with the widow who does the family washing, and to make her earn her dollar by a hard day's work, it is also thought to be a good thing to give a dollar without inquiry or equivalent to the widow who passes her days in idleness and her nights in debauchery. The fact that the first widow may in time come to contrast her lot with that of the second widow, and may prefer the latter, seldom occurs to the almsgiver, nor does he know how desperate a temptation he is presenting daily to his fellow men.

As a fact we have the miserable company of hopeless paupers that is imagined by the common mind, but it is most unfortunately not fixed in quantity; it is perpetually being augmented by the weak and foolish and wicked who have watched the course of benevolent persons and societies, and who can no longer resist the temptation constantly held out to them to give up the unpleasant struggle and accept the gift so freely offered of a living without labor. Therefore the problem before those who would be charitable, is not how to deal with a given number of poor; it is how to help those who are poor, without adding to their numbers and constantly increasing the evils they seek to cure.

Whatever the circumstances, whether in a sparsely settled neighborhood or in a crowded city, the principle adopted must be the same, although the action will have to be different.

The fundamental principle is that all charity must tend to raise the character and elevate the moral nature, and so improve the condition of those toward whom it is exercised, and must not tend to injure the character or condition of others.

Clinging to this principle as a guide, there are several rules which it is well to follow in practical work. I will mention some of the most important only.

The first is that each case is to be *radically* dealt with; that is, finding fellow beings in want and suffering, the cause of the want and suffering are to be removed if possible, even if the process be as painful as plucking out an eye or cutting off a limb.

The cause of distress is to be sought out and dealt with, or the distressed ones to be let alone, for only harm will result from unwise and ignorant meddling. Better leave people to the hard working of natural laws than to run the risk of interfering with those laws in a mischievous manner. This first rule, that each case must be radically dealt with and finally disposed of, shows one fundamental difference in the mental attitude of those who believe and who disbelieve in "dolegiving." The former regard it as a natural condition of things that a certain part of the community should not be self-supporting, they think it even desirable that there should be "the poor" to look after, they accept the degradation and suffering of other people with calmness, as inevitable facts and to satisfy their own feelings of pity they offer their inadequate doles, never casting a thought beyond the present day, or even inquiring whether permanent and efficient help might not be almost as easy to give.

The other class, on the other hand, regard each case of poverty as a wrong, an unnatural evil and one which they should use every effort to eradicate; it shocks them that men should be unable to live by their labor; but they do not give doles, knowing that this will often retard or entirely prevent the energetic action required on the part of the sufferers themselves to lift themselves out of their difficulties.

The dole-giving acts upon the receiver as insufficient watering in dry weather acts upon plants—they die because they are watered and are tempted to keep their roots near the surface, instead of plunging them deep down where they will find nourishment. With plants, you must either water thoroughly or not at all—with the human beings you must either care for them entirely or let them depend on themselves—to tempt them with a false hope that you will supply them with what they need, and then fail them, is cruelty.

The second rule is, that the best help of all is to help people to help themselves. That is, that instead of receiving the means of living, men should receive from the benevolent the means of earning a living—that the poor man or woman should have the road cleared so that they may themselves march on to success—that their brains should be released from ignorance, their hands freed from the shackles of incompetence, their bodies saved from the pains of sickness, and their souls delivered from the bonds of sin.

It seems most easy and natural and right in one's own neighborhood, where one knows everyone, to step into the house of a poor friend and give him the help he requires in his unexpected distress, and it is natural and right, provided one does know everyone; but gradually there come strangers, both rich and poor, to live in the village; suddenly the knowing everyone is discovered to have become a thing of the past, and the new rich neighbors upset the well considered plans that have been formed for the old poor neighbors, and the poor neighbors, hearing how much kindness there is in the town, ask also to share it, and suddenly the community awakes to the fact that they have a pauper class in their midst, and that some of their old inhabitants belong to it and the painful suspicion forces itself upon the benevolent that they have perhaps helped to drive them into it.

The only way to undo the harm is to regain by some means the advantage that the small community had without effort. The same intimate knowledge of those who have to be helped must be got in some way, and the only possible means of getting this knowledge, and of making it available to others, is that recommended by Dr. Chalmers and carried out in Glasgow and in Elberfeld, that is, of subdividing the labor among many willing hands.

A small association of men and women should be formed and a special territory assigned to each, so that he may become thoroughly acquainted with all who live within its limits.

Let this new association merely be a Friendly Society and let its objects be to work for the good of the whole town, to create a neighborly good feeling, to help forward all good objects and put down all bad ones, to see that the laws are enforced, sanitary regulations complied with, that the children attend school, and nuisances are abated. Such a society, acquainted with the town and all its people, would in great measure prevent the growth of pauperism, and it could give the wisest advice to private almsgivers were any almsgivers necessary, and it should make itself and its influence so prominent that all who wished to help others would come to it first for information and advice.

In a city no such simple means will suffice—for in every city the large multitudes of inhabitants and the complications of living make imposture easy, and unknown suffering a possibility, and a more complicated machinery is needed to defeat the one and discover the other. I believe a "Charity Organization Society" to be a necessity in order to check the growth of pauperism in cities, and to guide charity toward wise measures.

The ways of putting the rules of true charitable work into practice are as many as are the human beings who need help, but there are certain classes of sufferers, the members of each of which may be dealt with by very much the same means and these it seems worth while to describe.

The classes of cases where direct money help may be given are confined to those where the natural breadwinner is dead, or disabled by physical ailment, and these may be divided into permanent, long continued, and temporary disability. In all these cases, before any such help is decided on, it must be clearly understood that it is better, in the long run, better morally, better for themselves and the community, that the family should be held together; otherwise, whatever the suffering, entering an institution public or private, is the remedy for their trouble.

Old people, who through no fault of their own, have come to poverty, and who have no children who ought to help them, may be made recipients of a weekly or monthly pension, but it should be sufficient for a comfortable living and should be given by individuals, if possible, upon whom they have some claim. Each case must be judged on its own merits. These I call cases requiring permanent relief.

Widows with young children require long continued relief, and this should be given, but with the greatest care; no regular pension paid out week by week, without individual supervision, will suffice—such can not fail to injure both the mother and children especially if it is supplied from public funds.

We come now, however, to the most painful of all cases, those where the cause of suffering is moral, where the innocent suffer with the guilty, and where there seems almost nothing to be done. Often it is found that a whole family is suffering from the fault of the one man in all the world to whom they have a right to look for support and protection, and here the process of cure, if cure be possible, will be painful to all alike. The first thing to be understood, however, is that the wife and children of a drunkard *must* suffer, no power can prevent that; the only question presented is as to the kind of suffering. Shall the man be encouraged in his vileness, shall his children be exposed to the almost unimaginable horrors, moral and physical, which are inevitable so long as they live in the same house with him, shall there be children born yearly who will inherit broken health and depraved minds and bodies, and all this fostered by benevolence? Or shall the mother be forced, by her desire to see her children fed, to save them from this fate? Many good people call it a cruelty to refuse help to the family of a drunkard, but where the father and mother are cruel, no outside help will save the children from suffering, while to refuse outside help may do so.

I have not the slightest doubt that it is a *wrong,* and a great wrong, to give help to the family of a drunkard or an immoral man who will not support them. Unless the woman will remove her children from his influence, it should be understood that no public or private charity, and no charitable individual, has the right to help perpetuate and maintain such families as are brought forth by drunkards and vicious men and women.

The answer to objections on moral grounds that a woman has a duty to her husband which she must perform, is conclusive. She has no right to sacrifice her children to her husband—they are helpless and dependent upon her—he can reform if he chooses, or can at least voluntarily enter an institute where he will be helped to reform, and the strongest possible motive that he can have to reform is that his wife and children will suffer if he does not, or will leave him.

In case a woman does leave her husband from principle, she should be protected from him and should be treated as though she were a widow. In the case of drinking women, the rules should be the same, and every effort made to save the husband and children from the discomforts and suffering consequent on her vice.

Of course, where it is possible, the man should be dealt with by law and forced to support his family, but where he has escaped entirely, the mother and children should be left to be maintained by the constituted authorities, and the family broken up and distributed in different institutions, unless they can support themselves. It ought to be understood in every community that where a man deserts his wife and children and neglects his most pressing duties to them and to the public, that they will be left to suffer the fate he has prepared for them.

Help by means of employment is one of the natural devices of those who wish to aid the poor without demoralizing them, but unfortunately, this method, like many other good things is open to abuse, and can not be carelessly resorted to. In order to judge of the wisdom of supplying artificial work as a permanent means of relieving the poor, the whole question of poverty must be looked at broadly. We have to go so far back as to`ask, "What does the poverty of the worthy poor mean?" It can mean nothing else than that there are too many people in the community where the poverty exists. Sober, industrious men and women are poor only because their wages are low. If they can not get work it is because no one needs them, and if wages are low it is because there is such competition among the workers that they underbid each other. There is a congestion of workers wherever the "worthy poor" are suffering. For this state of things there seem but two remedies, one to create a genuine demand for their work on the spot where they are, and the other to send them to some place where a demand already exists. To undertake, however, to make artificial work for them, to supply charity sewing, or open a charity woodyard, is only to make matters worse than they were before, for the original poor people still remain where they were, and others, moreover, will probably come also to ask for employment, attracted by the offer of work, which is a great inducement to many who would scorn to ask or accept open charity.

The second rule is that the best help of all is to help people to help themselves, and it follows that no amount of thought or time or money can be too much to spend on such help as this, and that all plans for starting provident schemes, for encouraging thrift, for teaching providence and self-control, for establishing schools for industrial training and the teaching of skill, especially such as will help not only that residuum which we technically call "the poor" but the whole community, are the best manifestations of true charity.

We have, then, our guiding principle:

That charity must tend to develop the moral nature of those it helps, and must not tend to injure others; and our two rules:

That each case must be dealt with radically, and a permanent means of helping it be found, and that the best way to help people is to help them help themselves—and these seem simple enough, but to carry them out requires an amount of principle and character, of work and devotion, which it sometimes seems almost impossible to find. Besides the intimate knowledge of the suffering people which I have mentioned already as the necessary preliminary to all efficient help, the main instrument to be depended on to raise the standard of decency, cleanliness, providence and morality among them must be personal influence, which means that a constant and continued intercourse must be kept up between those who have a high standard and those who have it not, and that the educated and happy and good are to give some of their time regularly and as a duty, year in and year out, to the ignorant, the miserable and the vicious. In a Christian community it ought not to be difficult to find those ready to undertake such a task, and unless they are found (men and women both), vice and crime will continue to grow by the side of poverty and wretchedness in the rich cities of our favored land.

2

Tramping with Tramps: Josiah Flynt tells their story

Few among the poor were as marginal to American society as the hobo, the tramp who rode the boxcars, who panhandled first in one town and then moved on to another. Sensing a good story and aware of the growing number of transient poor, Josiah Flynt masqueraded as one of them. He traveled, talked, and lived among the transients, and he then wrote one of the most personal accounts we have of these men on the move. Flynt's book was well read, probably more for its rather exotic tales than for a sensitivity to the plight of the transient. Still it helped to publicize the condition of a very commonplace and yet unknown group among the poor.

It was about five o'clock on the afternoon of a cool September day that I left my friend's home clad as a tramp, and started for the night boat for Albany. I wore an old suit of clothes, a flannel shirt, a good pair of shoes, and a respectable hat. I had paid special attention to the shoes and hat, for it is a piece of tramp philosophy that the two extremities of a beggar are first looked at by the person of whom he is begging. While riding from Harlem down to the landing-place of the steamer, I laughed to myself while thinking how the tramps would envy me my nice head-

Josiah Flynt, *Tramping with Tramps* (New York, 1899), excerpts from pp. 164-165, 268-290.

and foot-gear. I wondered, too, whether I should be allowed to return with these coverings.

I sauntered lazily over to West Albany, for it was still early, and arrived as the people were lighting their breakfast fires. I waited until it seemed that the fires should have done their duty, and then began. I visited several houses. Sometimes the man of the house said that his wife was sick, or that he was out of work himself; and sometimes they told me to get out—that they had already fed one tramp.

My fifth call was at the home of a German woman who claimed that she had fed beggars in the Fatherland. She invited me in, placed a nice warm breakfast before me, and then we began a conversation in German about life, labor, and beggars. She was sorry for me, and said that I looked too young to be a beggar. I told her a tale. It was one of those stories in which the ghost of a truth still lingers—such as tramps know so well how to tell. I shall never know exactly how much of it she believed, or what she thought of me, as I told her that I was the outcast of a *hochwohlgeboren* family in Germany. I know, however, that she was sympathetic, and that she took me in, whether she did the same for my romance or not.

After breakfast I started for Troy. I knew that I should meet with plenty of loafers during the walk, and I preferred chatting with them on or near the highway. For Albany has a penitentiary. There is not a well-informed tramp in the United States that does not know about that prison; it has punished many a vagrant, and the Albany policemen are no friends to beggars. Syracuse Tom will bear me out in this statement, for he winters in Albany with his kid every year; but he does this simply because he is so well posted. Of course other tramps visit Albany as well, for it is a well-known town for "refreshments"; but only a few can thrive long there by begging only for money.

On my way to Troy I found a camp of thirty-three tramps. They were living off the charity of Albany. They had all been in for breakfast, and were now returned to the hang-out to chat and scheme. Some were discussing Albany prisons, its policemen, saloons, and general hospitality. Others had built a fire, and were boiling their shirts in a borrowed kettle to kill the vermin. Still others were planning Southern tours. Some had decided to winter in St. Augustine, some in Jacksonville, and a few were talking of the best routes to New Orleans.

One of the fellows recognized me. He must needs know where I had been so long, and why my hands were so white. "Cigarette," he said, "have you been a-doin' time? Where did you get yer white colors?" I told

Yorkey that I had been sick, and had been back on the road only a few days. He would not believe me, and I am afraid that he took me for a "crooked man," for he said: "Cig, you've not been in the sick-lugger all this while, and I hain't seen your register for many a day. No, my young bloke; you can't fool me. You've been up a tree, and you can't deny it."

I could not convince him of my innocence, so we dropped the subject, and I told him that I was bound for Buffalo, where I had friends who would help me to brace up and get off the road. I assured him that I knew now what a foolish business "bumming" was, and that I was going to make a grand effort to get work. Even this he would not believe, and he insisted that I was going West to some town where I knew that the tramps were going to have a "drunk." He tried to persuade me to go South with him, and claimed that Yonkers Slim was going to meet him in Washington with some money, and that the bums intended to have a great "sloppin'-up" (drinking-bout). I made him understand that I was determined to go West. Then he gave me some advice which was typical.

"Young feller, you're goin' to a pretty poor country. Why, when I left Buffalo two weeks ago, the bulls [police] were more than pinchin' the tramps right in the streets, and givin' them ninety days. The only decent thing about a journey up that way is the New York Central Railroad. You can ride that to death. That's the only godsend the country has. Jes let me tell you, though, what towns it cuts through, and then you'll squeal. Now, there's Schenectady. You can chew all right there, but divil a cent can you beg. Then comes Fonda, and you must know what a poor town that is. Then you've got Utica, where you can feed all right, for any fool can do that, but you can't hit a bloke for a dime in the streets without a bull seein' you and chuckin' you up for fifty-nine days in Utica jail. And you must know well enough what that jail is this time o' year—it's jes filled with a blasted lot o' gay-cats [men who will work] who've been on a booze. After Utica there's Rochester, a place that onc't was good, but isn't worth pawin' now since that gay-cat shot a woman there some time ago. After Rochester, what you got? Buffalo—the most God-forsaken town a bum ever heard of."

Here I interrupted my lecturer to say that I had heard of Buffalo as a good "chewing town." He turned upon me fiercely. "What d' you want? D' you only want to chew? Don't you want boodle, booze, togs, and a good livin'? Of course you do, jes like ev'ry genooine hobo. It's only a blasted gay-cat that'll fool around this country now. Cig, you'd better come South with us. Why, las' year the blokes more than sloughed in money around the Ponce de Leon Hotel in St. Aug'stine. We kin git there in a week if we ride passenger-trains. You'll hustle for an overcoat if you stay here much longer, an' I'll bet my Thanksgivin' dinner that every bloke you meet up the road is bound South. You'd better foller their coat-tails." I thanked Yorkey, but satisfied him that I was determined to get to Buffalo. "Well, so long, Cigarette," he said, when I left the camp for Troy.

Between Troy and Cohoes I found another camp of tramps. Here were forty-two men and boys who were enjoying what tramps termed a "sloppin'-up." Some of them had just returned from the hop-country, and had gathered together the fellows in their vicinity, and were now drinking keg after keg of beer. Thirteen kegs had already been emptied. These men seemed well satisfied with their treatment around Troy, and the majority of them had been there for nearly a week. One half-drunken loafer from Milwaukee was so anxious to praise the town's hospitality that he was haranguing some of his comrades most zealously. "I've boozed around this town," he said, "off and on for the last seven years, and I've not been sloughed up yet. There's only one or two bulls in the town that's after tramps, and if a bloke is anyway foxy he can slip them all right. Two years ago I fooled around here for two months, and had my three square meals every day, and booze too, and I was never touched. You can't hustle pennies, o' course, as well as you can down in the City [New York], but you can batter for clothes, chuck, and booze all right enough. I know as many as ten saloon-keepers in the town that'll give me a drink and ask no questions. Yes; Troy's all right, and it's only a rotten gay-cat that 'u'd say it wa'n't. The only mean thing about the town is that it's slow. Us hoboes must be on the march, and it's not in us to fool round a jerk town like this 'un too long. It's tiresome, blokes."

A hunt for supper in Cohoes afforded me a great deal of amusement, for I was entertained by an alderman's wife. At any rate, she told me, while I was eating my supper in the large restaurant dining-room, that her husband, eating his supper in a private room on the floor below, was a village father and a hater of tramps. "But don't worry," she said; "he shall not bother you while I'm around. I always feed a hungry man, and I always shall. I can't understand how some people can turn away from the door any one who claims to be hungry. If I should do this, I would expect to be hungry myself before long." A freight-train passed by the house while I was at the table, and my hostess noticed my anxiety to be aboard of it. "Never mind," she said; "there'll be plenty of freights along a little later, and this is a good place to catch them, for there is a grade here, and you can keep away from the station, where you might be arrested." I remembered this woman throughout my journey, and every tramp that I met bound in this direction was advised of her house. I think it would hardly be so good another year.

From Cohoes to Schenectady is only a short ride, and it seemed as if I had been asleep in the box-car only a few minutes when Ohio Red, who was with me, cried out, "Cigarette, we're in the yards; let's get out." We slept in a box-car overnight. This is an odd way of resting. The coat, vest, and shoes are taken off, then the shoes are made into a pillow, the vest is laid over them, and the coat is thrown over the shoulders. So sleep most of the tramps during the warm months.

After an early breakfast, we went over to the hang-out on the eastern side of the town. Thirteen rovers were already there, cooking a conventional meal. They had begged meat, potatoes, bread, and coffee, and had stolen some other vegetables, besides a kettle, and were now anxiously watching the fire. Two more vagrants, who had been looking for cigar-stubs in the town, came in later. Their pockets were well filled, and they divided equally their findings. This "snipe" chewing and smoking is the most popular use of tobacco in trampdom, and is even preferred to "store brands" of the weed, which are easily begged. About dinner-time a man came out to the camp, and offered every one of us the job of shoveling sand for a dollar and a half a day, the work to continue into November. He might better have stayed away. The tramps told him that they had just left as good a job as that in Buffalo, and were now looking for three dollars a day!

At nightfall sixteen tramps, including myself, boarded a freight-train bound west. I was now on the main line of the New York Central, and had no further need to fear any large amount of walking.

In Utica I made the acquaintance of a roadster called "Utica Biddy." I met him at the tramp camp just outside of the town, near the R.,W.&O.R.R. tracks, where twenty-six other loafers were waiting for three of their fellow-travelers to return from the hop-country, in order to help spend their money. Biddy is one of the best-known tramps on the New York Central, and he gave me more information about the districts around Syracuse and Utica than I could possibly have accumulated single-handed. While riding in a box-car from Utica to Syracuse we had a long conversation, and the following is the substance of what he told me:

"I've been a bum on the division of this railroad from Albany to Syracuse for the last four years. I've had my three squares every day, and in winter I've had a bed every night. I know you'll hardly believe this, for some of you beggars come up to this country and curse it because you don't get on the spot what you want. Now, I'll give you a few pointers about these towns. We've just left a town [Utica] where I can go to over a score of houses and get a square meal whenever I want it. Of course I was born there, and that may make a bit o' difference, but I can do the same in Rome, Albany, and Syracuse. I've been on this beat so long and have watched my chances so carefully that I know now just where to go when hungry. I hear a great many tramps kick about Utica, its policemen and snide houses. But if a lad will just knuckle down for a month or so and hunt out the good houses, make himself acquainted with the tough policemen and keep out of their way, find good barns for a doss at night, and make a business of bummin' carefully, there's not a town on the Central that ain't good. The trouble with you strange blokes is this: you come up here, booze, draw your razors when you're drunk, do too much crooked work, and o' course the people get hostile. Why, see how many lads are workin' my racket over in Pennsylvania. You know yourself that on the Pennsy [Pennsylvania Railroad] line there are tramps who not only bum within a division, but inside of subdivisions, and can chew whenever they like. But they do this 'cause they're foxy and have had their boozin' knocked out of them. Now, those lads that we left back in Utica will more than likely get sloughed into jail when they get to boozin'. You can't expect the people to stand such stuff as that. And these are the kind of fellows, too, who jigger our ridin' on this railroad. They get drunk, and if they want to ride and can't find an empty car, they break a seal [a car seal], and then there's the devil to pay about the tramps tryin' to rob the cars. If the bums would only keep sober once in a while, there wouldn't be a tramp pinched once a month. The bulls around here don't care to yank a tramp unless they have to. But what can they do when they find a bloke paradin' the streets with a jag on? They pull him in, o' course, or else the people would kick. I'll gamble that he wouldn't be touched, though, if he were simply huntin' a meal."

A great many tramps loaf around the hop-country in the vicinity of Syracuse and Utica during the early autumn, in order to drink at the expense of the too light-hearted hop-pickers. The nationality of these men, so far as I could judge from pronunciation, some of their own statements, and their professional names, were almost entirely American. I met one German loafer called "Dutchy," and he was the only recognized foreigner that I found. The others may have had parents born in other countries, but they themselves were certainly Americanized. A good test of a tramp's nationality is his professional name. For every genuine hobo couples the name of his birthplace with whatever other name he chooses, and the reader will find, if he will visit watering-tanks or other available stationary railway property in his vicinity, like section-houses, shanties, etc., where tramps "sign," that the names registered there indicate, in the great majority of cases, a birthplace in the United States.

That tramps are expensive no one will deny, but how much so it is difficult to decide. I have tried to show that a large number of them eat and wear things which certainly cost somebody considerable money, but a careful census of the vagabond population alone can estimate the amount. No one can tell exactly what this tramp population numbers, but I think it safe to say that there are not less than sixty thousand in this country. Every man of this number, as a rule, eats something twice a day, and the majority eat three good meals. They all wear some sort of clothing, and most of them rather respectable clothing. They all drink liquor, probably each one a glass of whisky a day. They all get into jail, and eat and drink there just as much at the expense of the community as elsewhere. They all chew and smoke tobacco, and all of them spend some of their time in lodging-houses. How much all this represents in money I cannot tell, but I believe that the expenses I have enumerated, together with the costs of conviction for vagrancy, drunkenness, and crime, will easily mount up into the millions. And all that the country can show for this expenditure is an idle, homeless, and useless class of individuals called tramps.

3

The New Industrial Poverty: A Senate committee interviews mill workers

In 1883, the United States Senate undertook one of the first extensive investigations of conditions facing American workingmen. Attempting to evaluate the effects of industrialism on the laborer and to understand the implications of the new concentrations of capital in large manufac-

Report of the Committee of the Senate upon the Relations between Labor and Capital (Washington, 1885), Vol. 3, excerpts from pp. 451-457.

turing enterprises, the committee interviewed a wide range of employers and employees. *That path-breaking effort gave the working class the opportunity to publicize the marginal circumstances in which they lived. Their testimony belied several popular myths. The workingman, on being asked why he did not escape industrial poverty by moving west, answered succinctly and accurately: "I can't see how I could get out West. I have got nothing to go with." Americans' education about their poor had begun.*

Thomas O'Donnell examined.

By the Chairman:

Question. Where do you live?—Answer. At Fall River.

Q. How long have you lived in this country?—A. Eleven years.

Q. Where were you born?—A. In Ramsbotham, England.

Q. Have you been naturalized here?—A. No, sir.

Q. What is your business?—A. I am a mule-spinner by trade. I have worked at it since I have been in this country—eleven years.

Q. Are you a married man?—A. Yes, sir; I am a married man; have a wife and two children. I am not very well educated. I went to work when I was young, and have been working ever since in the cotton business; went to work when I was about eight or nine years old. I was going to state how I live. My children get along very well in summer time, on account of not having to buy fuel or shoes or one thing and another. I earn $1.50 a day and can't afford to pay a very big house rent. I pay $1.50 a week for rent, which comes to about $6 a month.

Q. That is, you pay this where you are at Fall River?—A. Yes, sir.

Q. Do you have work right along?—A. No, sir; since that strike we had down in Fall River about three years ago I have not worked much more than half the time, and that has brought my circumstances down very much.

Q. Why have you not worked more than half the time since then? —A. Well, at Fall River if a man has not got a boy to act as "back-boy" it is very hard for him to get along. In a great many cases they discharge men in that work and put in men who have boys.

Q. Men who have boys of their own?—A. Men who have boys of their own capable enough to work in a mill, to earn 30 or 40 cents a day.

Q. Is the object of that to enable the boy to earn something for himself?—A. Well, no; the object is this: They are doing away with a great deal of mule-spinning there and putting in ring-spinning, and for that reason it takes a good deal of small help to run this ring work, and it throws the men out of work because they are doing away with the mules and putting these ring-frames in to take their places. For that reason they get all the small help they can to run these ring-frames. There are so many men in the city to work, and whoever has a boy can have work, and whoever has no boy stands no chance. Probably he may have a few months of work in the summer time, but will be discharged in the fall. That is what leaves me in poor circumstances. Our children, of course, are very often sickly from one cause or another, on account of not having sufficient clothes, or shoes, or food, or something. And also my woman; she never did work in a mill; she was a housekeeper, and for that reason she can't help me to anything at present, as many women do help their husbands down there, by working, like themselves. My wife never did work in a mill, and that leaves me to provide for the whole family. I have two children.

And another thing that helped to keep me down: A year ago this month I buried the oldest boy we had, and that brings things very expensive on a poor man. For instance, it will cost there, to bury a body, about $100. Now, we could have that done in England for about £5; that would not amount to much more than about $20, or something in that neighborhood. That makes a good deal of difference. Doctors' bills are very heavy—about $2 a visit; and if a doctor comes once a day for two or three weeks it is quite a pile for a poor man to pay.

Q. Will not the doctor come for a dollar a day?—A. You might get a man sometimes, and you sometimes won't, but they generally charge $2 a day.

Q. To operatives?—A. Oh, all around. You might get one for $1.50 sometimes.

Q. They charge you as much as they charge people of more means? —A. They charge as much as if I was the richest man in the city, except that some of them might be generous once in a while and put it down a little in the end; but the charge generally is $2. That makes it hard.

I have a brother who has four children, besides his wife and himself. All he earns is $1.50 a day. He works in the iron works at Fall River. He only works about nine months out of twelve. There is generally about three months of stoppage, taking the year right through, and his wife and his family all have to be supported for a year out of the wages of nine months—$1.50 a day for nine months out of the twelve, to support six of them. It does not stand to reason that those children and he himself can have natural food or be naturally dressed. His children are often sick, and he has to call in doctors. That is always hanging over him, and is a great expense to him. And then if he does not pay the bill the trustee law comes on him. That is a thing that is not properly looked after. A man told me the other day that he was trusteed for $1.75, and I understood that there was a law in this State that a man could not be trusteed for less than $10. It seems to me there is something wrong in the Government somewhere; where it is, I can't tell.

Q. How much money have you got?—A. I have not got a cent in the house; didn't have when I came out this morning.

Q. How much money have you had within three months?—A. I have had about $16 inside of three months.

Q. Is that all you have had within the last three months to live on? —A. Yes; $16.

Q. How much have you had within a year?—A. Since Thanksgiving I happened to get work in the Crescent Mill, and worked there exactly thirteen weeks. I got just $1.50 a day, with the exception of a few days that I lost—because in following up mule-spinning you are obliged to lose a day once in a while; you can't follow it up regularly.

Q. Thirteen weeks would be seventy-eight days, and, at $1.50 a day, that would make $117, less whatever time you lost?—A. Yes. I worked thirteen weeks there and ten days in another place, and then there was a dollar I got this week, Wednesday.

Q. Taking a full year back can you tell how much you have had? —A. That would be about fifteen weeks' work. Last winter, as I told you, I got in, and I worked up to about somewhere around Fast Day, or may be New Year's day; anyway, Mr. Howard has it down on his record, if you wish to have an exact answer to that question; he can answer it better than I can, because we have a sort of union there to keep ourselves together.

Q. Do you think you have had $150 within a year?—A. No, sir.

Q. Have you had $125—A. Well, I could figure it up if I had time. The thirteen weeks is all I have had.

Q. The thirteen weeks and the $16 you have mentioned?—A. Yes, sir.

Q. That would be somewhere about $133, if you had not lost any time?—A. Yes, sir.

Q. That is all you have had?—A. Yes, sir.

Q. To support yourself and wife and two children?—A. Yes, sir.

Q. Have you had any help from outside?—A. No, sir.

Q. Do you mean that yourself and wife and two children have had nothing but that for all this time?—A. That is all. I got a couple dollars' worth of coal last winter, and the wood I picked up myself. I goes around with a shovel and picks up clams and wood.

Q. What do you do with the clams?—A. We eat them. I don't get them to sell, but just to eat, for the family. That is the way my brother lives, too, mostly. He lives close by us.

Q. How many live in that way down there?—A. I could not count them, they are so numerous. I suppose there are one thousand down there.

Q. A thousand that live on $150 a year?—A. They live on less.

Q. Less than that?—A. Yes; they live on less than I do.

Q. How long has that been so?—A. Mostly so since I have been married.

Q. How long is that?—A. Six years this month.

Q. Why do you not go West on a farm?—A. How could I go, walk it?

Q. Well, I want to know why you do not go out West on a $2,000 farm, or take up a homestead and break it and work it up, and then have it for yourself and family?—A. I can't see how I could get out West. I have got nothing to go with.

Q. It would not cost you over $1,500.—A. Well, I never saw over a $20 bill, and that is when I have been getting a month's pay at once. If some one would give me $1,500 I will go.

Q. Is there any prospect that anybody will do that?—A. I don't know of anybody that would.

Q. You say you think there are a thousand men or so with their families that live in that way in Fall River?—A. Yes, sir; and I know many of them. They are around there by the shore. You can see them every day; and I am sure of it because men tell me.

Q. Are you a good workman?—A. Yes, sir.

Q. Were you ever turned off because of misconduct or incapacity or unfitness for work?—A. No, sir.

Q. Or because you did bad work?—A. No, sir.

Q. Or because you made trouble among the help?—A. No, sir.

Q. Did you ever have any personal trouble with an employer?—A. No, sir.

Q. You have not anything now you say?—A. No, sir.

Q. How old are you?—A. About thirty.

Q. Is your health good?—A. Yes, sir.

Q. What would you work for if you could get work right along; if you could be sure to have it for five years, staying right where you are?

—A. Well, if I was where my family could be with me, and I could have work every day I would take $1.50, and be glad to.

Q. One dollar and fifty cents a day, with three hundred days to the year, would make more than you make now in three or four years, would it not?

A. Well, I would have no opportunity then to pick up clams. I have had no coal except one dollar's worth since last Christmas.

Q. When do the clams give out?—A. They give out in winter.

Q. You spoke of fuel—what do you have for fuel?—A. Wood and coal.

Q. Where does the wood come from?—A. I pick it up around the shore—any old pieces I see around that are not good for anything. There are many more that do the same thing.

Q. Do you get meat to live on much?—A. Very seldom.

Q. What kinds of meat do you get for your family?—A. Well, once in a while we gets a piece of pork and some clams and make a clam-chowder. That makes a very good meal. We sometimes get a piece of corn beef or something like that.

Q. Have you had any fresh beef within a month?—A. Yes; we had a piece of pork steak for four of us yesterday.

Q. Have you had any beef within a month?—A. No, sir. I was invited to a man's house on Sunday—he wanted me to go up to his house and we had a dinner of roast pork.

Q. That was an invitation out, but I mean have you had any beef-steak in your own family, of your own purchase, within a month?—A. Yes; there was a half a pound, or a pound one Sunday—I think it was.

Q. Have you had only a pound or a half a pound on Sunday?—A. That is all.

Q. Has there been any day in the year that you have had to go without anything to eat?—A. Yes, sir, several days.

Q. More than one day at a time?—A. No.

Q. What have the children got on in the way of clothing?—A. They have got along very nicely all summer, but now they are beginning to feel quite sickly. One has one shoe on, a very poor one, and a slipper, that was picked up somewhere. The other has two odd shoes on, with the heel out. He has got cold and is sickly now.

Q. Have they any stockings?—A. He had got stockings, but his feet comes through them, for there is a hole in the bottom of the shoe.

Q. What have they got on the rest of their person?—A. Well, they

Women at work: the cigar factory. Photographer Lewis Hine was one of the first to use a camera to record working conditions in American factories. His sympathetic portraits convey a clear sense of what it meant to labor at the machine. Photograph by Lewis Hine, National Archives.

have a little calico shirt—what should be a shirt; it is sewed up in some shape—and one little petticoat, and a kind of little dress.

Q. How many dresses has your wife got?—A. She has got one since she was married, and she hasn't worn that more than half a dozen times; she has worn it just going to church and coming back. She is very good in going to church, but when she comes back she takes it off, and it is pretty near as good now as when she bought it.

Q. She keeps that dress to go to church in?—A. Yes, sir.

Q. How many dresses aside from that has she?—A. Well, she got one here three months ago.

Q. What did it cost?—A. It cost $1 to make it and I guess about a dollar for the stuff, as near as I can tell.

Q. The dress cost $2?—A. Yes.

Q. What else has she?—A. Well, she has an undershirt that she got given to her, and she has an old wrapper, which is about a mile too big for her; somebody gave it to her.

Q. She did not buy it?—A. No. That is all that I know that she has.

Q. Are you in debt?—A. Yes, sir.

Q. How much?—A. I am in debt for those funeral expenses now $15—since a year ago.

Q. Have you paid the rest?—A. Yes, sir.

Q. You live in a hired tenement?—A. Yes; but of course I can't pay a big rent. My rent is $6 a month. The man I am living under would come and put me right out and give me no notice either if I didn't pay my rent. He is a sheriff and auctioneer man. I don't know whether he has any authority to do it or not, but he does it with people.

Q. Do you see any way out of your troubles—what are you going to do for a living—or do you expect to have to stay right there?—A. Yes. I can't run around with my family.

Q. You have nowhere to go to, and no way of getting there if there was any place to go?—A. No, sir; I have no means nor anything, so I am obliged to remain there and try to pick up something as I can.

Q. Do the children go to school?—A. No, sir; they are not old enough; the oldest child is only three and a half; the youngest one is one and a half years old.

Q. Is there anything else you wanted to say?—A. Nothing further, except that I would like some remedy to be got to help us poor people down there in some way. Excepting the Government decides to do something with us we have a poor show. We are all, or mostly all, in good health; that is, as far as the men who are at work go.

Q. You do not know anything but mule-spinning, I suppose?—A. That is what I have been doing, but I sometimes do something with pick and shovel. I have worked for a man at that, because I am so put on. I am looking for work in a mill. The way they do there is this: There are about twelve or thirteen men that go into a mill every morning, and they have to stand their chance, looking for work. The man who has a boy with him he stands the best chance, and then, if it is my turn or a neighbor's turn who has no boy, if another man comes in who has a boy he is taken right in, and we are left out. I said to the boss once it was my turn to go in, and now you have taken on that man; what am I to do; I have got two little boys at home, one of them three years and a half and the other one year and a half old, and how am I to find something for them to eat; I can't get my turn when I come here.

He said he could not do anything for me. I says, "Have I got to starve; ain't I to have any work?" They are forcing these young boys into the mills that should not be in mills at all; forcing them in because they are throwing the mules out and putting on ring-frames. They are doing everything of that kind that they possibly can to crush down the poor people—the poor operatives there.

4

The Almshouse Solution:
Amos Warner surveys the traditional practice

The mainstay of public charity in late-nineteenth-century America was the almshouse. The poor, in order to gain relief, had to leave their families and communities to become inmates. When the almshouse solution first grew popular in the 1830's, it represented reformers' grand hopes for rehabilitating the poor. Within the walls of an almshouse, the dependent classes were to acquire the habits of order, discipline, and steady labor. By the 1870's, however, the almshouse had become custodial, a convenient place to support the aged, the orphan, and the hapless immigrant. The reliance on the almshouse almost to the exclusion of other types of relief emerges in Amos Warner's study of American charities. Warner, at one time secretary of the Baltimore Charity Organization Society and later a professor of economics, was an energetic and diligent researcher, and his 1894 volume was an accurate and intelligent account of the state of American public relief.

The almshouse is the fundamental institution in American poor-relief. It cares for all the abjectly destitute not otherwise provided for. Outdoor relief, although preceding it in point of time, is the resort of those who still, nominally at least, need only temporary assistance or partial support at home. Since the almshouse is the guarantee against starvation which the State offers to all, no matter how unfortunate or degraded, its inmates are often the most sodden driftwood from the social wreckage of the time. It is ordinarily a depressing experience to visit an almshouse,

Amos Warner, *American Charities* (New York, 1906, rev. ed.), excerpts from pp. 195-201, 204-206, 216-217, 223-225.

and accordingly we find it an institution that even the benevolent willingly forget. In many of the country almshouses no clergyman comes the year round; and no friendly visitor appears to encourage the superintendent to be faithful, or to bring to light abuses that may exist. Yet, since the institution is so fundamental, and since the number of its inmates is necessarily considerable, it may be doubted whether a more profitable work can easily be found than the right organization and proper management of almshouses. The benevolent too frequently hurry away to make excellent provision for special classes, leaving to the maladministration of the local almshouse a large assortment of destitute people under evil conditions.

In New England, except New Hampshire, where there are both county and town institutions, the town (township) is the local political unit to which the care of the poor is intrusted, and the almshouse is accordingly managed by the town officers. In the other States the almshouse is usually a county institution. It is not uncommon for several townships or counties to form themselves into an association, and establish what is called a district almshouse.

The tendency since 1890, especially in States where the town system of control prevails, is more toward the consolidation of small almshouses than toward the building of new ones. Of the 2373 almshouses enumerated at that time, 200 have since been discontinued, while the actual growth of such institutions has been slight.

In 1880 there were 66,203 inmates of almshouses in the United States, or one almshouse pauper to 758 inhabitants; in 1890 there were 73,045 almshouse inmates, or one to 857 inhabitants; in 1903 there were 81,764 almshouse inmates, or one to 920 inhabitants. The decrease in proportion to population does not necessarily indicate a general diminution of pauperism, but merely that a historical development, already in progress, has been continued. When the work of relief is first begun by the newly formed political units of an American settlement, it is usual to board out such dependents as must be supported entirely. Farmers or others are paid to care for old people, for imbeciles, and even for sick persons who have no homes of their own. Chiefly with a view to providing a place for the better care of the dependent sick, especially incurable cases, and also to economy, a public almshouse is established. During the first stage of its development, it acts as the charitable catch-all for the community. Idiots, epileptics, incurables, incompetents, the aged, abandoned children, foundlings, women for confinement, and a considerable number of the insane, the blind, and the deaf and dumb are all dumped together into some old farmhouse that has been bought by the authori-

The female almshouse at Blackwell's Island, New York. Unable to receive adequate relief in the community, the widowed, the sick, the aged, and the helpless had no choice but to pass their last days within this institution. Photograph by Jacob A. Riis. The Jacob A. Riis collection, Museum of the City of New York.

ties, and put to this use. The public then goes on its way, and thinks as little about the institution as possible, only grumbling annually at the expenses perhaps, when it happens to review public accounts.

In some populous cities even yet the almshouses are hardly more than enlarged specimens of this same type. The different classes of dependents are still assembled in one great institution, and the public assumes it has discharged its whole duty by giving enough food and fuel to keep the individuals that make up the incongruous mass from hunger and cold.

The next stage in institutional development has been described in the following words:—

When this humble home was out-grown or worn-out in the older States about the middle of the century and for a generation later, a new almshouse would be built; and the stage exemplified by the new building may be called that of the 'imposing edifice.' The architecture of this period was from the outside in; the building was planned for the admiration of the passers-by rather than for the comfort of the inhabitants. It was generally four or five stories high, regardless of the infirmities of its inmates; perfectly symmetrical, though the male population was generally two or three times the female, and in other respects planned without apparent reference to the uses to which it was to be put.

A third stage, as regards architecture, entered upon in the last quarter of the nineteenth century, is the cottage plan,—a plan which seems to combine the advantages without the defects of the older practice. It is, concisely speaking, a group of houses, sometimes connected by passages, permitting the complete separation of the sexes, separate hospital cottages, and a central administration building. To this class belongs the New York City Farm Colony established on Staten Island as a branch of the Home for the Aged and Infirm.

While this evolution of the almshouse buildings has been taking place, a much more important movement to differentiate the inmates has been developed. The classification of the inmates may be divided into two parts—the drafting out of the almshouse those who do not belong in it, and the differentiation of those that do belong in it. In the first division stand three groups which are gradually being taken over into institutions where they can receive more appropriate care. The first group includes all those requiring special scientific treatment; of these the defective classes of teachable age, the deaf, the dumb, and the blind, were the first to be drafted off to educational institutions, usually supported by the State. Next an effort was made to have the State take care of the insane. This is now usually done so far as the acute insane are concerned, but the great expense of providing for the increasing numbers of the chronic insane led to a suspension of their transfer from the almshouses to specialized asylums. The State of New York, as a result of the Willard report in 1865, determined to remove all insane from almshouses to State institutions, but the great expense of their transfer checked the movement, and it was thirty years before it was able to assume the exclusive care of all insane not in private hospitals. In 1900 Massachusetts provided that all insane should be cared for by the State. The Commissioners of Public Charities of Illinois in 1907 made a thorough report on the conditions surrounding the insane in county almshouses. Among the fifteen reasons for complete State care, they enumerate the following:—

Because, while this General Assembly has been sitting, a girl in an Illinois almshouse has been hobbled with chains, padlocked to her bare ankles, because her stamping disturbed other inmates in the insane department.

Because, . . . a rude box, with wooden slats across the top, supplied with iron hinges, hasps, and bolt, is ready, in a certain almshouse, to receive any insane man who becomes unruly, a service it has performed for others.

Because, to-day there are almshouses in Illinois where steel handcuffs, barred cells, cages, and padlocks are in service when required to restrain the insane. Imagine an insane girl 20 years old locked in a steel cage! This happened recently in Stark County.

Because, in 54 almshouses there is no provision to separate the insane from plain paupers.

Because, any insane resident of Illinois should have just as good care as any other insane resident.

The State of Illinois is, however, no worse than a number of others in respect to abuses in almshouses. In a thorough and impartial investigation of the almshouses of Missouri, Professor Ellwood found over 1177 insane persons—about one-third of all inmates—in almshouses, and a tendency toward an increased almshouse care of the indigent lunatic.

Of the treatment of the insane he says:—

I learned of one almshouse superintendent who declared that he found the horsewhip to be the most efficacious means of quieting insane inmates. In another, I found that an insane woman had been strapped in bed for over six years. According to the first annual report of the Missouri State Board of Charities, on one county poor-farm an insane man was found who had been kept in a stockade, open to the sky, winter and summer, with hardly a shred of clothing on him, for several years. According to the same report another insane man was found chained to a stump in a poorhouse yard. . . . In general, my investigation disclosed that in a majority of Missouri almshouses there are cells for their confinement; that in many cases manacles and chains were put on the insane, under which restraint they are kept for years; and that they are, if not brutally treated, grossly neglected.

Professor Ellwood places the responsibility for this condition of things where it belongs, when he says that the superintendents have to manage as best they can the persons turned over to them by the county authorities, and that the blame ultimately rests with the people of the whole State, who permit by law the commitment of the indigent insane to almshouses.

Many States have entered upon a policy of State care, and then failed to make appropriations large enough to carry out such a policy. The result has been that, after some State institutions were built, a large number of insane still remain in the almshouses, because the special institutions are overcrowded and can receive no more. This is practically the situation in Illinois. In California the lunacy commissioners frequently refuse to adjudge an almshouse inmate insane, because the State institutions are so overcrowded that they say he is better left in the almshouse.

A group which should manifestly be excluded from the almshouse is the pauper-delinquent. In most States, tramps and disorderly persons are accommodated here because of the lack of any place of safe-keeping between the almshouse and the jail. In the more advanced States such persons are sent to workhouses or reformatories. The disgrace that attaches to almshouse relief will not be lifted until differentiation has been carried a step farther, and there is some classification of inmates on the basis of character as disclosed in individual and family history. Reformatory institutions to which habitual drunkards, prostitutes, and other misdemeanants can be sent, and in which they must remain until reformation or death supervenes,, would relieve the almshouse of many inmates, and the worthy poor of a very considerable portion of the disgrace which attaches to going there.

The effect of the drafting off of the special classes to other institutions is seen in the altered character of the residuum. The general average age of 81,412 paupers admitted in 1904 was 49.4 years—much higher than formerly; the largest proportion admitted in 1904 is found in the age group, 60 to 64 years, and 36 percent of the total admissions were above 60. Of the paupers in all almshouses in the United States in 1904, 43 percent were over 60 years of age; while in Missouri, where the inmates of almshouses are still of all classes, the percent of persons over 60 is only 37.

When carried far enough the policy of differentiation leaves in the almshouses only the infirm and incapable.

A classification on the basis of habits, character, and a degree of refinement is usually not attempted, although it is of great importance to the inmates. It is a great hardship for the respectable who have seen better days to associate with the intemperate, diseased, and disreputable; but aside from this obvious demarcation, the almshouse inmate is often sensitive about social distinctions and has as strong preferences as to companionship as other people. Such peculiarities must be considered if the inmates are to be kept comfortable, and the utmost tact, patience, and ingenuity are required to adjust these relations satisfactorily. In the San Francisco almshouse, instead of wards they have a large number of rooms—a form of construction which is undesirable, but which was at one time used to good purpose to give the self-respecting and improvable cases a semi-privacy which they valued.

A very prevalent evil in the management of American almshouses is lack of a work test, and a failure to enforce proper discipline among the inmates. While in some places an energetic and specially capable official may overcome all obstacles and enforce discipline and compel work, yet such an undertaking is usually discouraged, or at least not encouraged, by the authorities, and the sentiment of the community and the nature of legislation are usually such as to make this course difficult. Under the average superintendent, as a rule, it costs more to set the inmates of an almshouse to work than their work is worth. That is, a given number of inmates can be supported more cheaply in idleness than when they are put to work. It is for this reason that the labor in the English "workhouse" has degenerated so persistently into mere task-work.

The principal advantage in obliging all inmates capable of doing anything to work consists in the deterrent influence of this policy upon would-be applicants. Its influence is especially valuable in preventing tramps from using the institution as a winter club-house. In most almshouses the main part of the work that can be offered to men is on a farm or in the garden. This kind of work is unavailable in the winter, just at the time when a rigid work test is most essential. In many institutions no inmate is required to work unless he is willing to do so. Some superintendents seem to think it is the height of brutality to ask an inmate to do anything against his will; and such service as can be utilized is usually obtained by offering extra rations of food and tobacco. The amount of patience, ingenuity, and energy necessary to make such work profitable, and to fit such laborers—who for the most part have failed to fit anywhere else in the industrial world—into some task suited to their limited capacity, requires a degree of ability and moral fibre rarely to be found in an almshouse official. Under the management of Mrs. Ellen Armstrong Weaver, the women of San Francisco almshouse reached a high degree of industrial efficiency, considering their capacities. A prostitute nursed a bedridden girl to whom she had become attached; a deaf and difficult old woman washed, dressed, and fed, as if she were a baby, a deaf, dumb, and blind girl; a woman nearly blind and knotted with rheumatism braided rag rugs; a feeble-minded Swedish woman made fine lace; a well-educated woman did fine sewing and read the daily paper aloud to the women in the sewing room. All the sewing and mending for the 900 inmates, and all the cleaning of the women's wards, was done by the women.

From the side of the inmates, work for all is desirable because they are happier for having it. About the only happy persons one finds in an almshouse are those who are occupied. Idleness conduces to restlessness, sensuality, bad temper, and various forms of nervous disorder. In alms-houses, as well as in prisons, insane asylums, and other kinds of institu-tions, discipline is doubly hard when the inmates are idle. That idleness in and of itself brings misery, can be seen by any one who passes through one of our Soldiers' Homes, especially the magnificent one for soldiers of the regular army at Washington. So well is this fact now ascertained that special societies are formed in the large cities for giving employment to the inmates of the great public institutions. Efforts in this direction were begun in 1893 at the City Hospital on Blackwell's Island, New York, by the County Visiting Committee of the State Charities Associa-tion, and during the last three years the work has been greatly enlarged. Teachers have been sent to municipal hospitals and homes for the aged and infirm to instruct the inmates in a variety of handicrafts. The effect of employment in Ward L, a ward at the home for the aged and infirm on Blackwell's Island, is thus described:—

Ward L is the ward devoted to the crippled, paralyzed, rheumatic, epileptic cripples. . . . I found sixty men sitting there doing nothing, the very picture of desolation. . . . To speak a cheery word in such an atmosphere seemed mockery. . . . There has come about, in process of time, what I call the transformation or the transfiguration of Ward L, and all this has taken place through the introduc-tion of the bead work. . . . With some persuasion, they induced one or two to enter into the work. The interest spread until 20 out of the 60 were engaged in it. . . . They were impatient when the supply of beads gave out. The clamor was for more beads and more looms. The whole character of the ward was changed. A joke was in order, cheeriness and good will were the rule.

Many other handicrafts have been introduced: one man illuminates texts; another has earned a phonograph for the ward by his knitting; others make raffia and osier baskets, Smyrna rugs, and carved wooden articles. The disciplinary and curative results of the work are highly encouraging, and the avenues for the development of the work are many. There ought to be similar societies, or at least similar work done, in our rural communities; if it accomplished nothing else, it would at least interest some of the influential classes in the neglected institutions of the locality.

It is evident that many of the abuses which we have been discussing will still occur even when capable and conscientious officials are in charge, primarily because of neglect by the general public. Professor Ellwood suggests three lines of effort toward correction: the visitation of almshouses by local boards of visitors, inspection of state officials, *i.e.*

Board of Charities, and mandatory and prohibitive legislation. The three methods will naturally be evolved and become effective in the order indicated. Following the example of English administration, there is some tendency in America to State control of almshouse administration.

If there could be in American almshouses thorough investigation of all applicants for admission and all applications for dismissal; if within the institution there could be a thorough discipline and an intelligent and kindly application of the work test to all capable of doing anything at all, there would be no danger that almshouses would be overcrowded; if in addition there could be a higher class of officials in charge, if the standard of medical care and nursing could be raised to that of the general hospital, and if some means of relieving the dreary monotony of the life were afforded, the almshouse would afford cleanly and honorable relief to the real children of misfortune.

Part Two

---

*THE URBAN POOR
IN THE PROGRESSIVE ERA*
1890–1920

5

Rediscovering Poverty:
Robert Hunter's contribution

*The most important, cogent, and well-documented Progressive state-
ment on dependency was made by Robert Hunter in his deservedly
famous study,* Poverty. *An associate of Jane Addams at Hull-House,
chairman of the Child Labor Committee in New York, and head of the
city's University Settlement House, Hunter was well equipped to undertake this effort. The results, published in 1904, startled and persuaded
many of his readers and moved them to action. His estimates on the
number of poor in America, his conception of the life cycle of poverty,
his analysis of the causes of the problem, and his recommendations for
amelioration were imaginative and intelligent. His book stands in the
best Progressive tradition of meticulous accumulation of facts and a
clear-headed analysis.*

There are many people in the world who believe that the provisions of
charity are in the present day so generous and varied that no one need
suffer; but, even if this were true, it would not materially lessen the
sorrow of the poor. To thousands and thousands of working-men the
dread of public pauperism is the agony of their lives. The mass of
working-men on the brink of poverty hate charity. Not only their words
convey a knowledge of this fact, but their actions, when in distress, make
it absolutely undeniable. When the poor face the necessity of becoming
paupers, when they must apply for charity if they are to live at all, many
desert their families and enter the ranks of vagrancy; others drink themselves insensible; some go insane; and still others commit suicide.

These are the terrible alternatives which the working people in
poverty accept in preference to pauperism, and yet it is a curious fact,

Robert Hunter, *Poverty* (New York, 1906), excerpts from pp. 2-3, 46-66.

which psychology alone explains, that the very men who will suffer almost anything rather than become paupers are often the very ones who never care to be anything else when once they have become dependent upon alms. When a family once become dependent, the mental agony which they formerly had disappears. Paupers are not, as a rule, unhappy. They are not ashamed; they are not keen to become independent; they are not bitter or discontented. They have passed over the line which separates poverty from pauperism.

This distinction between the poor and paupers may be seen everywhere. There are in all large cities in America and abroad, streets and courts and alleys where a class of people live who have lost all self-respect and ambition, who rarely, if ever, work, who are aimless and drifting, who like drink, who have no thought for their children, and who live more or less contentedly on rubbish and alms.

There are many, many thousand families who receive an income adequate enough to supply the necessities of physical life, but who, for one reason or another,—drink, ignorance, sickness, extravagance, misfortune, or weakness,—do not manage to obtain the essentials for maintaining physical efficiency. There are also many, many thousand families who receive wages so inadequate that no care in spending, however wise it may be, will make them suffice for the family needs. If every penny were spent judiciously, the income would not be sufficient to provide enough of the necessaries to maintain in efficient working order the various members of the family. Such wages are neither "fair" nor "living" wages: they are poverty wages.

It is obvious enough that it is impossible to determine a sum which may be called a "fair" or "living" wage, and which will apply with equal justice to the various parts of the country. There are at least two reasons for this. First, the prices of commodities differ greatly in so large and varied a country. The cost of necessaries is much lower in the South than in the North, and lower in Boston than in New York, and lower in Fort Wayne than in Chicago. When the cost of living in rural and urban districts is compared, it will be found that rents are perhaps responsible for the most considerable difference, and the prices of food and fuel also vary. This variation in the cost of living renders any fixed estimate of a necessary wage for the whole country practically valueless. There is a second element which is sometimes suggested as important when making estimates of the necessary cost of living. If it were indeed an important element, it would make any computation of a necessary income in this country almost impossible. The foreign peoples represented among our working classes are said to require various standards of living. The Jews, for instance, seem to thrive in the most insanitary tenements, despite poor food and insufficient clothing. The Italians and Hungarians seem to do as well as the Irish on a much more limited diet. The Jews, who are most saving and economical in their ways of living, do unquestionably manage to live better on a smaller income than many other races; and in so far as this is true of any race, that race, of course, will be able to live better than another which is less wise in its economies. The same thing is true of different families. But the income of any family must increase with the increase of physical expenditure. And for all races the increase of physical expenditure in the industrial life of America, over what they were formerly required to make in their native countries, is the principal reason for an increased standard of living, and consequently for an increased income. The element of the exhaustion of the physical energies by work must enter into all calculations concerning a required income.

But the Italian, the Jew, or the Hungarian will need good food, warm clothing, and a sanitary tenement, if he is to be paced by the swiftest workman, and rushed by a machine, which must be tended and cannot be stopped to permit a full breath or a moment's rest until the day's labor is done. The present industrial life "takes it out of a man," as the saying is, and it must be put back into a man, or the human machine depreciates and degenerates. It is hardly to be doubted that nearly all men, exhausting themselves at the same rate, require very much the same necessities to keep them in working order. For these reasons I do not consider that there should be different wage standards established for the different nationalities, although, unquestionably, the standards for the varying parts of the country should vary in relation to the varying cost of commodities, etc.

Without regard to these apparent differences in the standards of living required by different races and the varying costs of commodities, there are, nevertheless, a number of opinions concerning the necessary income for a family of average size. It was shown by the Massachusetts Bureau of Statistics that it takes $754 a year for a family of five persons to live on. John Mitchell has said that a minimum wage of $600 a year is necessary in the anthracite district for a worker with a family of ordinary size. The New York Bureau of Labor considers that $10 a week or $520 a year is inadequate for city workmen. It is unnecessary to say that, if any one of these estimates were taken as the standard necessary wage, an enormous number of working people, practically all of the unskilled and a considerable percentage of the skilled, would fall under the poverty line. However desirable and however socially valuable an

Room in a tenement flat, 1910. The cramped, airless, overcrowded conditions in which immigrants lived, bed squeezed next to bed, around a primitive gas stove, emerge vividly in such pictures as this. Photograph by Jessie Tarbox Beals. The Jacob A. Riis Collection, Museum of the City of New York.

income of $754 a year for each family would be, it is unquestionably too high for a fair estimate of the minimum necessary one. While $624 a year is probably not too much for New York City, in view of the excessive rents (consuming in some cases 40 percent of the income) and other almost inevitable expenses such as car fare, etc., it is, nevertheless, an estimate which could not apply, with equal fairness, to all of the industrial states of the North. When one gets below these figures, however, every dollar cut off may mean depriving a family of a necessity of life, in times of health even, and unquestionably in times of sickness.

While the above figures are altogether too inadequate to permit us to base upon them any estimate as to the extent of poverty, it seems reasonable to assume that the wages of the unskilled laborers in this country rarely rise above the poverty line. A certain percentage are doubtless able to maintain a state of physical efficiency while they have work, but when unemployment comes, and their wages cease, a great mass of the unskilled workers find themselves almost immediately in poverty, if not indeed in actual distress.

It can be assumed, therefore, fairly, I think, that the problem of poverty in this country is in ordinary times confined to a certain percentage of the unskilled laborers who have employment, to most unskilled laborers without employment, and to many unemployed skilled workers. In addition to these workers in poverty, there are those who are weak, infirm, unfortunate, the widows, the families of the sick or the injured, and those who are too incompetent, drunken, or vicious, etc., to be reliable workmen. These are, in the main, the classes of persons in poverty in this country.

It is safe to say that a large number of workers, the mass of unskilled and some skilled workmen with their families, fall beneath the poverty line at least three times during their lives,—during childhood, in the prime of life, and at old age. Mr. Rountree, as a result of his inquiries in York, has made the following diagram which illustrates this fact: —

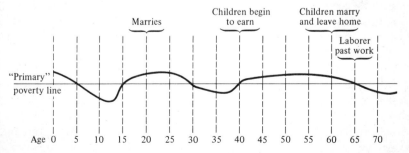

The ordinary increase of family numbers, and the increase or decrease in the family or the capacity for earning, forces the ordinary
working-class family above and beneath this line at certain periods,
despite their will. Some families may always remain beneath the line by
reason of individual or social causes. The curve may at any moment drop
to the bottom by reason of unemployment, infirmity, sickness, exhaustion, or accident. There are many observations of fundamental social
importance that might be made upon the significance of this diagram.
The things of real significance are, however, that the laborer in childhood, when he most needs upbuilding, is in poverty; the wife, when she
is bearing children,—a time when she most needs good food and relief
from want and worries,—is in poverty; the aged, when they should be
in peace and comfort, are in poverty. The reason for this is that the wages
of the ordinary unskilled workman are sufficient to support him and his
wife, and perhaps one or two children. As more children arrive, the
income gradually becomes less and less adequate to meet their needs. The
family drops below the poverty line. They are unable to get sufficient
necessaries. They drop lower and lower as the children grow and larger
supplies of food and clothing and more house-room are needed. Then as
the children begin to earn, the family rises out of poverty again, but it
remains above the poverty line only until the children leave home or
marry, or for some other reason may not continue to aid in the support
of the family. At about this time the father's earnings are likely to drop
off through age or infirmity, and again the parents are in poverty. In this
way laborers of the poorest class pass backward and forward over the
poverty line. The coming of children, the leaving of children, the periods
of employment and of unemployment, the days of health, the days of
sickness, the coming of infirmity, the hour of death,—all of these things
either force the workers of this class backward, or carry them forward
over the poverty line. A large immigration, insanitary tenements, dangerous trades, industrial changes, panics and bankruptcies—in a word, the
slightest economic disturbance or rearrangement—may precipitate them
into misery. The margin of life upon which many of them live is so
narrow that they must toil every possible hour of working time, and the
slightest economic change registers its effect upon this class of workers.

Any one going carefully through the figures which have been given
will agree that poverty is widespread in this country. While it is possible
that New York State has more poverty than other states, it is doubtful
if its poverty is much greater proportionately than that of most of the
industrial states. On the whole, it seems to me that the most conservative
estimate that can fairly be made of the distress existing in the industrial

states is 14 percent of the total population; while in all probability no less than 20 percent of the people in these states, in ordinarily prosperous years, are in poverty. This brings us to the conclusion that one-fifth, or 6,600,000 persons in the states of New York, Massachusetts, Connecticut, New Jersey, Pennsylvania, Ohio, Illinois, Indiana, and Michigan are in poverty. Taking half of this percentage and applying it to the other states, many of which have important industrial communities, as, for instance, Wisconsin, Colorado, California, Rhode Island, etc., the conclusion is that not less than 10,000,000 persons in the United States are in poverty.

The conclusion that about 10,000,000 persons in the United States are in poverty is, of course, largely based upon the figures of distress and of unemployment which have been given; and it would be warranted, were there no other indications of widespread poverty. However, many indications lend themselves to the support of this conclusion. A very large proportion of the working classes are propertyless; a very large mass of people, not only in our largest cities, but in all industrial communities as well, live in most insanitary conditions; there is a high death-rate from tuberculosis in most of our states; a large proportion of the unskilled workers receive, even when employed, wages insufficient to obtain the necessaries for maintaining physical efficiency; from all indications, the number injured and killed in dangerous trades is enormous; and, lastly, there is uncertainty of employment for all classes of workers. About 30 percent of the workers in the industrial states are employed only a part of each year, and, in consequence, suffer a serious decrease in their yearly wages, which, in the case of the unskilled, at least, means to suffer poverty. Nevertheless, the estimate that somewhat over 10,-000,000 persons in this country are in poverty does not indicate that our poverty is as great proportionately as that of England. But it should be said that a careful examination would, in all probability, disclose a greater poverty than the estimate indicates.

There is unquestionably a poverty which men deserve, and by such poverty men are perhaps taught needful lessons. It would be unwise to legislate out of existence, even were it possible to do so, that poverty which penalizes the voluntarily idle and vicious. In other words, there are individual causes of poverty which should be eradicated by the individual himself, with such help as his family, the teachers, and the preachers may give him. For him society may be able to do little or nothing. The poor which are always to be with us, are, it seems to me, in poverty of their own making.

But as surely as this is true, there are also the poor which we must not have always with us. The poor of this latter class are, it seems to me, the mass of the poor; they are bred of miserable and unjust social conditions, which punish the good and the pure, the faithful and industrious, the slothful and the vicious, all alike. We may not, by going into the homes of the poor, be able to determine which ones are in poverty because of individual causes, or which are in poverty because of social wrongs; but we can see, by looking about us, that men are brought into misery by the action of social and economic forces. And the wrongful action of such social and economic forces is a preventable thing. For instance, to mention but a few, the factories, the mines, the workshops, and the railroads must be forced to cease killing the father or the boy or the girl whose wages alone suffice to keep the family from poverty; or, if the workers must be injured and killed, then the family must at least be fairly compensated, in so far as that be possible. Tenements may be made sanitary by the action of the community, and thereby much of this breeding of wretched souls and ruined bodies stopped. A broader education may be provided for the masses, so that the street child may be saved from idleness, crime, and vagrancy, and the working child saved from ruinous labor. Immigration may be regulated constructively rather than negatively, if not, for a time, restricted to narrower limits. Employment may be made less irregular and fairer wages assured. These are, of course, but a few of the many things which can be done to make less unjust and miserable the conditions in which about 10,000,000 of our people live.

6

How the Other Half Lives: Jacob Riis describes New York's Lower East Side

Of all the people who described urban poverty in the Progressive era, Jacob Riis was probably the best known and the most widely read. Himself an immigrant to this country from Denmark, Riis became a police reporter for a New York newspaper, and his pursuit of a story

Jacob A. Riis, *How the Other Half Lives: Studies Among the Tenements of New York* (New York, 1890), pp. 104–105, 121–126, 130–135.

*frequently led him from police headquarters into the slums. In countless
articles and books he reported on the poverty and the wretchedness he
found there. A man of incredible energy and great talents, he not only
roused the conscience of the nation but helped secure a good deal of
ameliorative legislation. He did not altogether escape some of the prejudices of his new country, but on balance, his was a positive and major
contribution to the Progressives' efforts to improve the lot of the poor.*

The tenements grow taller, and the gaps in their ranks close up rapidly
as we cross the Bowery and, leaving Chinatown and the Italians behind,
invade the Hebrew quarter. Baxter Street, with its interminable rows of
old clothes shops and its brigades of pullers-in—nicknamed "the Bay"
in honor, perhaps, of the tars who lay to there after a cruise to stock up
their togs, or maybe after the "schooners" of beer plentifully bespoke in
that latitude—Bayard Street, with its synagogues and its crowds, gave
us a foretaste of it. No need of asking here where we are. The jargon of
the street, the signs of the sidewalk, the manner and dress of the people,
their unmistakable physiognomy, betray their race at every step. Men
with queer skull-caps, venerable beard, and the outlandish long-skirted
kaftan of the Russian Jew, elbow the ugliest and the handsomest women
in the land. The contrast is startling. The old women are hags; the young,
houris. Wives and mothers at sixteen, at thirty they are old. So
thoroughly has the chosen people crowded out the Gentiles in the Tenth
Ward that, when the great Jewish holidays come around every year, the
public schools in the district have practically to close up. Of their thousands of pupils scarce a handful come to school. Nor is there any suspicion that the rest are playing hookey. They stay honestly home to
celebrate. There is no mistaking it: we are in Jewtown.
    A friend of mine who manufactures cloth once boasted to me that
nowadays, on cheap clothing, New York "beats the world." "To what,"
I asked, "do you attribute it?" "To the cutter's long knife and the Polish
Jew," he said. Which of the two has cut deepest into the workman's
wages is not a doubtful question. Practically the Jew has monopolized
the business since the battle between East Broadway and Broadway
ended in a complete victory for the East Side and cheap labor, and
transferred to it the control of the trade in cheap clothing. Yet, not
satisfied with having won the field, he strives as hotly with his own for
the profit of half a cent as he fought with his Christian competitor for
the dollar. If the victory is a barren one, the blame is his own. His price
is not what he can get, but the lowest he can live for and underbid his

neighbor. Just what that means we shall see. The manufacturer knows it, and is not slow to take advantage of his knowledge. He makes him hungry for work by keeping it from him as long as possible; then drives the closest bargain he can with the sweater.

Many harsh things have been said of the "sweater," that really apply to the system in which he is a necessary, logical link. It can at least be said of him that he is no worse than the conditions that created him. The sweater is simply the middleman, the sub-contractor, a workman like his fellows, perhaps with the single distinction from the rest that he knows a little English; perhaps not even that, but with the accidental possession of two or three sewing-machines, or of credit enough to hire them, as his capital, who drums up work among the clothing-houses. Of workmen he can always get enough. Every ship-load from German ports brings them to his door in droves, clamoring for work. The sun sets upon the day of the arrival of many a Polish Jew, finding him at work in an East Side tenement, treading the machine and "learning the trade." Often there are two, sometimes three, sets of sweaters on one job. They work with the rest when they are not drumming up trade, driving their "hands" as they drive their machine, for all they are worth, and making a profit on their work, of course, though in most cases not nearly as extravagant a percentage, probably, as is often supposed. If it resolves itself into a margin of five or six cents, or even less, on a dozen pairs of boys' trousers, for instance, it is nevertheless enough to make the contractor with his thrifty instincts independent. The workman growls, not at the hard labor, or poor pay, but over the pennies another is coining out of his sweat, and on the first opportunity turns sweater himself, and takes his revenge by driving an even closer bargain than his rival tyrant, thus reducing his profits.

The sweater knows well that the isolation of the workman in his helpless ignorance is his sure foundation, and he has done what he could —with merciless severity where he could—to smother every symptom of awakening intelligence in his slaves. In this effort to perpetuate his despotism he has had the effectual assistance of his own system and the sharp competition that keeps the men on starvation wages; of their constitutional greed, that will not permit the sacrifice of temporary advantage, however slight, for permanent good; and above all, of the hungry hordes of immigrants to whom no argument appeals save the cry for bread. Within very recent times he has, however, been forced to partial surrender by the organization of the men to a considerable extent into trades unions, and by experiments in co-operation, under intelligent leadership, that presage the sweater's doom. But as long as the ignorant crowds continue to come and to herd in these tenements, his grip can never be shaken off. And the supply across the seas is apparently inexhaustible. Every fresh persecution of the Russian or Polish Jew on his native soil starts greater hordes hitherward to confound economical problems, and recruit the sweater's phalanx. The curse of bigotry and ignorance reaches halfway across the world, to sow its bitter seed in fertile soil in the East Side tenements. If the Jew himself was to blame for the resentment he aroused over there, he is amply punished. He gathers the first-fruits of the harvest here.

The bulk of the sweater's work is done in the tenements, which the law that regulates factory labor does not reach. To the factories themselves that are taking the place of the rear tenements in rapidly growing numbers, letting in bigger day-crowds than those the health officers banished, the tenement shops serve as a supplement through which the law is successfully evaded. Ten hours is the legal work-day in the factories, and nine o'clock the closing hour at the latest. Forty-five minutes at least must be allowed for dinner, and children under sixteen must not be employed unless they can read and write English; none at all under fourteen. The very fact that such a law should stand on the statute book, shows how desperate the plight of these people. But the tenement has defeated its benevolent purpose. In it the child works unchallenged from the day he is old enough to pull a thread. There is no such thing as a dinner hour; men and women eat while they work, and the "day" is lengthened at both ends far into the night. Factory hands take their work with them at the close of the lawful day to eke out their scanty earnings by working overtime at home. Little chance on this ground for the campaign of education that alone can bring the needed relief; small wonder that there are whole settlements on this East Side where English is practically an unknown tongue, though the people be both willing and anxious to learn. "When shall we find time to learn?" asked one of them of me once. I owe him the answer yet.

Take the Second Avenue Elevated Railroad at Chatham Square and ride up half a mile through the sweater's district. Every open window of the big tenements, that stand like a continuous brick wall on both sides of the way, gives you a glimpse of one of these shops as the train speeds by. Men and women bending over their machines, or ironing clothes at the window, half-naked. Proprieties do not count on the East Side; nothing counts that cannot be converted into hard cash. The road is like a big gangway through an endless work-room where vast multitudes are

Ready for the Sabbath eve in a coal cellar, Ludlow Street on the Lower East Side, early 1890's. Jacob Riis publicized the plight and dignity of the immigrant poor, not only through his writings but with his photographs. Diligently and imaginatively he recorded scenes of ghetto life, making his countrymen see the poor as people. Photograph by Jacob A. Riis. The Jacob A. Riis Collection, Museum of the City of New York.

forever laboring. Morning, noon, or night, it makes no difference; the scene is always the same. At Rivington Street let us get off and continue our trip on foot. It is Sunday evening west of the Bowery. Here, under the rule of Mosaic Law, the week of work is under full headway, its first day far spent. The hucksters' wagons are absent or stand idle at the curb; the saloons admit the thirsty crowds through the side-door labelled "Family Entrance;" a tin sign in a store-window announces that a "Sunday School" gathers in stray children of the new dispensation; but beyond these things there is little to suggest the Christian Sabbath. Men stagger along the sidewalk groaning under heavy burdens of unsewn garments, or enormous black bags stuffed full of finished coats and trousers. Let us follow one to his home and see how Sunday passes in a Ludlow Street tenement.

Up two flights of dark stairs, three, four, with new smells of cabbage, of onions, of frying fish, on every landing, whirring sewing machines behind closed doors betraying what goes on within, to the door that opens to admit the bundle and the man. A sweater, this, in a small way. Five men and a woman, two young girls, not fifteen, and a boy who says unasked that he is fifteen, and lies in saying it, are at the machines sewing knickerbockers, "knee-pants" in the Ludlow Street dialect. The floor is littered ankle-deep with half-sewn garments. In the alcove, on a couch of many dozens of "pants" ready for the finisher, a bare-legged baby with pinched face is asleep. A fence of piled-up clothing keeps him from rolling off on the floor. The faces, hands, and arms to the elbows of everyone in the room are black with the color of the cloth on which they are working. The boy and the woman alone look up at our entrance. The girls shoot sidelong glances, but at a warning look from the man with the bundle they tread their machines more energetically than ever. The men do not appear to be aware even of the presence of a stranger.

They are "learners," all of them, says the woman, who proves to be the wife of the boss, and have "come over" only a few weeks ago. She is disinclined to talk at first, but a few words in her own tongue from our guide set her fears, whatever they are, at rest, and she grows almost talkative. The learners work for week's wages, she says. How much do they earn? She shrugs her shoulders with an expressive gesture. The workers themselves, asked in their own tongue, say indifferently, as though the question were of no interest: from two to five dollars. The children—there are four of them—are not old enough to work. The oldest is only six. They turn out one hundred and twenty dozen "knee-pants" a week, for which the manufacturer pays seventy cents a dozen. Five cents a dozen is the clear profit, but her own and her husband's work brings the family earnings up to twenty-five dollars a week, when they have work all the time. But often half the time is put in looking for it. They work no longer than to nine o'clock at night, from daybreak. There are ten machines in the room; six are hired at two dollars a month. For the two shabby, smoke-begrimed rooms, one somewhat larger than ordinary, they pay twenty dollars a month. She does not complain, though "times are not what they were, and it costs a good deal to live." Eight dollars a week for the family of six and two boarders. How do they do it? She laughs, as she goes over the bill of fare, at the silly question: Bread, fifteen cents a day, of milk two quarts a day at four cents a quart, one pound of meat for dinner at twelve cents, butter one pound a week at "eight cents a quarter of a pound." Coffee, potatoes, and pickles complete the list. At the least calculation probably, this sweater's family hoards up thirty dollars a month, and in a few years will own a tenement somewhere and profit by the example set by their landlord in rent-collecting. It is the way the savings of Jewtown are universally invested, and with the natural talent of its people for commercial speculation the investment is enormously profitable.

We have reached Broome Street. The hum of industry in this six-story tenement on the corner leaves no doubt of the aspect Sunday wears within it. One flight up, we knock at the nearest door. The grocer, who keeps the store, lives on the "stoop," the first floor in East Side parlance. In this room a suspender-maker sleeps and works with his family of wife and four children. For a wonder there are no boarders. His wife and eighteen-year-old daughter share in the work, but the girl's eyes are giving out from the strain. Three months in the year, when work is very brisk, the family makes by united efforts as high as fourteen and fifteen dollars a week. The other nine months it averages from three to four dollars. The oldest boy, a young man, earns from four to six dollars in an Orchard Street factory, when he has work. The rent is ten dollars a month for the room and a miserable little coop of a bedroom where the old folks sleep. The girl makes her bed on the lounge in the front room; the big boys and the children sleep on the floor. Coal at ten cents a small pail, meat at twelve cents a pound, one and a half pound of butter a week at thirty-six cents, and a quarter of a pound of tea in the same space of time, are items of their housekeeping account as given by the daughter. Milk at four and five cents a quart, "according to quality." The sanitary authorities know what that means, know how miserably inadequate is the fine of fifty or a hundred dollars for the murder done in cold blood by the wretches who poison the babes of these tenements with the stuff that is half water, or swill. Their defense is that the demand is for "cheap milk." Scarcely a wonder that this suspender-maker will hardly be able to save up the *dot* for his daughter, without which she stands no chance of marrying in Jewtown, even with her face that would be pretty had it a healthier tinge.

Up under the roof three men are making boys' jackets at twenty cents a piece, of which the sewer takes eight, the ironer three, the finisher five cents, and the buttonhole-maker two and a quarter, leaving a cent and three-quarters to pay for the drumming up, the fetching and bringing back of the goods. They bunk together in a room for which they pay eight dollars a month. All three are single here, that is: their wives are on the other side yet, waiting for them to earn enough to send for them. Their breakfast, eaten at the work-bench, consists of a couple of rolls at a cent a piece, and a draught of water, milk when business has been very good, a square meal at noon in a restaurant, and the morning meal over again at night. This square meal, that is the evidence of a very liberal disposition on the part of the consumer, is an affair of more than ordinary note; it may be justly called an institution. I know of a couple of restaurants at the lower end of Orchard Street that are favorite resorts for the Polish Jews, who remember the injunction that the ox that treadeth out the corn shall not be muzzled. Being neighbors, they are rivals of course, and cutting under. When I was last there one gave a dinner of soup, meat-stew, bread, pie, pickles, and a "schooner" of beer for thirteen cents; the other charged fifteen cents for a similar dinner, but with two schooners of beer and a cigar, or a cigarette, as the extra inducement. The two cents had won the day, however, and the thirteen-cent restaurant did such a thriving business that it was about to spread out into the adjoining store to accommodate the crowds of customers. At this rate the lodger of Jewtown can "live like a lord," as he says himself, for twenty-five cents a day, including the price of his bed, that ranges all the way from thirty to forty and fifty cents a week, and save money, no matter what his earnings. He does it, too, so long as work is to be had at any price, and by the standard he sets up Jewtown must abide.

It has thousands upon thousands of lodgers who help to pay its extortionate rents. At night there is scarce a room in all the district that has not one or more of them, some above half a score, sleeping on cots, or on the floor. It is idle to speak of privacy in these "homes." The term carries no more meaning with it than would a lecture on social ethics to an audience of Hottentots. The picture is not overdrawn. In fact, in presenting the home life of these people I have been at some pains to avoid the extreme of privation, taking the cases just as they came to hand on the safer middle-ground of average earnings. Yet even the direst apparent poverty in Jewtown, unless dependent on absolute lack of work, would, were the truth known, in nine cases out of ten have a silver lining in the shape of a margin in bank.

These are the economical conditions that enable my manufacturing friend to boast that New York can "beat the world" on cheap clothing. In support of his claim he told me that a single Bowery firm last year sold fifteen thousand suits at $1.95 that averaged in cost $1.12½. With the material at fifteen cents a yard, he said, children's suits of assorted sizes can be sold at wholesale for seventy-five cents, and boys' cape overcoats at the same price. They are the same conditions that have perplexed the committee of benevolent Hebrews in charge of Baron de Hirsch's munificent gift of ten thousand dollars a month for the relief of the Jewish poor in New York. To find proper channels through which to pour this money so that it shall effect its purpose without pauperizing, and without perpetuating the problem it is sought to solve, by attracting still greater swarms, is indeed no easy task. Colonization has not in the past been a success with these people. The great mass of them are too gregarious to take kindly to farming, and their strong commercial instinct hampers the experiment. To herd them in model tenements, though it relieve the physical suffering in a measure, would be to treat a symptom of the disease rather than strike at its root, even if land could be got cheap enough where they gather to build on a sufficiently large scale to make the plan a success. Trade schools for manual training could hardly be made to reach the adults, who in addition would have to be supported for months while learning. For the young this device has proved most excellent under the wise management of the United Hebrew Charities, an organization that gathers to its work the best thought and effort of many of our most public-spirited citizens. One, or all, of these plans may be tried, probably will. I state but the misgivings as to the result of some of the practical minds that have busied themselves with the problem. Its keynote evidently is the ignorance of the immigrants. They must be taught the language of the country they have chosen as their home, as the first and most necessary step. Whatever may follow, that is essential, absolutely vital. That done, it may well be that the case in its new aspect will not be nearly so hard to deal with.

Evening has worn into night as we take up our homeward journey through the streets, now no longer silent. The thousands of lighted windows in the tenements glow like dull red eyes in a huge stone wall. From every door multitudes of tired men and women pour forth for a half-hour's rest in the open air before sleep closes the eyes weary with incessant working. Crowds of half-naked children tumble in the street and on the sidewalk, or doze fretfully on the stone steps. As we stop in front of a tenement to watch one of these groups, a dirty baby in a single brief garment—yet a sweet, human little baby despite its dirt and tatters —tumbles off the lowest step, rolls over once, clutches my leg with unconscious grip, and goes to sleep on the flagstones, its curly head pillowed on my boot.

7

Law and Order in the Slums:
Robert Woods surveys Boston's immigrants

Part of the contribution of settlement-house workers like Robert Woods was to educate the American public to life in the immigrant ghettos. The founder of Boston's South End House (1892) and organizer of the National Federation of Settlements (1911), Woods not only created and administered clubs for the young and classes for their parents but sparked a good deal of research into conditions in the city's slums. On the whole, the investigators drew sympathetic portraits, empathizing with the immigrants and the difficulties they confronted. But as Woods's descriptions below reveal, an undercurrent of anxiety for the stability of American communities and a fear of the disruptiveness of immigrant behavior were also common. Americans in Process illuminates both the experience of poverty and the complex attitudes of the Progressives toward it.

The outer aspect of great cities, even of contrasted American and European cities, grows less dissimilar year by year. Nevertheless, enough of the Old World can yet be found in some sections of the North and West Ends so that the stranger coming into these parts almost forgets that he is in America. The language heard on every side is in a foreign tongue, and the palpitating interest and variety of the street life give one a feeling that he is having a glimpse into some far-off town or village. A wealth of song and story is brought to mind by some word or gesture, a Neapolitan lilt or two belligerents biting thumbs even as did the ill-fated Montague and Capulet.

The light-heartedness of the Italians, and their keen love of pleasure, make an atmosphere so full of gayety that a spectator for the time is led to overlook the many discomforts which must naturally fall to the share of a people so closely crowded together. But perhaps these discomforts affect the Italians less than any other race, for they love the open air and

Robert Woods, *Americans in Process* (Boston, 1902) excerpts pp. 190-211, 224, 232-241, 244, 252-253.

the general fellowship of their kind, and every possible moment is spent beyond the confines of the house walls. The first glimpse of spring brings with it thronging streets, crowded doorways and well-filled open windows.

In winter the streets are comparatively quiet. Doorstep and window chats are transferred to the living-room. Small quarters do not limit sociability. It is rare that a family is permitted to spend the evening alone. Some lodger or boarder friend from the neighborhood drops in, and over the glass of wine or mug of beer tales of the home country are told. The men of the family enjoy the life of the neighboring saloon, where, aside from the social drink, various games can be played. It is at one of these saloons that the favorite game of peasant Italy, "bocce," is played almost every evening, and as this is the one place in Boston where it may be found, there are many spectators. The older people rarely mingle with people of another nationality, except the better educated ones, who sometimes go to enjoy a good play at one of the uptown theatres. The operas, too, and many of the best concerts are attended by those who can afford such luxuries. Those who saw the hearty and appreciative welcome which her countrymen in the upper gallery gave to Signora Duse will never forget it.

Jew and Italian are near neighbors in the North End. The two neighborhoods touch, but the line between them is sharp, the atmosphere of each absolutely alien to the other. The genial, carefree expression of the men in the Italian district is suddenly missed when the border-line into the Jewish quarter is crossed. There we find the shrewd yet ingratiating look which so often means financial gain at any cost, even at the cost of self-respect. This, in the long-bearded Jew of the older generation, is clothed with a cover of conscious martyrdom. Then, too, from the Italian woman, always hard worked, yet thoroughly alive to varying interests, we turn to the forlorn, almost degraded woman of the Jewish household, whose every action reveals the narrow, oppressive atmosphere which she has breathed for so many generations. The great intellectual gifts of this race have been far from equally shared between the sexes. Book learning for the Jewish woman has in the past been thought unnecessary, and the lack of education is keenly written in the faces of the older women.

Resemblance between these two localities lies merely in the crowding of the streets and the incessant trading thereon. While there is much that is of peculiar interest in Jewish life, there can be, where there is so much squalor, but little real beauty. On the streets the commercial instinct is everywhere evident. The dangling of old clothes, the pawnshop windows filled with everything that could possibly be turned into money, the baskets, barrels and carts of foul-smelling fish, do not add to the charm of the scene, and are hardly offset by the boxes of green vegetables and ripe fruits which border the sidewalk; but the human element, the owners of shops and wagons, with their forlorn expressions of anxiety to sell, the patriarchal old men, the intent, purchasing housekeepers, and the energetic young salesmen who do not hesitate to drag customers into the shops, are of never-failing interest. The general dinginess of the locality is perhaps centred in the unattractive Jewish restaurants and meat shops. The windows of the former are filled with indifferent eatables, and from the grimy ceilings often hang festoons of long sausages, while the meat shops display a great variety of fresh meats, some of the most loathsome parts of the fowls and carcasses being placed on the counters in such quantities as to lead one to suppose that they are in great demand, if not looked upon as delicacies. These eating saloons and meat shops contrast strangely with the occasional corner or basement where second-hand Hebrew books are sold, and where the beautiful parchment and leather bindings tempt one to dream of their scholarly past. Fine old brass candlesticks are often for sale in these places. It is to such bits of brightness that this region owes much of its small aspect of cheer.

During the warm weather the streets teem with life. Every doorway is crowded with the older people, while the sidewalks and highways are populous with children, some in an almost undressed condition. They are all great lovers of music, and the advent of any musical instrument sets the youthful feet at once to dancing. The Jewish children dance as if by instinct, and their correct ear for music makes them apt pupils in the sidewalk branch of the art.

There can be no greater contrast drawn between Jews and Italians than in their several ways of celebrating holidays and feasts,—the Italian seeking the air and sun on every occasion, the Jew finding sanctuary in his home for festival and rite; yet it is during the various holidays that the Jewish quarters appear to best advantage. These seasons first make themselves apparent to the Christian world by the festal gowns of the women and children. Among the older Jewish women, especially among those belonging to the Orthodox church, the married ones are easily distinguished by the coarse brown wig often made of some material other than human hair, the absence of which after marriage was formerly looked upon as a mark of immodesty. At times a kerchief or a piece of black cotton lace is used to take the place of the wig; but like many other customs, this of covering the head is disappearing before the general Americanizing tendency.

While the Jews are a people having large families, their inborn love of money-making leads them to crowd into the smallest quarters. Families having very respectable bank accounts have been known to occupy cellar rooms where damp and cold streaked the walls. Yet it is in their homes that the Jews rise to their best level. The family life is usually worthy of admiration. The parents are devoted guardians. The father feels strongly the responsibility of instructing his sons and daughters in the laws and customs of the faith. The mother is the affectionate and interested companion of her children, big or little. Even in the homes of the poorest, candles are always lighted for the Friday evening service, and the family assemble for the beginning of the Sabbath. On Saturday, after returning from the synagogue, the day is spent in visiting or receiving calls. The neighbor, with the ever-convenient shawl thrown over her head, comes to have a chat and a glass of tea from the steaming samovar.

There is one note always discernible in the daily life of the foreign peoples of the North and West Ends, and nowhere is it clearer than in their moments of leisure. In spite of the survival of types, in spite of the inevitable longing for the home country, in spite of all the differences of race and tradition, the strongest and most impelling of motives, the most cherished of ideals, is that of becoming American. Color, melody, comfort and content—indeed some of the sterner virtues themselves—are sacrificed before this Goddess of Democracy whose protecting arms, these people from foreign lands have been led to believe, will afford them and theirs a share in the joys of life. Not so ugly as it seems at first glance, then, is the ready adaptability with which the newcomers take on the least commendable of our customs. The Italian girl who forgets her cadenza and sings the most nasal of street songs, her mother who prefers the scrubbing of offices to the handicraft of her ancestors, her father who forsakes his native wines for beer, are unconscious idealists; and beneath one and all of these humble acts lies a meaning which we who are born to our inheritance would do well to prize. " 'Tis not the custom of the country" is a phrase that is changing the manners of the centuries and shaking the beliefs of ages past.

The North End, with the addition of the North Union Station and one half of the great market region near Dock Square go to make up Police Division 1.

It appears that out of the 4875 persons arrested in the division during the twelve months ending December 1, 1901, fully 3250 did not belong in Boston at all, and only about 825 resided at the North End. In view of the fact that this last-mentioned number comprises all who were arrested for any offense whatever, including drunkenness, in a population of nearly 30,000, it seems astonishingly small. According to the police showing, therefore, the North End, so far from being exceptionally lawless, is, on the contrary, law-abiding to a degree that is not generally supposed.

Certain measures recently taken by the police in the North End have had an important bearing on the moral welfare of this section of the city. One of these was the closing of the last of the dance halls in the spring of 1900. These dance halls for a number of years before they were shut up had been the sole survivals characteristic of that period in the history of the district when the moral tide was at its very lowest ebb. This period, which covered fifteen or twenty years from about the middle of the century which has just closed, presents a picture of vicious and criminal activity that seems incredible to one familiar with the North End of the present day.

The immigrants, who form the characteristic resident population of the North End, have brought certain evil ways of their own; they are also inevitably affected by the moral contagion in their surroundings. The Italian men, especially those of the so-called lower classes, are as a rule very lax morally, and the younger Jewish men are becoming so more and more. Dispensary doctors are able to give evidence of the serious inroads of sexual immorality among their Italian male patients, and to a less extent among their Jewish ones. Several Italians who are unmarried or without their wives may live with a common mistress, ostensibly the housekeeper of the group. This woman may be American or Irish, but is never an Italian.

The women of both races, on the other hand, are chaste with comparatively few exceptions. In the café of the hotel described, a Jewish girl rarely appeared, and an Italian girl almost never. No girl of either race frequented the dance halls. In the case of the Jewish women, chastity is due to religious and home influences; in that of the Italian, there is, in addition, the special protecting and avenging arm of the male members of the family. Any man attempting to lead an Italian woman astray is liable to be visited with a severe penalty from her father, brother or other male relative. Within a few years an Italian was murdered in the North End to prevent his returning to Italy, where he was likely to take up again an illicit relationship in which he had involved a kinswoman of the murderer. The custom still obtains among the Italians that a girl, especially if she is of marriageable age, shall never appear upon the street without a chaperon. The loyalty that goes with race seems to afford the Jewish girl, in a negative way, something of the same protection, for when she does lose her virtue it is seldom or never through a man of her own race. Although many of the Jewish men are bigamists, or at least are supporting more than one woman—one in Boston and one in New York or elsewhere—there is probably no instance in the North End where a Jewish woman is living with a man to whom, in her opinion, she is not properly married.

The number of liquor licenses held in Police Division 1 is 128. Of these, 10 are innholders' licenses, and the remainder, with the exception of 21, are ordinary saloon licenses. Saloons are situated on North street and one or two adjoining streets, and are resorted to for social as well as drinking purposes. Indeed, gaming rather than drinking seems to be their chief attraction. A man buys a glass of light wine or beer, and sitting down at one of the little tables, with which these saloons are well supplied, passes two or three hours in some game of chance with his companions, or in watching the play that may be going on.

The great bulk of saloon patronage at the North End is by nonresidents. The prohibition enactment in places on the north side of Boston sends into the North End by the ferries and the railroads entering the North Union Station a great crowd of people after liquor. These furnish the great majority of the men and women arrested for drunkenness. According to the average ratio between resident and non-resident offenders who fall into the hands of the police here, all but 450 of the 3124 persons taken into custody for drunkenness during the twelve months ending December 1, 1901, had their places of abode outside this section of the city.

Observation tends rather to confirm than to disprove the correctness of this estimate, low as it appears. Excessive drinking is not a characteristic either of the Jews or of the Italians. Indeed, instances of it among the former are extremely rare, and by no means common among the latter. The 3124 arrests for drunkenness referred to included no arrests of Jews and only five or six of Italians.

This moderation in the use of alcoholic drink is easily explained as part of the general frugality that characterizes both races. In the case of the Jews it has a further explanation in the habitual self-control of this people. Perhaps, also, the enlightenment of the race in the matter of health, resulting from the inculcation and observance of their dietary and other hygienic laws, serves as an additional restraint from immoderate drinking.

Strangely enough, crime at the North End, while comparatively small in amount, is to a considerable extent of the most serious character. Between such minor offenses as drunkenness, simple larceny or gaming, and the greatest of all crimes in the eye of the law, there are few gradations. During the last eight years twenty murders, whose perpetrators were found out and convicted, have been committed in this section of the city. Of these murderers fourteen had their homes here. During the twelve months so often referred to, three men were arrested for murder and four for assault with intent to murder—all residents of the North End. Thus a population that on the whole is orderly and law abiding almost to an exceptional degree includes an element of a strikingly different character.

But these murderers and would-be murderers are of a single race, —the Italian, and of the Sicilian or Calabrian branch of that race; and they by no means are representative of the population, or even of the Italian people. Moreover, while some of them premeditated their crimes, the majority acted on the impulse of the moment; hence are homicides rather than murderers. Of the twenty convicted of murder within the last eight years, only one was convicted of murder in the first degree. Some of the murders were to satisfy a blood feud perhaps of long standing, or to avenge an insult or injury to a kinswoman of the murderer. Indications of the Mafia are to be found at the North End, but none of the murders here have been traced directly or indirectly to that organization.

Other than murder, and assault with intent to murder, there is but little serious crime at the North End. Of course, where so many saloons stand open to the passing throngs, there are more or less assaults—289 in the year of which the police statistics have been given. Burglary is of infrequent occurrence, a district of this description offering but few inducements to the professional thief. Italian boys, and to a less extent Jewish boys, steal junk whenever an opportunity presents itself, and commit other minor offenses. In the Italian rising generation especially, an increasing spirit of lawlessness is very noticeable. Gangs of these boys are beginning to present a serious problem, the so-called "American spirit" appearing to have peculiar possession of them.

The Jews seldom fall into the hands of the police, but they cannot be called a race "void of offense against the public order and welfare." They are especially prone to contentions with one another, as well as with their Gentile neighbors. No other people come to the police station so often to make complaints and demand redress. The ground of their grievances is usually that of abusive or threatening language or some

form of personal violence. In nearly all cases their feelings have been hurt
more than their bodies. Either side will produce witnesses to almost any
number in support of its affirmations or denials. The readiness of the
Jews to commit the crime of perjury has passed into a proverb in this
part of the city. But the characteristic thrift of the race does not desert
the complainants even in the heated recital of their wrongs, real or
fancied; for unless they see in the satisfaction which they demand some
pecuniary gain to themselves, they usually drop their accusations. Isolated and aggravated cases of arson and swindling and other serious
crimes with a similar motive have occurred among the Jews in both the
North and West Ends. There are occasional instances of such crimes
which suspicion ascribes to them, but where evidence has been skillfully
covered up. In general, the law of the land is feared rather than respected
by Jewish immigrants; and a considerable proportion of them show a
tendency, in many petty ways, to violate its spirit while formally observ-
ing the letter. On the whole, however, the Jewish community is law
abiding to a marked degree.

8

Redefining Accidents:
Crystal Eastman recounts workers' experiences

*Until the Progressive era, industrial workers had almost no protection
against accidents. Although each year thousands of laborers were incapacitated or killed on the job, neither they nor their families could
obtain compensation. Curious and outmoded legal doctrines put all the
burdens on the worker. He had to sue his employer in court (a very
expensive procedure) and then prove not only that he and all other
workingmen involved were free from all fault for the accident, but that
his injury was not part of the risk he assumed by holding his job. Crystal
Eastman's study of work accidents helped transform Americans' think-*

Crystal Eastman, *Work Accidents and the Law* (New York, 1910), excerpts
from pp. 84-90, 99-104, 114-115, 223, 227, 232-233.

*ing and brought state legislation to the aid of the victims. It revealed how
accidents resulted from long working hours, from employers' negligence
in failing to train the worker or to protect him. It poignantly demonstrated how accidents ruined workers' lives, forcing them into poverty.*

To study industrial accidents from the "home" side has been my business
for a year. To acquaint myself daily with households doubly disabled by
sickness and loss of income, to see strong men just learning to face life
maimed, to visit home after home where sudden death has visited,—a
dreadful business, you might say. Yet it has left with me impressions of
personality, character, and spirit, which make the year's work a precious
experience.

The first thing brought home to me was that working people do not
have "the luxury of grief." The daily tyranny of hard work in their lives,
leaves little time for pondering the unanswerable "Why?" of sorrow.

For instance, Mrs. Dennison, the widow of a brakeman who was
killed on the Pennsylvania Railroad, spent no quiet days of solitary
mourning. She was left with six children, the oldest eleven. All the money
she had was $500 from the Railroad Relief Association, to which her
husband had belonged, $450 which the men on her husband's division
raised, and $30 which his own crew gave. The company gave her $20
toward the funeral.

With some of this money she rented and stocked up a little candy
and notion store, using the three rooms in the back to live in. Here she
tended store, and cooked, and sewed, and ironed, for herself and the six.
She would have done her own washing too, she told me, but she couldn't
leave the store long enough to hang her clothes up in the yard. She made
a reasonable success of the enterprise, enough to pay for rent and food,
until the hard times came. After that she steadily lost money. So now
she has put in her application for a chance to clean cars for the railroad
at $1.21 a day. For this privilege she must wait her turn among the other
widows; and when she gets it she must leave her children in one another's
care from six in the morning till six at night. They are now two, four,
six, eight, ten, and twelve, respectively. Mrs. Dennison will not have time
to sit down and grieve over the death of her husband for many years to
come.

One mother, whose thin face haunts me, has been able to endure her
tragedy only through this necessity of work. She had a daughter, just
seventeen, who was employed in the dressmaking department of one of
the big stores in Pittsburgh. This girl, Ella, was eager and gay, with a

heart full of kindness. She was everybody's favorite in the workroom; at home she meant laughter and good will for them all. To her mother, Ella was joy and gladness,—life itself. One morning this little dressmaker, after leaving her wraps on the eleventh floor, found that she was a few moments late. She ran for the elevator to go to her workroom above. The elevator was just starting up, with the door half closed. Ella tried to make it, slipped, and fell down the shaft.

This tragedy demoralized the working force of the store for two days. In the hunted, suffering eyes of the mother one reads that she cannot forget, night or day. She feels that Ella's employers were generous in giving her $500, but it would make no difference "if they gave her the whole store."

That poor people are used to trouble is a commonplace. I mean by "trouble," the less subtle disappointments of life, those which come with disease, injury, and premature death. Of all these rougher blows of fortune, the poor family gets more than an even share. This stands to reason, if experience has not already convinced one of it. To the ordinary causes of sickness,—unsanitary dwellings, overcrowding, undue exposure, overwork, lack of necessary vacation, work under poisonous conditions,—to all these, poor people are much more constantly exposed than others. To injury and death caused by accident they are also more exposed. Poor people's children play in dangerous places, on the street, near railroad tracks. The poor man's dwelling is not often fireproof. Poor people do most of the hazardous work in the world, and the accidents connected with work form the majority of all accidents.

Moreover, the poor family is, in a material way, less able to meet these disasters when they come than the well-to-do family. This is in some degree due to ignorance, for ignorance, whether as cause or result, almost always goes with poverty. In a very large degree, however, it is due to poverty itself. It is because they have no reserve fund to fall back on in emergencies. Suppose a young steel worker with a family gets a long, sharp chip of steel in his eye. He cannot go to the best specialist, to the man who knows all that anybody knows about saving eyes. Through ignorance or lack of interest on the part of the doctor who treats him, he loses his eye.

With these workers whom I met,—poor people, not as the charity visitor knows them, but poor as the rank and file of wage-earners are poor,—misfortune is almost part of the regular course of things. They are used to hard knocks, if not yet in their own lives, then in the lives of their relatives, friends, and neighbors. Consequently, there is often in their attitude toward trouble a certain matter-of-fact calmness which looks like indifference. Thus, I have had a mother tell me about her sixteen-year-old son's losing two fingers in the mill. She couldn't remember exactly how or when it happened; she thought he had lost only a week's work; and she had no comment upon it but that it might have been worse.

In every dangerous occupation there is not this sustaining common courage to help a man endure gaily a lifelong deprivation. A certain degree of independence and fraternity in a group is necessary to bring it about. Many go forth from the steel mills maimed for life, who have no such spirit to uphold them. I remember one night in Homestead seeing a boy on crutches, with one leg gone. He was about nineteen, with blue eyes and a shock of yellow hair falling down low on his forehead. In his face was that desperate look of defiance which comes with a recent deformity. He was trying with all his young will to be indifferent to the stares of the crowd, while in every nerve he felt them. All this and a weary hopelessness were written in his sullen childface.

I have shown how grief is crowded out of the lives of working people, and how their frequent experience of trouble gives them an ordinary manner in speaking of it. These things largely account for the opinion held by many, that working people do not feel their sorrows as keenly as others do.

"So you've come to Pittsburgh to study accidents, have you?" says the superintendent, or the claim agent, or the general manager, as the case may be. "Well, I've been in this business fifteen years and I can tell you one thing right now,—95 percent of our accidents are due to the carelessness of the man who gets hurt. Why, you simply wouldn't believe the things they'll do. For instance, I remember a man,"—and he goes on to relate the most telling incident he knows, to prove his assertion.

This is the almost invariable reaction of the Pittsburgh employer and his representatives to a query about industrial accidents. And the statements of such men are the chief source of effective public opinion on the subject in Pittsburgh. There are many people, to be sure, who view the whole situation through startling red headlines and whispered tales of horror,—who believe, for instance, that numbers of men are burned up in furnaces every year, the story of whose destruction never gets beyond the mill. There are also thousands of people, including most of the workingmen themselves, who think about each accident as a distinct and separate incident, without generalizing or drawing conclusions. Neither of these groups, however, forms an effectual element in public opinion; one is hysterical, the other inarticulate. Most of the men in the community whose opinions count, have made up their minds about this accident question from what they have heard employers, superintendents, casualty managers say. In other words, they believe that "95 percent of the accidents are due to the carelessness of the men." Those emphatic, reiterated assertions, those tales of recklessness often repeated, have grown into a solid, inert mass of opinion among business and professional men in the community, a heap of unreasoned conviction.

Whenever in any of the versions of the accident some responsibility was indicated, that indication is included in my tabulation. An accident is charged against the victim of it, if his act or omission in any way contributed to it, whether it was due to his carelessness, ignorance, or any other failing. The same rule is followed in the "fellow workmen" column. Between accidents attributable to the employer and those attributable to the superintendent or foreman, a rather sharp and arbitrary line was necessarily drawn. If the accident was due to some defective condition in the working plan or appliances, or to the furnishing of insufficient or inadequate material, it was checked in the "employer" column. But if the accident was due to some special failure in superintendence, as for instance, placing of ignorant men in dangerous positions, failure to warn, mistaken and dangerous orders, then it was charged, not against the employer, but against the superintendent or foreman.

In fact, considering all the evidence available, we had indication of some responsibility on the part of the victim in 132 out of 410 fatalities; of his sole responsibility in 68 fatalities. Even these 132 cases demand analysis. They represent not just "carelessness" as the word is commonly used, but a long list of human weaknesses, some common to us all, some resulting from special environment, some for which the man himself is not responsible, some for which he is.

Ignorance covers a large share of these cases, the ignorance of young boys, of those who are "green" at their job, of the tongue-tied alien, who finds himself for the first time a part of swift and mighty processes. In 22 out of 132 deaths in which the victim can be held accountable, he was "green." One was on his first night's work in a mill; one had been at his work four hours; another three days; eight, less than a month; four, less than two months; seven, less than six months. Nearly all these men were foreigners and eight of them had been among English-speaking people less than one year.

For example, in several cases where a miner was killed by a fall of slate, the evidence indicated that not enough posts had been used. In four such cases the man killed was a "greener." One had worked in a mine but two months.

Thirteen of the 132 who were in a measure responsible for their own deaths, were not men but boys. A fourteen-year-old assistant chemist was run over by an engine in the yards of a steel mill at night. A thirteen-year-old boy tried to pull up a freight elevator because one of the girls in the shop asked him if he could. It came up suddenly and fast, and struck him while he was leaning over. Two sixteen-year-old boys were killed while meddling with elevators. A newly landed Croatian lad of seventeen was killed by fooling with a switch with wet gloves on, watching the sparks fly.

In all these cases it could be said that there was no excuse. There was a path outside the tracks where the little chemist should have walked. The Croatian had been warned to keep away from the switch. The others had no business trying to run the elevators. It is all true, but they were children. We are too likely to think that a laborer must be grown up. We might expect that ten hours' work a day would take the nonsense out of any boy, but it doesn't.

Next there were 12 deaths due to a condition on the part of the man killed over which he had no immediate control. A repair man climbing to a high place became suddenly dizzy and fell, although there was a railing to protect him. A young lineman, with a weak heart, was electrocuted by taking hold of a wire supposed to be dead but which had crossed another wire carrying 250 volts,—not enough to kill an ordinary man. A brakeman was run down in the yards, because of slight deafness. One man, afflicted with epilepsy, fell in a fit upon a steam exhaust and inhaled steam until he died. Here it might be said with an air of finality, "While these men were not immediately responsible, they were responsible for selecting occupations for which they were unfit." Are we sure that they were responsible?

Such men as these are seldom in a position to choose an occupation suited to their handicap. Society might do well to protect them by a law setting certain physical standards for all those who seek employment in dangerous trades.

Many accidents for which a foreman is partly or wholly responsible are simply the result of mistakes on his part. Where several people are working together in a series of somewhat complicated operations, the first necessity is co-operation, perfect "working together." In many cases where a man is sent into a dangerous place to make repairs, it would seem that the foreman or superintendent should look out for his safety. At Rankin the ore is brought up from the ore beds to the "kipping buckets" in a chain of cars moved by an electric motor. One day the coupling between two of these cars broke, and George Schustic was sent by his foreman to fasten them together with a chain. Meanwhile the motorman, who had not been told that a man was working between the cars, started the motor which moved the chain. Schustic was killed. The foreman's responsibility seems unmistakable.

But it must not be forgotten that the foreman is human; his recklessness is largely the result of his environment; his powers of attention are often taxed beyond their endurance by the tension of work, by noise and heat, and by weariness. Moreover, the foreman is always under the greatest incentive to increase output. Pressure is brought to bear upon him in various ways. In the steel mills, for instance, bonus schemes, emulation, fear of discharge or desire for preferment, are constantly driving him. All this results in tremendous accomplishment, but it does not tend to make the foreman careful.

For an intelligent understanding of the "careless employer" one must consider not only his mental attitude, but also the actual mediums through which his intentions, good, bad or indifferent, must operate. In the first place, he does not exercise care directly, but through an army of superintendents, inspectors, foremen, etc. In the second place, his provisions for safety must very often depend upon the sufficiency of material things which, as we have suggested, it is always difficult and sometimes impossible to guarantee. The employer's "carelessness," then, is a matter not only of his own mental attitude, but of that of his agents, and sometimes of the "perversity of inanimate things."

Most of these 147 instances of negligence in employers come under failure in the "first duty"—to provide a safe place to work. They divide themselves into two main groups. In the first come those accidents which are due, strictly speaking, to defects; namely, some condition of plant or appliance which was not planned or intended.

Among the fatalities resulting from such defects, there were a few where the defect was perfectly plain, and a few where the accident was necessary to reveal it. But most of them can be laid to imperfect inspection. One story of a breaking scaffold has been already told; in another case four men were killed because a platform, ladder, or plank gave way under them. Twenty-two men were killed because something over their heads gave way and a heavy object fell upon them. The commonest instance of this is the breaking of crane chains. One man was killed by the falling of a coal trestle, another crushed by the collapse of the floor above him. A cracked grindstone, a steam-pipe valve which would not work, an electric wire with the insulation worn off, etc.—these are some of the other defects from which death resulted.

In so far as the employer's relation to industrial accidents is revealed by the history of this year's fatalities, we have found much deliberate disregard for safety in the construction of plant and equipment, and in the organization of work; we have found a long list of defects, not all of which the employer could have avoided, but most of which careful inspection would have revealed and immediate repair have rendered harmless; we have found those directly representing the employer in positions of authority often neglectful of safety; we have found cases of children regularly employed in work or in surroundings dangerous to them on account of their youth.

Were employers stimulated by a public opinion aroused in these various ways, they would more generally exert that determination to prevent accidents without which, as we have seen, the majority of accidents cannot be eliminated. And yet, in the face of the unremitting pressure for output, the motive for prevention can never be compelling until to each injury and death is affixed a uniform and unescapable penalty. If accidents became a heavy and determinable cost to the business not dependent upon the cleverness of lawyers, the leanings of judges, or the sympathies of juries, but directly proportioned to the number of deaths and the number and seriousness of injuries among the men on the payroll, then the prevention of them would become of direct economic interest to the employer. One economic motive would be set off against another. If safe, slow ways of producing involve a reduction in profits, we must see that the human waste resulting from dangerous, quick ways shall involve a greater reduction in profits. This is not because the employer is wicked and must be punished, but because he, like most of us, is held closely in the grip of economic motives.

Better factory and railroad acts, the public records of accidents, an intelligently aroused public opinion, a law making every serious accident a direct and unmistakable expense to the business,—these are some of the means of improving the employer's motive. Yet, with all these means, we shall not be able to make the protection of workmen his first interest, for clearly his first interest must be production. Herein lies the strong argument of the socialists. It will be impossible, they say, materially to modify the employer's motive so long as industry is carried on under a regime of competition; the law of the competitive struggle will prove stronger than any statutes which society may seek to superimpose upon it; legislation will, they maintain, make an employer stop for a moment to take thought for safety, but the force of competition will soon drive him on.

But the way is open for democracy to bring all these forces to bear upon the motives of the employer before accepting the conclusion that modern industry cannot be carried on under a competitive regime without the present wholesale destruction of the workers.

9

Family Life among the Poor: Margaret Byington visits Homestead's laborers

One of the most complete pictures of industrial poverty among both native white Americans and immigrants emerges from the famous Pittsburgh survey, a series of studies sponsored by the Russell Sage Foundation. Investigating Homestead, Pennsylvania, the home of the Carnegie Steel Corporation, researchers examined all facets of life in this major industrial setting. One of the most fascinating and insightful parts of the survey was Margaret Byington's close and sympathetic portrait of lower-class family life. She makes vividly clear the different styles of native whites and immigrants, and she illuminates the forces that would keep children of the second and third generations in the positions of their fathers.

THE ENGLISH SPEAKING AND NATIVE WHITE FAMILIES

In the families here, the women almost never go out to work—a marked contrast to cotton mill towns, for instance, where wives and daughters seek employment almost as a matter of course. This dependence on the men's wages is due not primarily to any theory as to woman's sphere, but to the simple fact that the one industry cannot use the work of women and children. Moreover, in this town where there are no marked differences in financial status and by far the larger number of housewives do all their own work, there is not much opportunity to obtain any form

---

Margaret Byington, *Homestead, The Households of a Mill Town* (New York, 1910), excerpts from pp. 107-113, 118-119, 125-128, 145-157.

of domestic service by the day. Women apparently think it wiser to save money by good housekeeping than to earn a little more and neglect the home. This feeling, combined with the difficulty in securing work, has developed the type of family in which the man's wages constitute almost the entire income.

Among the English-speaking and native white budget families only two women went out to do day's work. There were four of these families who took lodgers, but since the women were either widows who had no other means of income, or women who had no children, the presence of lodgers interfered very little with the household life. As these families averaged only 1.2 persons to a room their homes were not seriously overcrowded. For the most part the women, relieved from the task of increasing the income, use their time and interest to good purpose in developing in their households a distinctive quality of homelikeness.

The men are inclined to trust all financial matters to their wives. It is the custom in Homestead for the workman to turn over his wages to his wife on pay day and to ask no questions as to what it goes for. He reserves a share for spending money; otherwise his part of the family problem is to earn and hers to spend.

The thoughtful women are especially conscious that part of the responsibility for keeping the men away from the saloons belongs to them. The heat and thirst due to mill work, combined with the lack of other amusements, make the brightness and festivity of bar-rooms very appealing, and intemperance is consequently a serious evil in the town. The wives feel that they must help to overcome this temptation. One woman told me that she had been brought up to consider it wrong to play cards. She feared, however, that if she refused to have them in the house, her husband who was fond of playing would be tempted to go to the back rooms of the saloons for his entertainment. So, putting aside her scruples, she planned informal gatherings to play in the evenings. To her the drink evil was the more serious.

That home life has a strong hold and is a social force in keeping pure what we call the moral life of the town, is shown by the infrequency of immorality among these English-speaking families. There are instances, to be sure, of unfaithfulness among married people, and there are those who love to retail these bits of gossip. But even the way in which they are told reveals how strongly the general sentiment of the town condemns such moral laxity. It is very rare to hear of girls going wrong. These townspeople watch their daughters jealously, and make every effort to have the home the center of life so that the dangers almost inevitably attendant on public dances and skating rinks may not touch the girls of the family. I found it part of many a mother's problem to create such a household atmosphere that the children should find their happiness in the home rather than seek it in the doubtful amusements the town offers. They planned, for instance, to give the children music lessons so that in the evening they might enjoy such gayeties together. In one or two homes the children had learned to play on different instruments and had an embryo orchestra. These quiet family gatherings are apparently the source of much pleasure.

I have already noted that in this community of 25,000 there are over 50 saloons and other drinking places, ranging from "speak-easies" to the conventional bar-rooms with plate glass and bright lights. It was no part of my study to investigate the ownership or police surveillance of these establishments, the profits gathered in on pay nights, or the intoxication which, as we have seen, the courts prove so ineffectual in controlling. As places of relaxation, they fill a need not otherwise supplied. The Carnegie Library has a gymnasium and clubs, but, except for the saloons and the club rooms of one or two fraternal orders, there are no free and easy lounging places for refreshment and friendly intercourse. The Slavs bring much of the liquor they buy home and drink it sociably there, many of them being heavy drinkers. The budgets gave no basis for a conclusion that English-speaking Homestead men are hard drinkers. My inquiries naturally lay among men with families rather than among the unattached ones, who are the constant tipplers in all towns. In the homes on the hill streets I heard almost no complaints that men were drunkards, though many men undoubtedly, in good times, spent money that way that was needed for the household budget. An old resident said that among the older stock he could name perhaps a half dozen men known as drunkards in the town. With hot work to whet thirst, and with the natural rebellion of human nature against the tension of long hours, the liquor interests have exploited the needs of the adults for recreation and refreshment. It is true that they have not really met that need, and have exploited the opportunities they offer; but it is equally true that the need is met in no other way.

Outside of home festivities and the meagre or commercialized public provisions, the chief dependence for sociability is on the lodges, churches and other voluntary organizations.

In Homestead, as in other working communities, we find benefit organizations playing a prominent part. In one day's paper, 50 meetings of fraternal orders were scheduled for one week. Facts were secured concerning 23 out of the total of perhaps half a hundred lodges. The 23 had a membership in 1907 of 3663; of these 3400 were men. Almost all the organizations include both social and benefit features. The Order of Elks, which has no regular benefits and is a purely social organization, nevertheless gives generous assistance to members in distress. On the other hand the fraternal insurance orders, such as the Protected Home Circle and the Royal Arcanum, are important, not only because they help provide for the future, but because they provoke social intercourse in ways which help make this form of insurance popular.

Through children, more than through insurance, or savings, or even through home owning, does a workman's household lay claim upon the future. Here both the oldest instincts and new half-formulated ambitions find expression. They have asserted themselves even in a town where the men have submitted to exclusion from all control over their work, and where as we have seen they have failed to master the town's government as a whole. Here the community has set before itself what it feels to be high standards.

The working people of Homestead when talking of their children show a distinct recognition of the value of education and home training, as compared with the immediate money value of wages. English-speaking parents, at least, do not hurry their children to work the day they are fourteen years of age. Of the 17 boys between fourteen and twenty-one, in the English-speaking families from whom budgets were secured, 15 were at work; but of 16 girls, four were still at school and 12 were at home helping their mothers. This last figure is a striking one in view of the fact that in at least five of these families the man was earning less than $15 a week; yet even under such circumstances the parents did not seek to increase their income by sending the girls to work. A typical case is that of a girl of 18, the eldest of six children, in a family with an income of $14 a week. It was assumed to be her place to help her mother, rather than to supplement the father's wages. While the number of families studied is, of course, not large enough to warrant sweeping conclusions, their attitude in this matter corresponded with general impressions I received in visiting a much wider circle.

The parents' ambitions for their sons are, as a rule, very simple; usually to follow in their fathers' footsteps, getting from the practical work in the mill a training for future success. There is a fascination about the mill against which even unwilling mothers find themselves helpless to contend. One woman, whose husband had been a mill worker all his life and two of whose sons had worked up to responsible positions, had

had her fill of the terror of accidents which haunts many a Homestead woman. So she wished her third boy to do something else, and secured a place for him in a large department store. His wages seemed small compared with those received by his brothers, there was little prospect of promotion, and so he was soon hard at work in the mill. The fact that the best paid men, such as rollers and heaters, have worked up to these jobs through experience has increased the natural tendency to put sons directly into the mill rather than to give them a technical training. While occasionally a boy wishes to go to college, the general attitude of the community is one of scorn rather than of respect for academic education. There is a general belief that the college trained man, with all his theory, is less expert than the man who has learned the industry through work with his hands. As few men with technical training are at the start familiar with the processes of steel making, the value of their theoretical knowledge cannot overcome the prejudice created among the men by their early blunders.

Whatever its disadvantages the mill usually gives a boy a chance to earn a fair livelihood for a single man as a semi-skilled workman. Some want what are known as pencil jobs, weighing and marking steel, where the work is light and apparently considered more gentlemanly, though the pay is lower and the chances of mastering the business are less. The parents often accede to this desire. Others begin at regular boy's work, as messengers or door openers. Promotion is rapid in the beginning, and sometimes by the time a boy is eighteen he has already attained his maximum wage. One woman who regretted that her boy had not learned a trade, said that he was unwilling to go through a long period of apprenticeship as a mechanic, when at certain mill jobs he could earn good pay at once. Another woman told me that her brother early acquired dissipated habits because he earned man's wages while he still had a boy's lack of responsibility and self-control.

The sons may work a little further up than their fathers; a man told me with pride that his son, who was a foreman, had secured for him a job in the mill, and a mother was eager to relate how her boy had taught the new assistant superintendent the way to do his work. Only rarely, however, do they secure an education that fits them for an entirely different kind of labor.

Dynamic changes are affecting the town's growth, and the lives of the people composing it. It would be difficult to prophesy how far the children of the present steel workers will man the mills of the next generation; there is another stream of recruits coming in which as time goes on may more and more dispute with the native born and the sons of the old immigrant stock for place in the ranks of the semi-skilled and skilled. We must recognize the part the Slavs are to play. They today make up a full half of the working force of the plant. They already affect every phase of the town's life, as newcomers in the ranks of industry, as aliens from East Europe, and (the great majority of them) as day laborers at 16-1/2 cents an hour, whose earnings fall below what we have seen to be a living wage for a family.

THE SLAVIC COMMUNITY

One morning I entered a two-room tenement. The kitchen, perhaps 15 by 12 feet, was steaming with vapor from a big washtub set on a chair in the middle of the room. The mother was trying to wash and at the same time to keep the older of her two babies from tumbling into the tub full of scalding water that was standing on the floor. On one side of the room was a huge puffy bed, with one feather tick to sleep on and another for covering; near the window stood a sewing machine; in the corner, an organ,—all these, besides the inevitable cook stove upon which in the place of honor was simmering the evening's soup. Upstairs in the second room were one boarder and the man of the house asleep. Two more boarders were at work, but at night would be home to sleep in the bed from which the others would get up. Picture if you will what a week or a season means to a mother in such a home, the overwork, the brief respite from toil—to be increased afterward—when the babies come?

Not only is the mother too busy to give much time to her babies, but she also suffers from overwork during pregnancy and from lack of proper care afterward. Housework must be done, boarders must be fed, and most women work until the day of confinement. In accordance with their home customs, almost all of them employ midwives and call a doctor only in an emergency. I was told by a local physician that nearly half of the births in Homestead, the large proportion of them among the Slavic people, were attended by midwives. These women, who charge $5.00 or $10, include in their services the care of both woman and child for several days, and thus perform the services of trained nurse as well as doctor. While of the 21 midwives registered in Homestead, five or six have diplomas from schools of midwifery abroad, most of them are ignorant and are careless about cleanliness. In a paper before the Allegheny County Medical Society, Dr. Purman, a local physician, reported numerous instances where both mother and child had suffered serious injury from the ignorance of these women.

The necessity for mothers to be up and at work within three or four days adds to the harm. In at least 10 of the 29 Slavic families visited, special reference was made by the Slavic investigator to the ill health of the mother due to overwork and to lack of proper care during confinement. The strength to bear much doubtless comes to these women from years of work in the fields, but the change to the hot kitchens where their work is now done undoubtedly entails a strain which not only injures them but lessens the vitality of the children. This weakened condition at birth combines with the inadequate food and insufficient air and the neglect which comes through over-burdening the mother to produce the appalling infant death rate in these courts.

Even more serious is the injury to the moral tone of the Slavic community caused by the crowding together of single men and families. In only four instances in the courts studied were lodgers found in families where there were girls over fourteen, but even younger children learn evil quickly from the free-spoken men. With the husband at work on the night shift the situation is aggravated, and reports are current of gross immorality on the part of some women who keep lodgers; two or three actual instances came to my knowledge from unquestioned sources. Since half the families in the courts studied used the kitchen as a sleeping room, there was close mingling of lodgers and family among them. This becomes intolerable when families living in but two rooms take lodgers. This was true, as we have seen, in 71 instances. Even when extreme crowding does not exist, family and lodgers often all sleep in the kitchen, the only warm room, in winter.

Certainly there is little to quicken mental and spiritual development in these crowded tenements where there is neither privacy nor even that degree of silence necessary for reading. We agree in the abstract that the individual needs room for growth, yet complain of the stunted mental stature of these people who have the meagre development of seedlings grown in a mass.

Moreover, families who live in narrow quarters have no room for festive gatherings. In the evening a group often gathers around the stove gossiping of home days, playing cards, drinking, and playing simple musical instruments. On the Saturday after pay day the household usually clubs together to buy a case of beer which it drinks at home. These ordinarily jovial gatherings are sometimes interrupted by fights and the police have to be called in. One officer who had been on the force for nine years said that these men are generally good-natured and easy-going, and in all his experience he had never arrested a sober "Hunkie"; it was when they were drunk that the trouble began. The punishment usually inflicted for disorderly conduct in Homestead, a small fine, has little deterrent effect among the Slavs. It is indeed currently said that some are proud of having a large fine imposed, as they feel that it indicates increased importance. Usually, however, they gather without disturbance simply to chat and drink, to pass the hours after the day's work.

The women have few opportunities for relaxation. Sometimes they gossip around the pump or at the butcher's, but washing, ironing, cleaning, sewing and cooking for the boarders leave little time for visiting. The young people perhaps suffer most from the lack of home festivities. A two-room house has no place for games or "parties," or even for courting; there is not even space enough, to say nothing of privacy. So young folks are driven to the streets for their gayety. Almost the only time when the house is really the scene of festivity is when those primal events, birth, and marriage, and death, bring together both the old-time friends and the new neighbors.

Starting in with such a household as that described at the opening of this section, how far do any of these Slavic families succeed in working out ideals they have set for themselves?

If we turn from the crowded courts with their two-room tenements to the homes of some who have attained their ambitions, we find conditions that show an inherent capacity for advancement in the race. As an illustration, note the change in type in two houses, the homes of families from the same place in the old country, the one newcomers, the other among the "oldest inhabitants" of the Slavic community. The first family live in a one-room tenement, where even though the furniture includes only absolute necessities, it is hard to keep all the crowded belongings in order. On wash-day morning the disorder is increased. Nevertheless, the home is kept as neat as the circumstances permit, and the bright pictures on the wall are proof of a desire to make it attractive. As the man earns only $9.90 a week, they must keep their rent low if bills are to be paid and anything laid by for the future. In the other picture, the "front room" with its leather-covered furniture is in a five-room house which the family owns. The sacred pictures with their vivid coloring relieve the severity of the room while they also reveal the religious note in Slavic life, for if happiness is to stay with the family, the priest must come yearly to "bless the home." This family after many years in

America has, by hard work and thrift, succeeded in obtaining a real home.

Turning from this visible evidence of the way in which an individual Slavic family has prospered, we find in the mill census that the number of skilled, and therefore highly paid members of the race, are few. Of the 3603 Slavs in the mill in 1907, 459 were ranked as semi-skilled, 80 as skilled. The Slovaks from Austro-Hungary are the most numerous of the race in Homestead, and were the first of this stock to come here. Among them we find proportionately a slightly larger number of semi-skilled workers.

We have seen that of the budget Slavs still earning laborers' wages, a third had been here over ten years; it is apparent, however, that individuals are slowly making their way into skilled work—a movement which, as the older English-speaking men drop out, is probably bound to increase. In the 29 immigrant families keeping budgets all of the men who earned $12 or more a week had been here over five years. It is interesting to note that some had come here when they were very young, eleven, fifteen, sixteen, or seventeen years old; for example, a tonnage worker had been here ten years; a man at one of the furnaces earning $3.50 a day, seventeen years, and a machinist who earned about the same amount, eighteen years. Even with the higher wages, their families continue to make sacrifices to secure the desired property more rapidly. A helper at one of the open-hearth furnaces, who had been here for seven years, was earning $2.50 to $3.00 a day. The husband and wife still took in two boarders, so that with their two children there were six people in a two-room house, which was but scantily furnished. They had a bank account of at least $400. Another Slav, the head of a family of three, had been here ten years and was working on tonnage, in good times earning about $6.00 a day. They, too, lived in a two-room house, but it was neat and from their standpoint probably seemed large enough as they had no lodger. They had purchased the farm in the old country and besides had a $500 bank account.

It is by such thrift that some of the Slavs attain their ambition to own a home. An official in the foreign department of one bank said he knew of 25 Slavs who had purchased homes in 1907. Sometimes these families continue to live in the Second Ward. One family, for example, had bought an eight-room house on one of these busy streets. The four rear rooms they rented, but with evident regard for appearances lived themselves in the four that faced the front. With the aid of the rent from the rear tenement they had succeeded in freeing the house from the mortgage. The families more often, however, move further from the mill. One I knew bought a house on the hill with two porches and a big yard where they kept chickens. While they had only succeeded in paying $500 on the $1700 the place cost, now that a son was at work they hoped to be able to clear the debt. In the meantime they truly rejoiced in being on the hill above the smoke and away from the bustling courts.

For most Slavic households, however, the increased income which would make such increased expenditure possible must be looked for not from the man's wages, but, at least in the first years, from other sources. We have seen how the first recourse of the young couple is to keep lodgers and the cost to health and childhood that that involves. Time goes on, brings children, and household expenses rise, and even with increased earnings, tends to keep the couple at this double work.

10

Case Studies in Urban and Rural Poverty: The research of Katherine Anthony and E. Franklin Frazier

During the Progressive era, sociology for the first time became a rigorous and vitally important social science discipline. The first sociologists were acutely concerned with social problems; indeed, the line between sociology and social work was very thinly drawn. Eager to move away from the traditional philosophizing of social thinkers and to enter into the detailed examination of reality, sociologists relied heavily on case studies. They devoted a great deal of energy and enterprise to composing tightly drawn and detailed accounts of individual lives of the poor. Their work now provides us with the information from which to construct a complex picture of the attitudes and experiences of the lower classes. The first two

Katherine Anthony, *Mothers Who Must Earn* (New York, 1914), excerpts from pp. 178-181, 186-190; E. Franklin Frazier, *The Negro Family in the United States* (Chicago: University of Chicago Press, copyright 1939), excerpts from pp. 496-501.

cases below, written by Katherine Anthony, are of families in New York City's slums. The third, compiled by the noted black sociologist E. Franklin Frazier, is about a black tenant family in the South.

A HOME WHERE NOBODY SITS DOWN

Mrs. Fuhrmann lives "across the tracks" in one of the desolate tenements peculiar to the Eleventh Avenue quarter. The halls and stairways by which we reach the fourth floor where Mrs. Fuhrmann's flat is located are bare of any attempt at covering. A couple of lads race past us making a terrific din all the way down. However, the board flooring is well washed and the musty smell which pervades the carpeted hallways in the better tenements to the east is missing here. The Fuhrmann apartment, when we reach it, presents the same meager, well-scoured appearance. The afternoon sunshine pours into the kitchen, and as the apartment has "rooms through," the ventilation is not of the worst. Notwithstanding cleanliness and sunshine, the kitchen looks shabby and uninviting. Two or three straight chairs stand about in casual positions; but it is apparently a home in which nobody ever sits down.

The rent is high—too high for Mrs. Fuhrmann's income. She earns $9.00 a week by working every day including Sunday. During the last year she did not fail her job a single day out of the 365. Her earnings for the year, therefore, came to $468. Out of this, $144, or 31 percent, went into the rent. When she moved into these quarters her oldest son was earning also and the rent was less of a tax on the family income, but her son has died since, leaving Mrs. Fuhrmann with the two younger children, a girl of eleven and a boy of seven, to occupy the four rooms, and the mother to meet the rent alone with her slender earnings. She does not make a change, partly because with the entire seven days of the week given over to drudgery, little time is left for house-hunting and even less courage for making changes. Another fact which holds her fast is that the children are favorites "on the block." Hattie, who is rosy and healthy, is a favorite with Mr. Schmidt, the grocer, who says she looks as if she "hadn't long been over," and jokingly doubts Mrs. Fuhrmann's statement that the child was born in Fortieth Street. Little Walter, who looks anaemic and pale beside his buxom sister, has also his patron on the block, a detective, who promises to make of Walter a detective too some day. The housekeeper of the tenement tells the children when to start to school, for Mrs. Fuhrmann must be at her work an hour before it is time for school to begin.

It is characteristic that Mrs. Fuhrmann has never had "but the two jobs in her lifetime." At fourteen she went to work in a shirt laundry and stayed there until she married seven years later. The laundry itself changed management four times during this period and passed through a series of vicissitudes, none of which, however, were strong enough to dislodge the steady young collar starcher who went right ahead earning her twelve and fourteen dollars weekly.

At twenty-one she married. Her husband was a German cigar maker, who succeeded in supporting his family until his death eleven years later. They had 10 children, including two pairs of twins, but only three survived infancy. When Fuhrmann fell ill with tuberculosis, it became necessary for Mrs. Fuhrmann to look for work although she was then in the fourth month of her pregnancy. She found a place as scrubwoman in a large theater which employed six women to scour the premises—halls, floors, stairs and stage—on hands and knees. For seven days' work she was paid $7.00. On this she kept the family of four during her husband's last illness. After two months he died, and Mrs. Fuhrmann returned to work the day after the funeral. Her job was now more necessary than ever. She continued at it until the day before her baby was born. In her own words, she was "at work Saturday evening and Sunday the baby was there." This was her eighth confinement within ten years.

When the baby was one month old, she put him in the care of a neighbor, paying $1.50 a week for the service, and returned to her work, "thankful to get it again," as she says.

For eight years she has worked at this job. Her absence of a month when her baby was born, and two others, one of seven weeks and another of ten days, both due to sickness, are her only absences in the entire term of service. Her wages have been raised to $9.00 a week. There were a few years, after her eldest boy got his working papers, when his wages made things easier. But this son died at eighteen, and again Mrs. Fuhrmann became the sole wage-earner.

Mrs. Fuhrmann walks to and from her work, making two trips daily. She must be there at 8 o'clock in the morning and work until 1 o'clock. After walking home, she washes and irons and scrubs her own floors until 4:30 p.m., when it is time to start for Broadway again. At 6:30 she leaves the theater for the day. On Sunday she is not required to return in the afternoon. When we consider the character of the job itself, the four trips daily between Eleventh Avenue and Broadway, the cooking, washing, and ironing at home, it is not surprising that the Fuhrmann home has the air of one in which nobody ever sits down.

ONE FAMILY THAT HAS NOT FAILED

From a farm region in a remote corner of Hungary, the home of the Gravats, the Grubinskys have found their way into a West Side tenement. The transition was not made all at once, but by gradual stages. Martin Grubinsky was the son, and his wife the daughter, of farmer people. The first break with farm life occurred when Martin went to work on the railroad. He had charge of a gang of men going over the railroads and making repairs on the tracks. He lost his awe of travel. With the railroad, one could reach the city of Vienna in six hours! Soon the couple shifted there. Mrs. Grubinsky went to work in a factory as a wool spinner and her husband continued on the railroad. After six years they were ready for America. Mary Grubinsky, with their four children, returned to her father's farm and Martin took the immigrant's way to America. In less than a year his wife followed, but the children stayed on the farm where bread and milk and fruit were abundant. Mrs. Grubinsky found her husband at work as a machinist in a Passaic mill and found employment there herself as a spinner. A year in the Passaic mills was followed by removal to New York and the West Side.

For seven years the Grubinskys have been West Siders. Mrs. Grubinsky cooked in a restaurant until her first "American" baby came. It was a little girl, whom she named "Annie." The baby was cherished like a first-born, for the other four children on the remote Hungarian farm seemed almost lost by this time. The mother's devotion to little Annie, however, did not prevent her from going out to do a day's work as often as she could get it. Martin Grubinsky was then earning but $7.00 a week.

Since coming to the West Side, he has worked for the same firm— a factory where furniture is made. He never misses a day. If overtime is called for, Grubinsky jumps at the chance. If Sunday work is needed to fill a heavy order, he is the first man to report for it. If the firm gives out chair caning for home work, he sits over it all evening. His odd moments at home are rare, but they suffice for him to make a piece of furniture for his wife, to resole the children's shoes, or to patch a coffee pot for a neighbor. In this case, industry becomes almost a fault. "He would work all night," says his wife, with a shrug.

In seven years his wages have advanced from $7.00 to $11 a week. The increase came about once a year and amounted to 50 cents a week. But the Grubinsky family has also increased. Besides little Annie, three more "American" babies have been born. The children left in Hungary have begun to arrive one by one. Theresa, the eldest, came first. The second daughter soon followed. The family expenses have mounted with the advent of new babies and the arrival of the older children. One pays a friend or relative $20 for bringing a child from Hungary to New York, besides the passage money, which is also $20. The younger Grubinsky's have been brought into the world at much less cost, for their mother never had a doctor. The principal expense was her loss in wages.

There has never been any question in Mary Grubinsky's mind as to whether she should work. Her husband's uncommon industry and steadiness have brought him at the age of forty to where he is earning $11 a week with which to maintain a family of seven. Naturally, his wife must work. Besides, she has always worked. From the days when she toiled in her father's fields and went to service on a neighbor's farm, then later as a wool spinner in Vienna and Passaic, as cook in a restaurant, as charwoman by the day she has always worked, and worked to earn. As soon as each of her babies was a month old, she left it with a cousin and began to go out, securing a half day here, a whole day there, and gradually working up to an income of about $5.00 a week.

At home she is never idle. She helps her husband with the chair caning, makes the children's clothes, mends for her own family and also for hire, cooks, washes, irons, scrubs, tends her window boxes, minds the children of a neighbor who is doing a day's work, fetches ice from the brewery where it is thrown away, forages for kindling around warehouses, runs to the school when the teacher summons her—but a complete list of all that Mrs. Grubinsky does in the course of a week would be quite impossible. In her home, nothing is wasted, nothing lost. Even the feathers from a Thanksgiving turkey were made into cushions and dust brushes.

In short, Mrs. Grubinsky works as hard as her husband does. But she is by no means a spiritless drudge. She is enterprising and adaptable and takes the lead in Americanizing the family where Grubinsky lags behind. She collects green trading stamps diligently and has a clock secured with them. She never buys at the Eighth Avenue department stores, but always on Tenth Avenue where, as she says, rent is cheaper and prices are lower. But, she will tell you, it does not pay to buy things too cheaply. For instance, she paid a good price originally for her wash boiler, but has had it "since the President was elected." She not only bought a sewing machine, which is common enough among the West Side women, but she learned how to use it, which is uncommon.

Two months ago she moved her family from a two-room into a three-room apartment, thereby raising the rent from seven to nine dollars. This was done in the face of Martin Grubinsky's flat command to the contrary. There are many things Martin Grubinsky does not know about America. How should he? All day long he works on chairs in the factory. Every evening he sits at home and weaves chair seats of cane. How should he know that an American family must have a sitting room besides a bedroom and kitchen, or that Tessie must have white shoes like the other girls when she goes to the church to be confirmed? In these matters, Mary Grubinsky feels that she must decide and that Martin must accommodate himself.

In this home it is understood that some recreation is necessary. Neighbors drop in for a social evening, well-known neighbors who also came from Hungary. There are no less than seven families living in the same house who came from the same Hungarian district. In the Grubinsky kitchen they sit in a circle, husbands and wives together. Martin Grubinsky and his wife are each at work on cane weaving. The babies play on the floor in the middle of the circle. Perhaps a pail of mild beer is handed around once or twice, but not too often. The Grubinskys and their friends are temperate. Their men do not frequent saloons.

The Grubinskys have ideals and hopes. These all center around the possession of a little farm in New Jersey. One day, when Mary Grubinsky's parents die, she will have a small remittance from Hungary. Then, too, the children will be working and Mrs. Grubinsky will be able to go out more days in the week. When they get together $600 they will move to a little place on the other side of the Hudson. In the meantime, it is a sustaining hope equally for the husband and the wife, and unites them through every other difference.

A BLACK TENANT FAMILY WITH GRANDMOTHER AS HEAD

[There was one son and a grandson on the porch at the time the investigators came up. The son was married and lived a short distance from this place, while the grandson and another son lived with the grandmother. The grandchildren were aged ten and twelve, respectively, and in the first and third grades at school.]

When questioned about herself and family, Mrs. Griggs replied, "My mamma, she said I was born on ole man Chuma Crack's place on B____'s farm. After I married I left 'em, but I been here in the neighborhood nigh on about forty years. I been on this spot nigh about thirty years. My chillun done married off. I don' keep good health; I keep bad health. I want this ole house tore down. Mr. B____ own it in slavery time, an' he sold it to Miss J____ H____. She sold it to Miss B____

C____, then Mr. H____ got it. We been here through all that. This not quite a one-horse farm. But you got to work. The white man don't do nothin' but give you the land, and there it is.

"My mamma never did send me to school, but I tried to learn my chilluns. My mamma died this year; she were about 103 years old when she died. My papa used to tell me how the white folks did [in slavery days]—beat him and put hounds on him and work him. He was only married one time. Papa died about seven years ago. He was eighty some when he died. I don't know anything about my grandparents. Mamma said her mamma died with the small pox and they burn her up [in slavery time].

"I was the mother of fifteen chillun in all. I got six livin'. Some come live, but didn't live no time, yet three got to be big chillun walkin' about befo' dey dies. One boy got to be eighteen years old. He had that fever and from that spasms and chills, and from the spells he fell in the fire and got burnt and never did get over it. The other two just died with the fever. Charlie, he goin' on about three years old when he died with the fever, too. With the others I go about five months or six months and I lose 'em. I jest keep a losin' 'em. That the last one I saved right there [*pointing to the son*]. I had to work to save him. I had to go to the doctor. I got so weak I couldn't hold 'em." Speaking of the boys, she said concerning one that he was "cross-eyed or cock-eyed or somethin'. He can't see right good. But ain't nair one crippled. Nair one have fits. Andrew Potts got his eye might nigh knocked out years ago."

When asked if Mr. Griggs was the father of all her children, Mrs. Griggs answered: "No'm, he wasn't the father of 'em all. He was the father of Julia and Dan [the oldest boy in Montgomery]. Robert Potts is the father of de other four—Mae, Reginald, James, and Andrew. I was married to Griggs by Dick Brown. I wasn't never married to Potts.

"Charlie [grandson] was born here. My daughter were in Birmingham, but she came on here. She went back for a while and stay with her husband, then she sent him [Charlie] back and give him to me. Robert [speaking of another grandson] was born in Montgomery. Dan [Mrs. Griggs' son and Robert's father] give him [Robert] to me when he was three. Sam Brooks, Charlie's father, I don' know where he is at. His home, though, is in Birmingham. Mae Brooks, my daughter, and Sam was married right down there. Professor Cook married 'em. Lillie Page was Robert's mother. She an' Dan weren't married."

In regard to the children away, she said: "Mae, she married and went off from here before the boy was born. Mae ought to be about thirty-two years old. She been out here once this last year. She in Montgomery. Julia, she in Montgomery, too. She been out here twice. They stay in jinin' rooms. She been gone about eleven years. She stayed here a year after 'Miss' [Mae] married; washes some for the white peoples and cooks some, I reckon. James moved away year before last. He's married; ain't got no chillun. He's the oldest one. Reginald [Rooster], he live right over the hill. He been away [from the parent-home] five years; got three chillun. Dan, he in Montgomery. He been gone I don't know how long. He won't staying with me when he went off in the army. He been gone a long time. He been married twice. Had three chillun by his first wife, Alice Robinson. His second wife's Susie Black, but him and her ain't never found no chillun. Andrew's on Mr. B____'s place. He got four chillun. He been gone about nine years. He married Ruth Williams.

"Mr. Griggs [her husband], he stays up yonder to Liverpool. He married again to Mamie Wright. He tole me he want a divorce; I tole him he was welcome to it. Me and him was separated near about ten years before he did marry. He didn't work to suit me, and I didn't work to suit him." When asked if she put him out, she replied, "I didn't put him out, he walked on out I reckon. I didn't want no lazy man.

"We rent from Mr. H____; he ain't give us no advance in seven years. The place suits us and we jes' do the best us can. We made a sort of little crop last year, and then he went up on the rent this year. I guess he thought that would get that [all the crop]. We paid one bale [450 pounds] for rent and sold 1-1/2 bales. The money was divided between my boy and me and his wife, and he had three to look after and I had four, and there wasn't much left. We divided after paying $25.00 for the mule. We sold 1-1/2 bales of cotton for $50.00; paid $25.00 for the mule, and had $25.00 left, and this was divided.

"We ain't raised nothin' much but a little corn and a little syrup; about twenty-five bushels of corn, and we divided that. Then there was two small banks of 'taters. Last year it was so dry the 'taters didn't have time to get their growth. We got about twelve gallons of millet syrup." Speaking of the crop, she remarked, "The last two or three years the crop has been bad. Last year it wasn't so bad, but year before that, and the year before that, we didn't make the rent."

When asked if she had any farm implements, she replied, "Yes, ma'm, I got a couple of plows; ain't much; just nailed 'em up and pieced 'em up. If I make anything, I am going to buy me some plows."

Concerning the food, she said, "Ain't had nothin' today but meat and bread, and hardly had that; the garden done burn up so bad. For

Sunday, we had some fried inguns and flour bread and such as that. I milk every day. The cow can't give much, she might nigh dry, don' hav' nothin' much to give her. We have just one thing, and can't hardly get that. Times is hard and you have to scuffle yourself. White folks ain't gwine to give you nothin', jes' have to do the best you can. We killed the hog last year because she ate the chickens. Den we bought dis one an' she eat chickens. One of the grand children works for one of the neighbors. Charlie gets $0.50 a day from Edwin Work. He black, but a big man and sees after 'em, and he has somethin' to hire we with for the money. The rest of 'em ain't got nothin' to hire nobody." When questioned about expenditures for food and clothing, she answered, "Ain't got nothin' to spend. I work out and get a little something. I work for anybody, and get a half gallon of syrup or like dat. Dey ain't got nothin' to pay you with.

"This house been built about thirteen years. It done wore out one set of shingles. We got a privy but tain't no 'count. Got to get lumber to fix it up. We cook on a stove, but it done wore out now." When Mrs. Griggs was asked if she slept with the windows open, she replied, "No'm. I'm scared to stay in here with 'em open." In reply to the question of whether she liked the place, she said, "I likes here bettern any wheres else I know. I would have to go and get used to it, but I been here so long." When asked if there was anything wrong with the house, she replied, "There's nothing wrong if the white man would fix it. Yes'm, it leaks."

Concerning school expenditures, she said, "It takes all I can do to eat. This year I cut down to about $3.00 for the two chillun. Last year it was $4.00. I worried this year till they cut it down."

Concerning insurance, she said, "We ain't got no insurance; I was just in a society, but it got to the place where I could not keep it up, and I just got out. I wanted to try to stay in something so when I lay down and die, I have somethin' to bury me. If you don't pay the dues they just put you out. You can jine again, but you have to pay that back money. Societies done got to the place they don't help you none. All of them near 'bout done broke down. The treasurer, she said she had the money in the bank and the bank close down. I decided to let it alone. Don't care how much you have in there, you get behin', they goin' to turn you out. I was sick when the Red Cross was giving seeds. I went to the Health Department and some of them said if I tried to farm they wouldn't give you nothin'; jest help them what was caught.

"I don't know 'zackly how much I spent for clothes; it was such a little bit. I bought the chillun a little somethin'. I bought books and pay the teacher. If you don't pay the teacher, they send 'em back. I spent about $11.00 in buying them underwear and everything.

"Ain't spent nothin' for medicine more than a little Black Draught. If I had money I would go to the doctor. I'm old enough to cross over and it worries me. I ain't been to no doctor. I did say I was going to Dr. Davidson to see if he had anything. Last year the doctor give me some pills and liquory medicine for the fever. I sometime think I got something; I keep sick all the time, but they ain't never tell me what it is. It been near twenty years since I been to a doctor. I need to go a heap of times, but I don't have nothin' to go with. I keep puny and need medicine all the time, but I ain't had no money. My last blood that was drawn, I ain't got no hearin' from. The first time they say I had bad blood. I took seven shots, but the doctor said I was most too old, and he change up and give me medicine. Charlie took three or four shots, until they drawed his blood again, and did not get no hearin'. Robert took the shots."

When asked what she did for a good time, she answered, "I can't catch no fish. I jest stay here trying to clean up, patch up and do something or other."

Concerning how she got along with her neighbors, she said, "I don't worry nobody in the world but myself and Jesus and I have to beg him all the time to get some bread to eat. He sure will answer your prayers but look like it come so long, but he moves in his own time; got to keep on begging him to open a way for you; if he don't, someone gwine to perish. I belong to Damascus Church, but I go to all the churches, if I ain't too tired to walk." About paying dues, she said, "Yes, I paid 'em at first; womens pay $1.80. I didn't pay last year 'cause I didn't have it. Ain't paid nothin' this year. All I did is make out to live." When asked if the church helped her any, she replied, "My mamma was here; she was a hundred some odd years old and blind, and they didn't give her nothin'."

She said, concerning church membership, "I been belongst to church now near about thirty years. Where the Lord convert my soul? Right over yonder by dat dead tree, dat where the Lord convert my soul at about nine o'clock on a Thursday. I was over there praying; over by that tree was my praying ground. I know when the Lord poured his Holy Ghost around my soul. I knowed there was something doin' then 'cause I had been praying so long. He told me to go in all parts of the world and tell what he have done for my soul. I was baptized by John Woods

—old Pap Woods. I jined Damascus. That church been tore down three times. It started as a bush harbor, then a log cabin, then they built a little bit more."

11

The Social Settlement: Jane Addams establishes Hull-House

Jane Addams was undoubtedly the most imaginative and perceptive social reformer in the Progressive era. The founder of the Hull-House settlement in Chicago, a prolific writer on urban poverty, and an effective lobbyist for corrective legislation, she represented all that was generous and high-minded in Progressive sentiments and actions. Born in 1860 to a well-to-do Illinois family, she went to Rockford College and then on to medical school; but in 1883 her health broke, and for the next several years she traveled and recuperated in Europe. Returning to the United States in 1887, having been influenced by the social experiments taking place in England, she established Hull-House, and around her and this institution the most noted reformers of the period clustered. Her account of the enterprise, Twenty Years at Hull-House, *captures well her own enlightened sensitivity and the general spirit of reform.*

I think that time has justified our early contention that the mere foothold of a house, easily accessible, ample in space, hospitable and tolerant in spirit, situated in the midst of the large foreign colonies which so easily isolate themselves in American cities, would be in itself a serviceable thing for Chicago. I am not so sure that we succeeded in our endeavors "to make social intercourse express the growing sense of the economic unity of society and to add the social function to democracy." But Hull-House was soberly opened on the theory that the dependence of classes on each other is reciprocal; and that as the social relation is essentially a reciprocal relation, it gives a form of expression that has peculiar value.

Jane Addams, *Twenty Years at Hull-House* (New York, 1910), excerpts from pp. 89-112.

In our search for a vicinity in which to settle we went about with the officers of the compulsory education department, with city missionaries and with the newspaper reporters whom I recall as a much older set of men than one ordinarily associates with that profession, or perhaps I was only sent out with the older ones on what they must all have considered a quixotic mission.

In the early spring, on the way to a Bohemian mission in the carriage of one of its founders, we passed a fine old house standing well back from the street, surrounded on three sides by a broad piazza which was supported by wooden pillars of exceptionally pure Corinthian design and proportion. I was so attracted by the house that I set forth to visit it the very next day, but though I searched for it then and for several days after, I could not find it, and at length I most reluctantly gave up the search.

Three weeks later, with the advice of several of the oldest residents of Chicago, including the ex-mayor of the city, Colonel Mason, who had from the first been a warm friend to our plans, we decided upon a location somewhere near the junction of Blue Island Avenue, Halsted Street, and Harrison Street. I was surprised and overjoyed on the very first day of our search for quarters to come upon the hospitable old house, the quest for which I had so recently abandoned. The house was of course rented, the lower part of it used for offices and storerooms in connection with a factory that stood back of it. However, after some difficulties were overcome, it proved to be possible to sublet the second floor and what had been the large drawing-room on the first floor.

The fine old house responded kindly to repairs, its wide hall and open fireplaces always insuring it a gracious aspect. Its generous owner, Miss Helen Culver, in the following spring gave us a free leasehold of the entire house. Her kindness has continued through the years until the group of thirteen buildings, which at present comprises our equipment, is built largely upon land which Miss Culver has put at the service of the Settlement which bears Mr. Hull's name. In those days the house stood between an undertaking establishment and a saloon. "Knight, Death, and the Devil," the three were called by a Chicago wit, and yet any mock heroics which might be implied by comparing the Settlement to a knight quickly dropped away under the genuine kindness and hearty welcome extended to us by the families living up and down the street.

We furnished the house as we would have furnished it were it in another part of the city, with the photographs and other impedimenta we had collected in Europe, and with a few bits of family mahogany. While all the new furniture which was bought was enduring in quality, we were careful to keep it in character with the fine old residence.

Probably no young matron ever placed her own things in her own house with more pleasure than that with which we first furnished Hull-House. We believed that the Settlement may logically bring to its aid all those adjuncts which the cultivated man regards as good and suggestive of the best life of the past.

On the 18th of September, 1889, Miss Starr and I moved into it, with Miss Mary Keyser, who began by performing the housework, but who quickly developed into a very important factor in the life of the vicinity as well as in that of the household, and whose death five years later was most sincerely mourned by hundreds of our neighbors. In our enthusiasm over "settling," the first night we forgot not only to lock but to close a side door opening on Polk Street, and were much pleased in the morning to find that we possessed a fine illustration of the honesty and kindliness of our new neighbors.

Halsted Street has grown so familiar during twenty years of residence, that it is difficult to recall its gradual changes,—the withdrawal of the more prosperous Irish and Germans, and the slow substitution of Russian Jews, Italians, and Greeks.

The houses of the ward, for the most part wooden, were originally built for one family and are now occupied by several. They are after the type of the inconvenient frame cottages found in the poorer suburbs twenty years ago. Many of them were built where they now stand; others were brought thither on rollers, because their previous sites had been taken for factories. The fewer brick tenement buildings which are three or four stories high are comparatively new, and there are few large tenements. The little wooden houses have a temporary aspect, and for this reason, perhaps, the tenement-house legislation in Chicago is totally inadequate. Rear tenements flourish; many houses have no water supply save the faucet in the back yard, there are no fire escapes, the garbage and ashes are placed in wooden boxes which are fastened to the street pavements. One of the most discouraging features about the present system of tenement houses is that many are owned by sordid and ignorant immigrants. The theory that wealth brings responsibility, that possession entails at length education and refinement, in these cases fails utterly. The children of an Italian immigrant owner may "shine" shoes in the street, and his wife may pick rags from the street gutter, laboriously sorting them in a dingy court. Wealth may do something for her self-complacency and feeling of consequence; it certainly does nothing for her comfort or her children's improvement nor for the cleanliness of any one concerned. Another thing that prevents better houses in Chicago is the tentative attitude of the real estate men. Many unsavory conditions are allowed to continue which would be regarded with horror if they were considered permanent. Meanwhile, the wretched conditions persist until at least two generations of children have been born and reared in them.

In every neighborhood where poorer people live, because rents are supposed to be cheaper there, is an element which, although uncertain in the individual, in the aggregate can be counted upon. It is composed of people of former education and opportunity who have cherished ambitions and prospects, but who are caricatures of what they meant to be—"hollow ghosts which blame the living men." There are times in many lives when there is a cessation of energy and loss of power. Men and women of education and refinement come to live in a cheaper neighborhood because they lack the ability to make money, because of ill health, because of an unfortunate marriage, or for other reasons which do not imply criminality or stupidity. Among them are those who, in spite of untoward circumstances, keep up some sort of an intellectual life; those who are "great for books," as their neighbors say. To such the Settlement may be a genuine refuge.

Our "first resident," as she gayly designated herself, was a charming old lady who gave five consecutive readings from Hawthorne to a most appreciative audience, interspersing the magic tales most delightfully with recollections of the elusive and fascinating author. Years before she had lived at Brook Farm as a pupil of the Ripleys, and she came to us for ten days because she wished to live once more in an atmosphere where "idealism ran high." We thus early found the type of class which through all the years has remained most popular—a combination of a social atmosphere with serious study.

Volunteers to the new undertaking came quickly; a charming young girl conducted a kindergarten in the drawing-room, coming regularly every morning from her home in a distant part of the North Side of the city. Although a tablet to her memory has stood upon a mantel shelf in Hull-House for five years, we still associate her most vividly with the play of little children, first in her kindergarten and then in her own nursery, which furnished a veritable illustration of Victor Hugo's definition of heaven,—"a place where parents are always young and children always little." Her daily presence for the first two years made it quite impossible for us to become too solemn and self-conscious in our strenuous routine, for her mirth and buoyancy were irresistible and her eager desire to share the life of the neighborhood never failed, although it was often put to a severe test. One day at luncheon she gayly recited her futile attempt to impress temperance principles upon the mind of an Italian mother, to whom she had returned a small daughter of five sent to the kindergarten "in quite a horrid state of intoxication" from the wine-soaked bread upon which she had breakfasted. The mother, with the gentle courtesy of a South Italian, listened politely to her graphic portrayal of the untimely end awaiting so immature a wine bibber; but long before the lecture was finished, quite unconscious of the incongruity, she hospitably set forth her best wines, and when her baffled guest refused one after the other, she disappeared, only to quickly return with a small dark glass of whisky, saying reassuringly, "See, I have brought you the true American drink." The recital ended in seriocomic despair, with the rueful statement that "the impression I probably made upon her darkened mind was, that it is the American custom to breakfast children on bread soaked in whisky instead of light Italian wine."

The dozens of younger children who from the first came to Hull-House were organized into groups which were not quite classes and not quite clubs. The value of these groups consisted almost entirely in arousing a higher imagination and in giving the children the opportunity which they could not have in the crowded schools, for initiative and for independent social relationships. The public schools then contained little hand work of any sort, so that naturally any instruction which we provided for the children took the direction of this supplementary work. But it required a constant effort that the pressure of poverty itself should not defeat the educational aim. The Italian girls in the sewing classes would count that day lost when they could not carry home a garment, and the insistence that it should be neatly made seemed a super-refinement to those in dire need of clothing.

As these clubs have been continued during the twenty years they have developed classes in the many forms of handicraft which the newer education is so rapidly adapting for the delight of children; but they still keep their essentially social character and still minister to that large number of children who leave school the very week they are fourteen years old, only too eager to close the schoolroom door forever on a tiresome task that is at last well over. It seems to us important that these children shall find themselves permanently attached to a House that offers them evening clubs and classes with their old companions, that merges as easily as possible the school life into the working life and does what it can to find places for the bewildered young things looking for work. A large proportion of the delinquent boys brought into the juvenile court in Chicago are the oldest sons in large families whose wages are

needed at home. The grades from which many of them leave school, as
the records show, are piteously far from the seventh and eighth where
the very first instruction in manual training is given, nor have they been
caught by any other abiding interest.

In spite of these flourishing clubs for children early established at
Hull-House, and the fact that our first organized undertaking was a
kindergarten, we were very insistent that the Settlement should not be
primarily for the children, and that it was absurd to suppose that grown
people would not respond to opportunities for education and social life.
Our enthusiastic kindergartner herself demonstrated this with an old
woman of ninety, who, because she was left alone all day while her
daughter cooked in a restaurant, had formed such a persistent habit of
picking the plaster off the walls that one landlord after another refused
to have her for a tenant. It required but a few weeks' time to teach her
to make large paper chains, and gradually she was content to do it all
day long, and in the end took quite as much pleasure in adorning the
walls as she had formerly taken in demolishing them.

On our first New Year's Day at Hull-House we invited the older
people in the vicinity, sending a carriage for the most feeble and an-
nouncing to all of them that we were going to organize an Old Settlers'
Party.

Every New Year's Day since, older people in varying numbers have
come together at Hull-House to relate early hardships, and to take for
the moment the place in the community to which their pioneer life
entitles them. Many people who were formerly residents of the vicinity,
but whom prosperity has carried into more desirable neighborhoods,
come back to these meetings and often confess to each other that they
have never since found such kindness as in early Chicago when all its
citizens came together in mutual enterprises.

In those early days we were often asked why we had come to live
on Halsted Street when we could afford to live somewhere else. I remember one man who used to shake his head and say it was "The strangest
thing he had met in his experience," but who was finally convinced that
it was "not strange but natural." In time it came to seem natural to all
of us that the Settlement should be there. If it is natural to feed the
hungry and care for the sick, it is certainly natural to give pleasure to
the young, comfort to the aged, and to minister to the deep-seated
craving for social intercourse that all men feel. Whoever does it is rewarded by something which, if not gratitude, is at least spontaneous and
vital and lacks that irksome sense of obligation with which a substantial
benefit is too often acknowledged.

In addition to the neighbors who responded to the receptions and classes, we found those who were too battered and oppressed to care for them. To these, however, was left that susceptibility to the bare offices of humanity which raises such offices into a bond of fellowship.

From the first it seemed understood that we were ready to perform the humblest neighborhood services. We were asked to wash the new-born babies, and to prepare the dead for burial, to nurse the sick, and to "mind the children."

But in spite of some untoward experiences, we were constantly impressed with the uniform kindness and courtesy we received. Perhaps these first days laid the simple human foundations which are certainly essential for continuous living among the poor: first, genuine preference for residence in an industrial quarter to any other part of the city, because it is interesting and makes the human appeal; and second, the conviction, in the words of Canon Barnett, that the things which make men alike are finer and better than the things that keep them apart, and that these basic likenesses, if they are properly accentuated, easily transcend the less essential differences of race, language, creed and tradition.

Perhaps even in those first days we made a beginning toward that object which was afterwards stated in our charter: "To provide a center for a higher civic and social life; to institute and maintain educational and philanthropic enterprises, and to investigate and improve the conditions in the industrial districts of Chicago."

12

Rescuing Children from the Almshouse: The origins of aid to dependent children

The first White House Conference on the Care of Dependent Children, convened in 1909 by President Theodore Roosevelt, announced a new goal in the care of poor children: whenever possible the family should not be broken up because of poverty. To implement this program, the Conference recommended state pensions for needy widows with children, a measure that was rapidly adopted in many industrial states. It

Proceedings of the Conference on the Care of Dependent Children (Washington, 1909), 60th Congress, 2nd session, Senate Document No. 721, excerpts from pp. 5-7, 17-18, 43-50, 87-98.

represented the first break with the reliance on almshouse relief. Slowly over the next several decades, public programs attempted to relieve the poor within the community and not in custodial institutions.

To the Senate and House of Representatives:

On January 25–26, 1909, there assembled in this city, on my invitation, a conference on the care of dependent children. To this conference there came from nearly every State in the Union men and women actively engaged in the care of dependent children, and they represented all the leading religious bodies.

The subject considered is one of high importance to the well-being of the nation. The Census Bureau reported in 1904 that there were in orphanages and children's homes about 93,000 dependent children. There are probably 50,000 more (the precise number never having been ascertained) in private homes, either on board or in adopted homes provided by the generosity of foster parents. In addition to these there were 25,000 children in institutions for juvenile delinquents.

Each of these children represents either a potential addition to the productive capacity and the enlightened citizenship of the nation, or, if allowed to suffer from neglect, a potential addition to the destructive forces of the community. The ranks of criminals and other enemies of society are recruited in an altogether undue proportion from children bereft of their natural homes and left without sufficient care.

The interests of the nation are involved in the welfare of this army of children no less than in our great material affairs.

Notwithstanding a wide diversity of views and methods represented in the conference, and notwithstanding the varying legislative enactments and policies of the States from which the members came, the conference, at the close of its sessions, unanimously adopted a series of declarations expressing the conclusions which they had reached. These constitute a wise, constructive, and progressive programme of child-caring work. If given full effect by the proper agencies, existing methods and practices in almost every community would be profoundly and advantageously modified.

More significant even than the contents of the declarations is the fact that they were adopted without dissenting vote and with every demonstration of hearty approval on the part of all present. They constitute a standard of accepted opinion by which each community should measure the adequacy of its existing methods and to which each community should seek to conform its legislation and its practice.

Prayer time in New York's Five Points Nursery, 1889. The reliance on institutionalization affected the very young as well as the very old. Orphans and children deserted by their parents grew up in settings that were all too often rigid, fixed, and mechanical. Photograph by Jacob A. Riis. The Jacob A. Riis Collection, Museum of the City of New York.

The keynote of the conference was expressed in these words:

Home life is the highest and finest product of civilization. Children should not be deprived of it except for urgent and compelling reasons.

Surely poverty alone should not disrupt the home. Parents of good character suffering from temporary misfortune, and above all deserving mothers fairly well able to work but deprived of the support of the normal breadwinner, should be given such aid as may be necessary to enable them to maintain suitable homes for the rearing of their children. The widowed or deserted mother, if a good woman, willing to work and to do her best, should ordinarily be helped in such fashion as will enable her to bring up her children herself in their natural home. Children from unfit homes, and children who have no homes, who must be cared for by charitable agencies, should, so far as practicable, be cared for in families.

I transmit herewith for your information a copy of the conclusions reached by the conference, of which the following is a brief summary:

1. *Home care.*—Children of worthy parents or deserving mothers should, as a rule, be kept with their parents at home.

2. *Preventive work.*—The effort should be made to eradicate causes of depen-

dency, such as disease and accident, and to substitute compensation and insurance for relief.

3. *Home finding.*—Homeless and neglected children, if normal, should be cared for in families, when practicable.

4. *Cottage system.*—Institutions should be on the cottage plan with small units, as far as possible.

5. *Incorporation.*—Agencies caring for dependent children should be incorporated, on approval of a suitable state board.

6. *State inspection.*—The State should inspect the work of all agencies which care for dependent children.

7. *Inspection of educational work.*—Educational work of institutions and agencies caring for dependent children should be supervised by state educational authorities.

8. *Facts and records.*—Complete histories of dependent children and their parents, based upon personal investigation and supervision, should be recorded for guidance of child-caring agencies.

9. *Physical care.*—Every needy child should receive the best medical and surgical attention, and be instructed in health and hygiene.

10. *Cooperation.*—Local child-caring agencies should cooperate and establish joint bureaus of information.

11. *Undesirable legislation.*—Prohibitive legislation against transfer of dependent children between States should be repealed.

12. *Permanent organization.*—A permanent organization for work along the lines of these resolutions is desirable.

13. *Federal children's bureau.*—Establishment of a federal children's bureau is desirable, and enactment of pending bill is earnestly recommended.

14. Suggests special message to Congress favoring federal children's bureau and other legislation applying above principles to District of Columbia and other federal territory.

While it is recognized that these conclusions can be given their fullest effect only by the action of the several States or communities concerned, or of their charitable agencies, the conference requested me, in section 14 of the conclusions, to send to you a message recommending federal action.

There are pending in both Houses of Congress bills for the establishment of a children's bureau, i.e., Senate bill No. 8323 and House bill No. 24148. These provide for a children's bureau in the Department of the Interior, which

shall investigate and report upon all matters pertaining to the welfare of children and child life, and shall especially investigate the questions of infant mortality, the birth rate, physical degeneracy, orphanage, juvenile delinquency and juvenile courts, desertion and illegitimacy, dangerous occupations, accidents and diseases of children of the working classes, employment, legislation affecting children in the several States and Territories, and such other facts as have a bearing upon the health, efficiency, character, and training of children.

One of the needs felt most acutely by the conference was that of accurate information concerning these questions relating to childhood. The National Government not only has the unquestioned right of research in such vital matters, but is the only agency which can effectively conduct such general inquiries as are needed for the benefit of all our citizens. In accordance with the unanimous request of the conference, I therefore most heartily urge your favorable action on these measures.

THEODORE ROOSEVELT

Address of Mr. James F. Jackson, Superintendent Associated Charities, Cleveland

Mr. Chairman, ladies, and gentlemen, it has not always been possible for us to have the agreement of the church and the state relative to the care of children. To-day the state and the church have agreed as to what should be done for the child, as far as the question under consideration is concerned, and it simply rests upon laymen—the common, ordinary, every-day laymen in this tremendously democratic country of ours—to say that both the church and the state are just and wise and humane. And there is little more to say.

Civilization demands that a mother shall do more than bring up her child. When an animal is born and anything chances to happen to the mother, if it happens to find a foster mother that animal may grow up; if not, it will have to die. But with the human species, we demand that the mother shall do more than simply bring up animals of the human kind. We demand that they shall educate their offspring; that they shall train them to be good citizens. Morally, mentally, and physically children must be educated. That education chiefly falls to the mother, and therefore it has come about with us that the mother is not expected to become the breadwinner. When anything happens to the breadwinner, if the mother is capable, it seems to be perfectly clear that it is our business, either as a state or as individuals, to see that she has material support. Always there should be individual friendliness as a part of such aid. Either the state or the individual, or the two in cooperation, should see that the mother has the necessities of existence, has the raw material, we may say, with which to care for the children and provide the home where she may educate them. We make this demand upon her on the assumption that she has the capacity. Should she lack the capacity, if she is inefficient or below the community standard of morality, the mother is thereby unable to rear good men and women. Then we must help substitute capacity for her incapacity, or if that is impossible the children must be rescued from her.

The standard of the community in morality is easily stated, while its standard of efficiency is rather difficult to state. When a woman, after a few years of material aid, can not be taught to provide for her children, it usually indicates incapacity, and because of that incapacity it is not a good home for her children. Or if a woman becomes a beggar, her home is no better for the child than the home of an immoral woman, and the child has no better chance for good citizenship. Then it becomes necessary for us, under the adjudication made by the state and indorsed to-day by the church, to take away the child from the mother because she can not make a good citizen of that child. The question is, Will she develop a good citizen or a bad citizen?

As Mr. Scanlan has just said, it is up to us as individual societies. It is a work that can not remain entirely with the state; in fact, it is usually better for the state to take no part in the aid. It is the work of individual societies to see that she has a fair chance in the development of her child; that she not only has a fair chance, but has good backing, especially that she has friendship.

It seems to me, when we talk about starvation in this country, we must bear in mind that practically nobody starves in America who can digest food. But thousands are dying every year, morally and physically from the lack of friendship. The dependent parent or parents are entitled to our friendly aid and our material support until, they can prove whether or not they are capable of developing children to good citizenship. If they are incapable, then it is necessary that the children be taken from them.

I think there is one more point that may be fairly made. Whereas I think we all agree that the interests of the child entirely overbalance the interest of the parents, the welfare of the parents should be considered. When we take her children from a mother simply because of poverty, we subject her to temptations which frequently she is not able to bear. The child, in many instances, is the anchor that holds the woman to a good life, and in that good life she will herself bring up good children.

Then the mother has another interest which I think is perfectly fair to be considered; that is, the chance of being cared for in her old age. Every women makes an investment with each child for care in her old age. If we have taken the child from an efficient mother simply because of poverty, we have robbed her of possible care in old age, and the injustice is as great as in any form of robbery.

Mr. Chairman, I am glad that we are in accord—the state, the church, and the common democracy—in the conclusion that the home should not be broken up simply for reasons of poverty, and that children should be removed only for reasons of inefficiency or immorality. I thank you.

Address by Rabbi Emil G. Hirsch, D. D., LL. D., Ph.D., President National Conference of Jewish Charities, of Chicago

Mr. Chairman, ladies, and gentlemen: Of different religious beliefs, of various political creeds, and perhaps members of different economic and philosophical schools, yet are we all united by the magic power of certain convictions basic of our meeting here, to the effect that if it is worth while to conserve the natural resources of our country it is a thousand times more important to conserve the children of our nation.

Institutions represent the line of least resistance. But in morals the line of least resistance is never the first but always the last that ought to be chosen. Childhood is too sacred a possession and too mighty a potentiality to be handled on the ready-made plan. The best of institutions after all must neglect individual differences. They can not take account of personality. They deal with inmates. Discipline of military rigor is absolutely indispensable where hundreds and hundreds of children are herded together in one asylum. No account may be taken of individual needs and no patience can be shown individual idiosyncrasies. The inmates are of necessity trimmed and turned into automatons. The result is the institutional type. They who have had opportunity to observe the mental and perhaps also the moral strabismus, almost invariably characteristic of the young men and women fresh from these institutions, are familiar with the sad and depressing fact that it is symptomatic of the institutional type. They know that the type is marked by repression if not atrophy of the impulse to act independently.

At all events, the institution segregates its inmates. Segregation always results in creating specialized character which sets off the segregated apart from the community, while under normal conditions they would be, as they should be, part of the community. Class character is not necessarily of weaker moral texture than is the community's. Instances recur to mind where the reverse is true, class outshining the mass in certain regards. But segregation of the young into a class is always beset with peril to their morality.

Institutional life for the young would be less objectionable if society at large itself were institutionalized. Asylums and orphanages of necessity are organized on a plan which is not that of the world, which sooner or later their protégés have to reenter. Upon their wards thus at the period of their dismissal from the institutions is laid the burden of readjusting themselves to surroundings radically different from those in which they have been raised. And the wrong, the danger, and the strain are all the greater since this period, as a rule, is coincidental with that of puberty, the one period when drain of nerve force should be the least. The plight of those sent out is similar to that of the immigrant from another country. As all asylums must send their wards out into the noninstitutional world, if this word be permissible, institutional preparation is necessarily inadequate, to say the least. As now constituted, the basic rock on which society rests is the home. The family is the structural cell. It seems thus a very queer proceeding first to unhome the young when later they will have to do their part in a society founded on the home and rooted in the family.

That the home and not the institution is the normal environment for children they have recognized who have made strong efforts to modify the institutional policy, with a view to approximately reproducing the conditions of home surroundings for the dependent children. The cottage plan was devised to meet the shortcomings of the preceding institutional method. That it was a step forward is well assured. But even it is not free from the objections that lie against the institutional device. In the first place, the cottage as a rule is not a reproduction of the home. Families of over 30 children are certainly exceptional. Again, in the cottages as a rule the sexes are segregated, and that for good reasons, and indeed the children are classified according to age, members of this artificial family being selected for living together on account of correspondence of age. The normal family does not segregate the sexes nor does it classify by the age line.

More difficult are the cases where dependency is the result of abandonment or of parental viciousness and immorality. But again most cases of abandonment are due to wife desertion. Let the mother be aided to keep the family together under the same precautions as to guardians and visitations as have been outlined in the case of dependency due to the death of the parent. Mothers, in fact, should be pensioned when the alternative is placing the child into an institution and the mother going to work or the child's suffering for want of attention. By forcing the mother into the competitive struggle for wage harm is done to her and her child and to many others. The mother that devotes herself to her child and household renders social service of inestimable value. It is her right to expect compensation at the hand of society that ultimately and often immediately is the gainer by her maternal devotion. Let me suggest that the cause of unmarried mothers and illegitimate children is as yet too cruelly ignored. Even these children and mothers are worth saving, and their cause is not in essentials different from that of other helpless mothers and children. In the long run, pensioning mothers is cheaper than building almshouses and jails and reformatories. Keep the mothers at home and a long stride is taken on the road leading away from pauperism and that which causes it—alcoholism and domestic anarchy. I should never separate children from their parents or brothers and sisters from one another wherever it is possible to keep the family intact. In this work "preserve the family" must be our watchword. Where this is not given unto us, find another family that the child may come to its own, a healthy childhood under the inspiration of love and the sunshine of affection, with the freedom to find himself spontaneously both in play and in work.

Every consideration, then, points to the desirability of abandoning the institutional plan. Institutions for the care of dependent children should hereafter serve but one purpose; that of affording temporary shelter until homes are found for those that need them.

13

The Organization of Legal Aid:
Reginald Heber Smith describes the innovation

Another crucial though less well-known innovation of the Progressive era, was the creation of legal-aid societies. They sprang up in cities all over the nation, trying to extend legal services without cost to the poor, hoping that all classes would receive equal justice in the courts. The effort at first was limited, not covering, for example, criminal cases or divorce proceedings. But soon a program of public defenders for lower-class

Reginald Heber Smith, *Justice and the Poor,* Carnegie Foundation for the Advancement of Teaching, Bulletin No. 13 (New York, 1924), excerpts from pp. 8-12, 152-153.

criminals took hold, and the societies widened the scope of their operations. The goals of the legal-aid movement emerge clearly in the statement of one of its founders, Reginald Heber Smith.

The administration of American justice is not impartial, the rich and the poor do not stand on an equality before the law, the traditional method of providing justice has operated to close the doors of the courts to the poor, and has caused a gross denial of justice in all parts of the country to millions of persons.

Sweeping as this indictment may appear, it is substantiated by ample authority. A few statements deserve to be presented here.

If there is one sad anomaly that should stand out in our present days of conscientious self-searching, it is the harsh fact that, with all our prating about justice, we deliberately withhold it from the thousands who are too poor to pay for it.

The equal administration of the laws is a right guaranteed by the fundamental law of the land; and yet no person will deny that this privilege is more honored in the breach than in the observance; for there are very many people in every American community who, through ignorance of their rights or their inability to pay the imposts levied by the state as a condition precedent to the pursuit of justice in the courts, are constantly being denied that equal administration of the laws and the justice that is supposed, logically, to follow it.

The majority of our judges and lawyers view this situation with indifference. They fail to see behind this denial of justice the suffering and tragedy which it causes, the havoc it plays in individual lives, and its influence in retarding our Americanization program. "The judicial department," said Chief Justice Marshall, "comes home in its effects to every man's fireside. It passes on his property, his reputation, his life, his all." Because law is all-embracing, the denial of its protection means the destruction of homes through illegal foreclosures, the loss through trick or chicanery of a lifetime's savings, the taking away of children from their parents by fraudulent guardianship proceedings. Hundreds of thousands of men, many of them immigrants, have been unable to collect their wages honestly earned.

Denial of justice is not merely negative in effect; it actively encourages fraud and dishonesty. Unscrupulous employers, seeing the inability of wage-earners to enforce payments, have deliberately hired men without the slightest intention of paying them. Some of these employers are themselves poor men, who strive in this way to gain an advantage. The evil is not one of class in the sense that it gives the poor over to the mercies of only the rich. It enables the poor to rob one another; it permits the shrewd immigrant of a few years' residence to defraud his more recently arrived countrymen. The line of cleavage which it follows and accentuates is that between the dishonest and the honest. Everywhere it abets the unscrupulous, the crafty, and the vicious in their ceaseless plans for exploiting their less intelligent and less fortunate fellows. The system not only robs the poor of their only protection, but it places in the hands of their oppressors the most powerful and ruthless weapon ever invented.

The law itself becomes the means of extortion. As Lord Brougham said of the English administration of justice in 1800, it puts "a two-edged sword in the hands of craft and oppression." From the cradle to the grave the poor man is the prey of a host of petty swindlers, who find it easy, through such devices as fraudulent assignments, trustee process, or garnishment of wages for fictitious debts, to rob and despoil. There exist to-day businesses established, conducted, and flourishing on the principle that as against the poor the law can be violated with impunity because redress is beyond their reach. It is this situation which allowed such unrestrained abuse of the laws regulating the assignment of future wages that a sort of quasi-slavery resulted, which brought the loan shark into being, and permitted flagrant usury to grow into a monstrous thing.

The effects of this denial of justice are far reaching. Nothing rankles more in the human heart than the feeling of injustice. It produces a sense of helplessness, then bitterness. It is brooded over. It leads directly to contempt for law, disloyalty to the government, and plants the seeds of anarchy. The conviction grows that law is not justice and challenges the belief that justice is best secured when administered according to law. The poor come to think of American justice as containing only laws that punish and never laws that help. They are against the law because they consider the law against them. A persuasion spreads that there is one law for the rich and another for the poor.

How this comes about can be simply told. One afternoon, Arthur V. Briesen, President of the New York Legal Aid Society, took Theodore Roosevelt, then Police Commissioner of New York, to the Society's office to see what went on. They sat at the interviewing desk. A glazier came in and related that he had set twenty-two panes of glass in a barn and that the owner of the barn had refused to pay him $6.60, the agreed price. He had been out of work and needed this money to buy bread and milk for his family's supper. On his way home from the West Side, where he had worked, to the East Side, where he lived, he crossed Fifth Avenue at Forty-fourth Street and passed the luxurious restaurants on either corner. His own children went to bed supperless. The next morning he sought out a lawyer, who told him that to bring suit the costs and the fee would be ten dollars. This he could not pay. From there he went to the Municipal Court, originally known as "The Poor Man's Court," where he saw a judge, who was obliged to explain that he had neither the time, not the money, not the right to undertake the necessary proceedings; that as the man had no money, he could not prosecute the case; and that, inasmuch as the expenses would exceed the amount in dispute, he had better drop it. As the man told his story, sitting in the office of the legal aid society, he was an incipient anarchist.

The effect on the immigrant is peculiarly unfortunate. He comes to this country, often from lands of injustice and oppression, with high hopes, expecting to receive fair play and square dealing. It is essential that he be assimilated and taught respect for our institutions. Because of the strangeness of all his surroundings, his ignorance of our language and our customs, often because of his simple faith in the America of which he has heard, he becomes an easy prey. When he finds himself wronged or betrayed, keen disappointment is added to the sense of injustice. Through bitter disillusionment he becomes easily subject to the influences of sedition and disorder.

The essentially conservative bench and bar will vehemently deny any suggestion that there is no law for the poor, but, as the legal aid societies know, such is the belief to-day of a multitude of humble, entirely honest people, and in the light of their experience it appears as the simple truth. Consider, for example, this actual case. A woman borrowed ten dollars in 1914, and for two years paid interest at 180 percent. In 1916 a law was enacted fixing 36 percent as the maximum rate. The lender, by a device contrary to the statute, compelled her to continue paying 156 percent interest. The law also provided that if excess interest were charged, the loan would be declared void by a suit in equity. The law was on the books. The court house was open, the equity court in session with its judge on the bench and its officers in attendance. All that was of no avail to her, for the law could not bring its redress until five dollars was paid for service of process and entry fee, and ten dollars to an attorney to draw, file, and present the necessary bill of complaint. Fifteen dollars she did not have and, because of her condition, could not earn. For her there was no law.

Repeated warnings have come from sources entitled to respect that such a condition of affairs is capable of producing incalculable harm.

When litigation is too costly, the result for many persons is a denial of justice. Such denial or partial denial of justice engenders social and commercial friction. The sense of helplessness thus caused incites citizens to take the law into their own hands. It causes crimes of violence. It saps patriotism and destroys civic pride. It arouses class jealousies and breeds contempt for law and government.

The problem is fundamental. It strikes at the very root of our economic, social and political structure. The man or woman who has honestly toiled and cannot obtain the wages earned, loses faith in humanity and the efficacy of our laws and courts; is often turned out a beggar, vagrant, or criminal, or seeks redress by forcible means.

If ever a time shall come when in this city only the rich man can enjoy law as a doubtful luxury, when the poor who need it most cannot have it, when only a golden key will unlock the door to the court room, the seeds of revolution will be sown, the firebrand of revolution will be lighted and put into the hands of men, and they will almost be justified in the revolution which will follow.

In that direction we have imperceptibly, unconsciously, and unintentionally drifted. The end of such a course is disclosed by history. Differences in the ability of classes to use the machinery of the law, if permitted to remain, lead inevitably to disparity between the rights of classes in the law itself. And when the law recognizes and enforces a distinction between classes, revolution ensues or democracy is at an end.

Writing in the light of experience gained in a hundred thousand cases, the attorney for the New York Society thus expresses it:

What is Legal Aid Work? What kind of work do you do? How often these questions are asked each year, and surprising as it may be to some, there are thousands in this City of ours, who are not only unfamiliar with our purposes, but to whom our existence is unknown.

From birth to death, the poor man is the prey of a host of petty swindlers. He is educated to believe that justice is free and he finds that to get it, he must pay a lawyer a price he cannot afford. It has often been said that only the poor know the sorrows of the poor. This may be so, but I believe that only the Legal Aid Society knows their wrongs. Unless injuries and unfairness to the poor man are punished, he feels that justice is not for him, and that he has not the same opportunity and protection as the rich man; he becomes anarchistic. The fundamental object of our Society, therefore, is to see that all, no matter how poor, or how oppressed, shall get justice. We care nothing for race, sex, color, creed, or previous condition of servitude; we do believe that the laws mean something and our work is to see that they mean the same for the poor that they do for the rich. Let me emphasize that the Society does not give charitable support to needy persons, but only justice and the enforcement of just and honorable claims.

The scope of the work is confined to the field of legal action. The societies are engaged in the practice of law and not in social service work as that phrase is generally used. More closely than anything else, the work resembles the work of an attorney engaged in general practice, the chief points of difference being in the matter of fees and in the number of cases. To many of the innumerable questions which are asked the attorneys give answers based as much on common sense as on law, but the bar will admit that this is not a peculiarity confined to legal aid practice.

Proceeding to a more specific examination of just what cases are brought to the legal aid societies, it is at once apparent that claims for wages and domestic difficulties far outnumber any other classes of cases. Almost universally the collection of wages comprises the greatest work, then come the husband and wife difficulties with suits for separation (not divorce) and proceedings to enforce support, and beyond these two great groups the cases presented range widely over the whole field of civil law, except that poor corporations have not yet sought legal aid, so that there is little practice in corporation law.

Part Three

MARKING TIME
1920–1929

14

The Professionalization of Social Work:
Mary Richmond's definition

The new principles transforming social work in the 1920's received their clearest definition in Mary Richmond's What is Social Case Work? *One of the most diligent settlement-house workers in the Progressive era and a frequent lecturer at schools, Richmond tried to generalize relief methods and techniques into a system of social work. Her statements reveal not only the influence of Progressive benevolence but the newer intellectual currents as well, particularly the psychological doctrines of Sigmund Freud and his school. The attempt to be scientific and objective ran through Richmond's pages. But there was also a moralism in them that reflected some very traditional American attitudes toward the poor.*

It may be well, before attempting any description of social case work as practised in a genuinely professional spirit, to present some illustrations of such work and later compare illustrations with description. The purpose of this small book is not, however, to discuss method, but to inquire into *what* social case work is and *why* it is.

During the last decade social case work has had a rapid extension of its field of activity. At one time, as a vocation, its field was confined almost exclusively to the care of dependents and delinquents, just as the first savings banks were for dependents only and the first hospitals for the destitute sick. But today social case work in some form or other has become a necessary part of many of our courts, schools, hospitals, factories, workshops, compensation commissions, and of the hundred other places in which decisions affecting the welfare of individuals must be made.

Excerpted from *What is Social Case Work?* by Mary E. Richmond, © 1922 by Russell Sage Foundation, Publishers, New York, pp. 26-42, 87-99.

My first illustration of "case work in being" describes the social treatment given for four years to a Polish girl, who was under the care of a small private society having a staff of case workers and a school for difficult but not defective young girls. From this school its pupils are usually placed out in private families, where they continue to be under the careful supervision of the society's staff. Before the girl whose story I shall tell entered the school, she had been the charge for a short while of a probation officer of the court.

Maria Bielowski went to work in a factory when she was only fifteen. After many disagreements with her stepmother about the share of her wages to be turned over to the family and also about her habit of staying out late at night, she left home and began to live in lodging houses and cheap hotels. From one of these the girl was brought into court for stealing a few dollars from a fellow-boarder. To those who saw her just after her arrest she was a very unprepossessing sight. Her features were dark and heavy, her clothing ragged, dirty, and badly stained; her head was crowned with three strands of false hair, later found to be infested with vermin.

What did the probation officer discover as to her background? From two places of employment her record was that of an irregular worker. One hospital asked to examine her reported that she had good intellectual capacity but a psychopathic personality. As regards her family, the Bielowskis had come from Poland five years earlier—the father, his second wife, and four children. But the father had died three years after his arrival, and the stepmother, who could speak not a dozen English words, appeared, although a good woman, to have lost all control over the children. The two grown sons were away from home; the younger boy was in a reformatory. Should Maria, who had been found guilty by the court, be committed to a similar institution?

The social data obtained by the probation officer made it appear unwise to place the girl on probation in her own home. On the other hand, her record before she had gone to work did not seem to justify commitment to a reformatory. At school she had been a fair scholar; beginning with no knowledge of English whatever, she had completed the seventh grade in four years. Moreover, it was learned that she had been a popular member of a Girl Scout troop and of her Sunday school class. These facts suggested that probation under conditions which would assure a maximum of individualized care might bring good results. Accordingly, the officer sought the aid of the small private society already mentioned, and somewhat later, after Maria had been in its school a few months, one of their case workers became, with the sanction of the girl, the girl's family, and the court, her legal guardian. Under this guardianship her behavior and character have improved steadily.

From a careful reading in the original record of the treatment which followed and from conference with this guardian, I have been able to trace some of the steps by which the marked change in the girl's habits and in her relations to the world she lives in has been effected. There has been no element of the magical or the spectacular in her gradual development.

During the earlier stages of treatment careful attention had to be given to Maria's physical condition. Her scalp was cleansed and her teeth cared for. There was no evidence of irregular sex conduct, but she was found to have some symptoms of syphilis of origin unknown, and was taken regularly into the city for hospital treatments. A bad nose and throat condition was treated at the same hospital. Enuresis was controlled at the school by suggestion. Twice during the following year, at times of special discouragement, this symptom recurred, but it responded at once to any change of program which improved her mental attitude. Her other physical difficulties were soon remedied.

It was at the society's little school, with its less than twenty pupils, that Maria had her first contact with American standards of home life. Here she was given careful training in habits of personal cleanliness, in the care of her room, in mending and washing her clothing, in cooking, and in respect for the personal belongings of others. No borrowing was allowed; each girl had her own bureau and closet and her own small treasures. One day early in her stay, two little cakes from a new baking were missing from the kitchen pantry. Every girl denied taking them, so the whole group were deprived of their Christmas trip to town. Three days later Maria confessed to the head teacher, for whom she had learned to have a real affection, that she was the one at fault, and this was her last dishonest act. In one of the private homes in which she worked a year or two later, her employer reported her to be so honest that "she would not even borrow an ink bottle."

After eight months in the school and her completion of the eighth grade, Maria was sent as a mother's helper to a family at a summer resort. In the autumn of that year a position was found for her in another family, to help with the housework in exchange for her board and with the opportunity to enter the first-year class at the high school. She has continued her high school course with credit ever since, making one change of school, however, when transferred to another city. Here there was a chance to place her with a Polish professor and his wife, in whose family she has had many advantages in addition to her pleasure at being once more with compatriots. Each summer the society finds a place for her amid country surroundings, and each year it has arranged a vacation, once at a girls' camp. During the four years under guardianship she has worked in five different families. Though only two of the frequent changes were due to her own restlessness, Maria has at times been a troublesome charge, eager and demanding and inordinately fond of personal adornment.

These family placements, which were all made with the greatest care, have been valuable in giving the girl a chance to participate in American life and ways, but the most important influence in her improvement has continued to be that of the case worker appointed as her guardian. Without dwelling upon details, let me try to name some of the principles and processes of case work that Maria's history reveals.

Probably the case worker's ability to win her way with a difficult girl was due more to her imaginative sympathy than to any other one thing. But whether this quality was a native endowment or partly a result of experience with other girls, the outstanding fact of the record is that the guardian did contrive to see the world in somewhat the fashion that it appeared to her ward. Having some of the dangers of her own professional world in mind, perhaps, she was also careful to avoid that rigidity of mind, that tendency to inhibit the client's initiative, which is the too common reaction to irritating behavior. Thus she writes in a letter of explanation:

Whenever I can possibly let a girl do what she wants to, I agree to her doing it. The instances are so innumerable where we have to say "no" that I feel we must be on our guard against increasing them unnecessarily. This is not the same thing as giving in to a girl because she teases or insists on having her own way.

When Maria was troublesome, her guardian discriminated between the trouble that she caused and the real delinquency of which she had been, but was no longer, guilty. Her appeal was constantly to the girl's self-respect and ambition, though not so much in set terms as in acts which would stimulate these qualities. The society had Maria's earlier trials in mind when it allowed her a little more pocket-money than was granted to some of its other charges. Her clothes were never satisfactory to her; after a few months she tired of every purchase, no matter how much it pleased her at first. At one time the question of clothing versus schooling became so acute that she was given permission to leave school and take a short course which would fit her for office work. But when the girl actually realized that the break with school would be permanent, she changed her mind and asked permission to remain.

Closely related to this habit of introducing an element of give and take even into her admonitions, and bringing to mind Miss Sullivan's policy, was the case worker's determination to be honest and frank—to give the real reason for a decision wherever this was possible.

This habit of giving the true answer to questions did not mean that the guardian always told all she knew as soon as she knew it. On the contrary, she found that Maria's respect increased for her when she proved to be hard to deceive, when she was able occasionally to surprise her charge by a piece of information supposed to be undiscovered. To give all the freedom that by any chance her ward could make right use of, but to give this freedom under such conditions that she herself could get a pretty clear idea of what that use was, had proved the best policy. At one time, for instance, a young Pole appeared on the scene whom Maria threatened to marry unless she could have a new hat at once. By a judicious arrangement with her employer covering permitted calls and attentions from this young man, and by providing clothing in due season and not before, the small crisis was successfully passed.

This case worker's wise handling of Maria, however, all comes back to the gift of imaginative sympathy, such as was shown when she sent one of the girl's class compositions to a periodical for young people. The composition was accepted by the editor with a small payment in return, and its acceptance meant a great deal to the young writer.

One cannot help wondering what Maria would be like today if the court had treated the fact of larceny in a merely routine way, without taking into account the social background brought to light by the probation officer, and had pronounced the usual sentence for that particular offense. A very different girl would now be crossing the threshold into womanhood—untruthful, hard, perhaps depraved. As it is, she faces the future with the advantages of high school education, with good health, an attractive personality, and a number of real friends who trust her. She is not a perfect mortal, of course; she is still somewhat restless at times, still magnifies the importance of trifles, and is still too fond of finery. But on the whole her sense of values is an adjusted sense; her ideas are no longer confused and unreasonable.

The tentative definition of social case work which I am about to attempt will have no safer basis than my personal experience supplemented by a habit of reading many social case histories.

For this merely introductory description of case work, however, I have adopted the policy of exclusion, rejecting first of all and without question all those aimless dosings of social ills by inexperienced practitioners which are called social case work but have no relation to its theory or its practice. And for the present, at least, all short-term services to individuals are excluded, such as tiding them over a temporary period of stress, helping them to find some agency or some professional skill which they know they need, giving them advice upon a question which puzzles them, and so on. All of these services have social value, of course, but, without more follow-up work and more detailed knowledge of their clients than case workers engaged in this type of work usually have, the permanent values cannot well be measured.

It follows that this stage in my description is limited to skilled service in the first place, to long-term, intensive care of difficult cases in the second place, and to service rendered under relatively unhampered, independent auspices in the third place. Concentration upon this group should bring to light considerations of value to social treatment in general, for it is treatment of the intensive and long-continuing type which provides us with criticism of all our processes—with the most searching criticism, in fact, that we now have. It is easy to be pleased with the results of a social service when we measure them just after the first changes for the better, or when we see them from one angle and no more. But when we dare to examine them from the point of view of life as a whole, with the permanent welfare of the individual and of society in mind, we are applying a much severer test of values.

Let me, with such a test in mind, make the broadest generalization about social case work that I can. Its theories, its aims, its best intensive practice all seem to have been converging of late years toward one central idea; namely, toward the development of personality.

It is true that social case work has dealt and will continue to deal with questions of restoration to self-support, with matters of health and personal hygiene, and that each of these things has a direct relation to personality. But, in so far as each is a specialty (some are specialties demanding quite other forms of professional skill), social case work will be found to be coterminous with none of them, but to have, in addition to its supplementary value in these other tasks, a field all its own. That field is the development of personality through the conscious and comprehensive adjustment of social relationships, and within that field the worker is no more occupied with abnormalities in the individual than in the environment, is no more able to neglect the one than the other. The distinctive approach of the case worker, in fact, is back to the individual by way of his social environment, and wherever adjustment must be effected in this manner, individual by individual, instead of in the mass, there some form of social case work is and will continue to be needed. So long as human beings are human and their environment is the world, it is difficult to imagine a state of affairs in which both they and the world they live in will be in no need of these adjustments and readjustments of a detailed sort.

To state this in a more formal way is to arrive at my tentative definition:

Social case work consists of those processes which develop personality through adjustments consciously effected, individual by individual, between men and their social environment.

What do we mean by "social environment"? The dictionary defines environment as "the aggregate of surrounding things and conditions," but when we put "social" in front of it, it becomes evident at once that many persons and things have been excluded and many substitutes included; the environment ceases to be environment in space merely—it widens to the horizon of man's thought, to the boundaries of his capacity for maintaining relationships, and it narrows to the exclusion of all those things which have no real influence upon his emotional, mental, and spiritual life.

15

The Life of the Tenant Farmer:
A rural sociologist's investigation

The field of rural sociology grew popular in the 1920's, especially in universities interested in the broad area of agricultural research. Applying the tools of sociology to the particular question of rural organization and farm life, these researchers were among the first to explore the plight of the nonurban poor. In 1922, J. A. Dickey spent three months in North Carolina townships. After extensive interviews and first-hand observa-

J. A. Dickey and E. C. Branson, *How Farm Tenants Live,* University of North Carolina Extension Bulletin, Vol. 2, No. 6 (Chapel Hill, North Carolina, 1922), excerpts from pp. 7-9, 20-24, 35-37.

tions, he was able to describe convincingly the style of life and the outlook of tenant farmers.

THE MONEY THEY LIVE ON

What about marrying on $20 a month—really on $6.00 a month in money, the balance of your cash income being held back till the end of the year? On a money income of that sort, do you think you'd have the nerve to set about establishing a home, sheltering, feeding, clothing, and safe-guarding a family in sickness and in health, and giving the children a decent chance at life?

I shoved these questions at a young college graduate on the train the other day—a cotton buyer in a flourishing cotton-belt city.

He looked at me in amazement. Kidding me? said he. Looks like it. I'm getting $200 a month, and I can't get married. I'd be a fool to marry on any such income. It couldn't be done in my town.

But, said I, this is exactly what fifty-one farmers have had the nerve to do in one small corner of a mid-state county in North Carolina. Thirty-eight of them are tenants, who handled in 1921 a household average of $250.64 in cash in the run of the year or just a little more than $20 a month. Thirteen are croppers with a household average of $153.27 in cash or a little less than $13 a month. And they are not negro farmers. They are white farmers—tenants to be sure, but native born whites of your race and mine.

But say, said he, how do these people live? How do they keep soul and body together on an average of thirteen to twenty dollars a month in money? What are their standards of living? What are their notions of comfort and culture? They are not starved nor even half-starved in body, you say, but they must be wholly starved in mind—halt and maimed and blind in spirit! What can they look forward to? Can they ever hope to be anything but underling farmers, disadvantaged and under-privileged, they and their children and their children's children to the remotest generation?

All of which are tremendously important questions. They concern 63,487 white farm tenants in North Carolina. With their families they number 317,500 souls, or nearly one-fifth of the entire white population of the state. Who are these people? Why are they farm tenants instead of farm owners? On what level do they live? What are their hopes and fears? What chance have they to rise out of farm tenancy into farm ownership?

What we need is a close-up study of the 317,000 souls in the families of the white tenants of North Carolina. And it must be a keenly sympathetic study or we shall fail to understand and interpret aright the facts we find.

In order to supply this need, at least in part, Mr. J. A. Dickey, an A.M. graduate of the State University, spent the three summer months of 1922 in 329 farm homes of Baldwin and Williams townships in the northeast corner of Chatham county. They were the homes of practically all the farmers of this small area—the homes of owners and tenants, white and black.

The three hundred and twenty-nine families of Baldwin and Williams townships—the owners and tenants of both races—are scattered throughout 104 square miles of territory. Whites and blacks are nearly equal in number, and their farms are small, averaging less than thirty cultivated acres each. They dwell in solitary farmsteads with wide spaces between, and farming is by nature a solitary business. The unit of economic production is the family, and the father is the over-lord of the group, in the ancient patriarchal fashion of family life. He may not have his legs under his own table, as the Danes say, but where he sits is the head of it, and nobody in the family is in doubt about it. Such is the type of rural family life in Chatham county, the State, and the South as a whole.

Within family groups in the country regions autocracy is the rule; between family groups democracy is the unquestioned order. The farmer is the best in his own group and accounts himself equal to the best in any other farm group. So it is in the rural civilization of almost all the countries of the new world. In almost all old-world countries the farmers dwell together in farm villages, and the extremes of individualism are softened by the intimate social contacts and the common concerns of hamlet households.

As a result American farmers are bred to think privately and locally in terms of the family and the neighborhood. They do not easily think in terms of the community and the commonwealth. The private-local mind of the farmer in the South is the ultimate obstacle to country community life and coöperative farm enterprise; also it is the ultimate problem in county government and in commonwealth development.

Our study discloses the social aloofness of the farm tenant—the great distances to town centers, until recently in Chatham the absence of improved public highways, the rarity of telephones and motor cars—there are only two of each in fifty-one tenant homes, the fourth and fifth grade levels and limits of school culture in a majority of the families, the small average number of household newspapers, magazines, and books. The epoch-making events of the big wide world break in tiny ripples on the far distant shores of farm tenant lives only after many days—here and everywhere else in the South.

Social contacts and social occasions in the tenant households of this territory consist mainly of the inter-family affairs and events of the local church and school neighborhoods. In the order of frequency they are (1) preaching days in the country churches and commencement occasions in the country schools, (2) mutual visits between the homes of owners and tenants of each race on the basis of democratic equality—assumptions of family superiority are almost unknown, (3) the neighborly exchange of labor in pinches produced by seasonal stresses—plowing, harvesting, threshing, corn shucking seasons and the like, (4) dogs, guns, and hunting parties—in these fifty-one tenant households there are fifty guns and forty-six dogs, (5) picnics which are usually school events, (6) holiday occasions and neighborhood gatherings, mainly during the Christmas season—parties or sociables as they are called, (7) occasional neighborhood fairs, usually at the school buildings, (8) other events— barbecues, opossum suppers and so on. The most common entry in the schedule blanks is "visiting, talking, telling jokes, hunting, fishing, eating, watermelons."

Practically everybody goes to church, every household hunts and fishes, and every family but one exchanges visits. The tenant families that have no part in the inter-family life of this territory are as follows: sixteen exchanged no labor during the year, eighteen attended no picnics, six took no part in holiday events, twenty-nine attended no sociables, and forty-two stayed away from the infrequent neighborhood fairs. No family attended a circus, and only one looked in at a film picture in the run of the year. Nowhere did we find a trace of dancing as a neighborhood event.

Children's plays around the home are primitive and in twenty-one homes they are altogether absent. Base, tag, dog-on-wood, hide-and-seek, cat, ball-over, stick-it-to-him, pitching horse-shoes, marbles, dolls, mud pies, riding sticks, red bugs, gully bugs, jack-in-the-bush, checkers, and rook are the home games of country children in this territory—dolls in only one tenant family, checkers in one, and rook in two. No cards were in evidence anywhere; but also Mother Goose is everywhere unknown. The home groups are too small for lively fun among the young people, and the one-teacher schools are too small to develop the values of team-play. Besides, the unconscious assumption is that children are born to work not to play. In listing for us the children's games in the various homes, one tenant housewife said with spirit, "I wants you to understand that we works hereabouts; we ain't no sportin neighborhood." There is abundant seasonal leisure in farm tenant homes, but no leisure-time philosophy of life. Salvation for young people lies in work, and getting together for a good time is an evidence of mortal sin of some sort.

And such is the unconscious assumption of the country churches. In no instance did we find any evidence that they were concerned about wholesome recreation in the countryside. Not social affairs in this world but salvation in the next world is the core of religious consciousness in our country regions. Rural religion is not annointed with "the oil of gladness" that David prayed for. Fun and frolic are tolerated with qualms of conscience or viewed with vague suspicion as essentially evil. And so the country church resigns country recreation to the Devil and all his works.

Life in solitary farmsteads, a few to the square mile, in the vast open spaces of America, is in itself a denial of a primary social instinct—the craving for companionship, and the farm family group fails to satisfy this craving. As a result, lonesomeness alone plays a large part in the cityward drift of country populations; it plays the largest part in the exodus of farm boys and girls in their teens. There has been a steady movement of country people out of Baldwin and Williams townships for thirty years; since 1890 the population of Baldwin had dwindled from 2068 to 1439, and Williams has dropped from 2760 inhabitants to 1517. More than a third of all the people of these two townships have moved out in a single generation. Soon or late, a steady decrease in population produces static or stagnant social areas. Such is the net result of economic and social disadvantages, of life and livelihood under uninspiring or dispiriting influences; and in the last analysis it is social disabilities that destroy values of every sort, economic, civic and religious alike—farm values and incomes, store business and profits, neighborhood life and enterprise, community morals, law and order, county government efficiency and church development. Such are the pressing issues of existence for farmers and storekeepers, teachers and preachers to consider in Baldwin and Williams townships. More and better roads, better market facilities, larger cash incomes, more efficient schools and churches, more books, newspapers and magazines, greater attention to sanitation and hygiene, a braver attitude toward community morals, law and order, and a more intimate acquaintance with county office affairs—such are the foundations of a fuller life in the territory surveyed in Chatham county.

We can know about the gross money incomes of farmers. That information is as simple as abc's. We know about the gross money incomes of 329 farmers in two Chatham county townships in 1921— about (1) the cash incomes sourced in farm activities and interests, and (2) the casual money received from all other sources.

And no matter what their net incomes were, their gross incomes in money were a beggar's pittance, ranging from eight cents a day per person in the household of white croppers to 34 cents per person in the household of white farm owners.

Let us now turn our attention to the 51 white tenants alone, and ask who they are, how they live.

These fifty-one white tenants fall into three classes, (1) twenty-five renters living on and cultivating family lands, (2) thirteen renters with no landowning ancestry—with one exception the sons of landless tenant farmers, and (3) thirteen croppers who are without neighborhood kinship in land tenures—pilgrims, strangers and sojourners in the land, with little or no workstock and farm implements of their own, and a minimum worldly wealth in household goods and utensils or with an average of only $426 per family, which is only $17 more than that of the 66 negro renters alongside whom they struggle for existence.

(1) The twenty-five white renters living on family lands are distinctly a preferred class of tenant farmers—here as everywhere else in the South. They are the sons, sons-in-law, or nephews of their landlords. They rent on favorable terms, they share in small or large measure in the properties and products of tribal farming—in fruits, vegetables, poultry, butter and eggs, in milk animals, workstock and implements, in automobiles and buggies in trips to town on week days and to church on Sundays, and so on and on. What they need they borrow from the homefolks. They belong to the landed gentry. They enjoy the social estate of the land owners.

(2) The thirteen white renters who are not living on family lands are all—or all but one—the sons of renters or croppers. They were not born to landownership. If ever they own farms of their own, they must depend on self-effort alone—on industry, thrift, sagacity, sobriety and integrity. Their lot in life is toil. With only two exceptions, their wives are hoe-hands in the fields, from eight to ten hours a day during periods ranging from thirty to two hundred days of the year according to family circumstances. One of these women is a mother fifty-one years old. The un-

broken rule is to send the children, both boys and girls alike, into field work at seven or eight years of age—so because there is no hired labor to be had and no money with which to pay such labor.

(3) The thirteen white croppers are in a different category in many or most particulars. And mind you, they are a fourth of the white tenants in this territory. They lack industry in the area surveyed; as shown by the fact that their average annual cash income per family is $44 less than that of the black croppers, nearly $100 less than that of white renters, and $136 less than that of the black renters. They lack aspiration, as shown by the fact that they own little or no workstock and farm tools, without which they could not hope to rise out of tenancy into ownership. They lack the home-owning aspirations and virtues of the thirteen self-help farmers in the class next above them. Their standards of living are higher but their levels of life are lower than those of the black farmers alongside whom they live and work; inevitably so because their average cash income is less—22 percent less than that of the black croppers, 47 percent less than that of the black renters, and 74 percent less than that of the black owners. They suffer in personal and in family pride. They move from pillar to post from year to year. They are a migratory type of farmers. They are cursed with the restless foot of the Wandering Jew. They lack identity with the community in which they live. They lack abiding citizenship and a sense of proprietary interest in schools and churches and neighborhood enterprises. They lack a sense of responsibility for community morals, law and order. They live on an average cash income of eight cents a day per family member in the area surveyed and upon some such pauper wage the South over. They are unduly tempted into the business of making and vending illicit liquors. They furnish a disproportionate percent of the white cases on the criminal court dockets. They are satisfied with their landless lot in life. They are a contented not a bold peasantry, in Goldsmith's phrase, but they are not their country's pride. As a class they are a doubtful economic asset and a distinct social menace. Or so they are as a rule in Chatham, in every other county of the state—in this state and in every other state of the cotton and tobacco belt.

From this point on we group both types of white renters together, because they live on almost exactly the same social level. The differences are trivial and not worth noting. From time to time we deal with the white croppers separately because they are a class occupying a distinctly lower level of existence.

The households of the thirty-eight white renters number 178 souls.

The children number 101 and sixty of these are children of school ages. The dwellings they live in are usually of board and timber construction, a few are old log houses, the left-over remains of former days. Six of them let in the weather through the roofs or the floors and walls. Twenty have 203 window lights out and ten have shutters off. In more than half of these dwellings it is possible to study astronomy through the holes in the roof and geology through the cracks in the floor. There is a separate dwelling for each family, and the 38 dwellings are scattered throughout 104 square miles of territory or close to three square miles for every family. There is no lack of elbow-room for family life in this farm area.

On an average these dwellings are thirty years old; nearly half of them have faced the elements for a quarter century or more. Only four have been built within the last four years. How can farm owners with a gross money income averaging $629 a year build new tenant houses or keep the old houses in proper repair?

Nor is there any lack of elbow space within the tenant dwellings. There are 164 rooms and 147 beds for the 178 occupants. The bed rooms number 124 or more than three per household on an average. Of one-room shacks there are none, and of two-room shanties only four. Eleven dwellings have four rooms each, and fifteen contain from five to six rooms each. These last were the homes of farm owners in by-gone days, now abandoned to tenants. The crowding of humans as in city tenements is a thing unknown in the country regions of the South. Parlors are rare —there are only two in all the thirty-eight dwellings. There are no separate sitting rooms. Bed rooms and sitting rooms are one and the same, and kitchens are invariably used as dining rooms. Only seven of the dwellings are ceiled or plastered, only ten are painted or white-washed, and only thirteen evidence care on part of the occupants.

Only eight families have out-door closets, and these are all used by both sexes. None of the out-houses are fly-proof or water-tight, all are open to the poultry and pigs, none are ever cleaned, and three of them are drained toward the water supply. The bushes and the barn lot build-ings are the screens of family privacy for thirty homes. Soil pollution by bodywaste is the rule here as elsewhere throughout the country regions of the United States. Kitchen waste in all the dwellings is fed to the hogs in the nearby pens, and on six lots the pens are drained toward the water supply.

A doctor's office is on an average of eight miles away from the homes of these thirty-eight farm tenants. And so only seventeen families called in physicians during the year.

16

Aftermath of a Riot:
Chicago blacks evaluate urban life

*At the end of World War I, the country that had fought to make the
world safe for democracy experienced a series of major race riots. One
of the fiercest and most tragic of the riots occurred in Chicago in 1919.
It was touched off when a black youth accidentally swam into the un-
marked white section on a bathing beach; the whites stoned him and he
drowned. For two days, whites and blacks battled each other, and when
they finished, there were 38 persons dead, 537 injured, and 1000 homeless. In an effort to understand this tragedy and to forestall another,
government officials undertook an extensive investigation. In the course
of their efforts, they learned much about the lives of Chicago's blacks.
In fact, despite the horror of the riot and the pain of their poverty, the
blacks preferred the northern urban scene to the southern rural one. The
testimony below clarifies their feelings.*

During the period 1916–18 approximately a half-million Negroes suddenly moved from southern to northern states. This movement, however,
was not without a precedent. A similar migration occurred in 1879, when
Negroes moved from Mississippi, Louisiana, Texas, Alabama, Tennessee, and North Carolina to Kansas. The origin of this earlier movement,
its causes, and manner resemble in many respects the one which has so
recently attracted public attention.

    The migration of 1916–18 cannot be separated completely from the
steady, though inconspicuous, exodus from southern to northern states
that has been in progress since 1860, or, in fact, since the operation of
the "underground railway." In 1900 there were 911,025 Negroes living
in the North, 10.3 percent of the total Negro population, which was then
8,883,994. Census figures for the period 1900–1910 show a net loss for
southern states east of the Mississippi of 595,703 Negroes. Of this number 366,880 are found in northern states. Reliable estimates for the last
decade place the increase of northern Negro population around 500,000.

Chicago Commission on Race Relations, *The Negro in Chicago* (Chicago, 1922),
excerpts from pp. 95-100, 103, 165, 169-173.

The 1910–20 increase of the Negro population of Chicago was from 44,103 to 109,594, or 148.5 percent, with a corresponding increase in the white population of 21 percent, including foreign immigration. According to the Census Bureau method of estimating natural increase of population, the Negro population of Chicago unaffected by the migration would be 58,056 in 1920, and the increase by migration alone would be 51,538.

The migration to Chicago.   Within a period of eighteen months in 1917–18 more than 50,000 Negroes came to Chicago according to an estimate based on averages taken from actual count of daily arrivals. All of those who came, however, did not stay. Chicago was a re-routing point, and many immigrants went on to nearby cities and towns. During the heaviest period, for example, a Detroit social agency reported that hundreds of Negroes applying there for work stated that they were from Chicago. The tendency appears to have been to reach those fields offering the highest present wages and permanent prospects.

At the time of the migration the great majority of Negroes in Chicago lived in a limited area on the South Side, principally between Twenty-second and Thirty-ninth streets, Wentworth Avenue and State Street, and in scattered groups to Cottage Grove Avenue on the east. State Street was the main thoroughfare. Prior to the influx of southern Negroes, many houses stood vacant in the section west of State Street, from which Negroes had moved when better houses became available east of State Street. Into these old and frequently almost uninhabitable houses the first newcomers moved. Because of its proximity to the old vice area this district had an added undesirability for old Chicagoans. The newcomers, however, were unacquainted with its reputation and had no hesitancy about moving in until better homes could be secured. As the number of arrivals increased, a scarcity of houses followed, creating a problem of acute congestion.

During the summer of 1917 the Chicago Urban League made a canvass of real estate dealers supplying houses for Negroes, and found that in a single day there were 664 Negro applicants for houses, and only fifty houses available. In some instances as many as ten persons were listed for a single house. This condition did not continue long. There were counted thirty-six new neighborhoods, formerly white, opening up to Negroes within three months.

At the same time rents increased from 5 to 30 and sometimes as much as 50 percent. A more detailed study of living conditions among the early migrants in Chicago was made by the Chicago School of Civics and Philanthropy. The inquiry included seventy-five families of less than a year's residence. In the group were sixty married couples, 128 children, eight women, nine married men with families in the South. Of these migrants forty-five families came from rural and thirty-two from urban localities. The greatest number, twenty-nine, came from Alabama; twenty-five were from Mississippi, eleven from Louisiana, five from Georgia, four from Arkansas, two from Tennessee, and one from Florida. Forty-one of these seventy-five families were each living in one room. These rooms were rented by the week, thus making possible an easy change of home at the first opportunity.

Reasons for the ready acceptance of lodgers in Negro dwellings were apparent, among them friendship and the desire to be obliging and to assist others in a new environment. Most Negroes would regard it as a breach of good faith to encourage friends and relatives to come to Chicago from the South and then fail to help them after their arrival. This accounts for the frequent designation of "relatives" and "friends" among the lodgers. Sometimes these lodgers seemed to be permanent, but often they were taken only until they could adjust themselves.

During the period of greatest migration, 1915–20, hundreds of unattached men and women could be seen on the streets as late as one or two o'clock in the morning, seeking rooms shortly after their arrival in Chicago. One instance was reported of a family to whose house four men came at midnight looking for rooms. Lack of lodging-houses or of hotels where accommodations could be had at reasonable prices was partly responsible for this swarm of migrants seeking shelter in private homes. The meager provision of such places for the accommodation of unattached Negroes has been a factor in the lodger problem.

The following experience of one or two families from the many histories gathered, while not entirely typical of all the migrants, contain features common to all:

The Thomas family.   Mr. Thomas, his wife and two children, a girl nineteen and a boy seventeen, came to Chicago from Seals, Alabama, in the spring of 1917. After a futile search, the family rented rooms for the first week. This was expensive and inconvenient, and between working hours all sought a house into which they could take their furniture. They finally found a five-room flat on Federal Street. The building had been considered uninhabitable and dangerous. Three of the five rooms were almost totally dark. The plumbing was out of order. There was no bath, and the toilet was outside of the house. There was neither electricity nor gas, and the family used oil lamps. The rent was $15 per month. Although the combined income of the family could easily have made possible a better house, they could find none.

Mr. and Mrs. Thomas were farmers in the South. On the farm Mrs. Thomas did the work of a man along with her husband. Both are illiterate. The daughter had reached the fourth grade and the boy the fifth grade in school. At home they belonged to a church and various fraternal orders and took part in rural community life.

On their arrival in Chicago they were short of funds. Father and son went to work at the Stock Yards. Although they had good jobs they found their income insufficient; the girl went to work in a laundry, and the mother worked as a laundress through the first winter for $1 a day. She later discovered that she was working for half the regular rate for laundry work. Soon she went back to housekeeping to reduce the food bill.

All the family were timid and self-conscious and for a long time avoided contacts, thus depriving themselves of helpful suggestions. The children became ashamed of the manners of their parents and worked diligently to correct their manner of speech. The children attended Wendell Phillips night school in the hope of improving their community status.

The freedom and independence of Negroes in the North have been a constant novelty to them and many times they have been surprised that they were "not noticed enough to be mistreated." They have tried out various amusement places, parks, ice-cream parlors, and theaters near their home on the South Side and have enjoyed them because they were denied these opportunities in their former home.

The combined income of this family is $65 a week, and their rent is now low. Many of their old habits have been preserved because of the isolation in which they have lived and because they have not been able to move into better housing.

The Jones family.   Mr. Jones, his wife, a six-year-old son, and a nephew aged twenty-one, came from Texas early in 1919. Although they arrived after the heaviest migration, they experienced the same difficulties as earlier comers.

They searched for weeks for a suitable house. At first they secured one room on the South Side in a rooming-house, where they were obliged to provide gas, coal, linen, bedding, and part of the furniture. After a few weeks they got two rooms for light housekeeping, for $10 a month. The associations as well as the physical condition of the house were intolerable. They then rented a flat on Carroll Avenue in another section. The building was old and run down. The agent for the property, to induce tenants to occupy it, had promised to clean and decorate it, but failed to keep his word. When the Jones family asked the owner to make repairs, he refused flatly and was exceedingly abusive.

Finally Jones located a house on the West Side that was much too large for his family, and the rent too high. They were forced to take lodgers to aid in paying the rent. This was against the desire of Mrs. Jones, who did not like to have strangers in her house. The house has six rooms and bath and is in a state of dilapidation. Mr. Jones has been forced to cover the holes in the floor with tin to keep out the rats. The plumbing is bad. During the winter there is no running water, and the agent for the building refuses to clean more than three rooms or to furnish screens or storm doors or to pay for any plumbing. In the back yard under the house is an accumulation of ashes, tin cans, and garbage left by a long series of previous tenants. There is no alley back of the house, and all of the garbage from the back yard must be carried out through the front. Jones made a complaint about insanitary conditions to the Health Department, and the house was inspected, but so far nothing has been done. It was difficult to induce the agent to supply garbage cans.

Jones had reached the eighth grade and Mrs. Jones had completed the first year of high school. The nephew had finished public-school grades provided in his home town and had been taught the boiler trade. He is now pursuing this trade in hope of securing sufficient funds to complete his course in Conroe College, where he has already finished the first year. The boy of six was placed in a West Side school. He was removed from this school, however, and sent back south to live with Mrs. Jones's mother and attend school there. Mrs. Jones thought that the influence of the school children of Chicago was not good for him. He had been almost blinded by a blow from a baseball bat in the hands of one of several older boys who continually annoyed him. The child had also learned vulgar language from his school associates.

The Jones family were leading citizens in their southern home. They were members of a Baptist church, local clubs, and a missionary society, while Jones was a member and officer in the Knights of Tabor, Masons, and Odd Fellows. They owned their home and two other pieces of property in the same town, one of which brought in $20 a month. As a boiler-maker, he earned about $50 a week, which is about the same as his present income. Their motive in coming to Chicago was to escape from the undesirable practices and customs of the South.

They had been told that no discrimination was practiced against Negroes in Chicago; that they could go where they pleased without the embarrassment or hindrance because of their color. Accordingly, when they first came to Chicago, they went into drug-stores and restaurants. They were refused service in numbers of restaurants and at the refreshment counters in some drug-stores. The family has begun the re-establishment of its community life, having joined a West Side Baptist church and taking an active interest in local organizations, particularly the Wendell Phillips Social Settlement. The greatest satisfaction of the Joneses comes from the "escape from Jim Crow conditions and segregation" and the securing of improved conditions of work, although there is no difference in the wages.

MIGRANTS IN CHICAGO

Migrants have been visited in their homes, and met in industry, in the schools, and in contacts on street cars and in parks. Efforts have been made to learn why they came to Chicago and with what success they were adjusting themselves to their new surroundings.

Some of the replies to questions asked are given:

Question: Why did you come to Chicago?

Answers:

1. Looking for better wages.
2. So I could support my family.
3. Tired of being a flunky.
4. I just happened to drift here.
5. Some of my people were here.
6. Persuaded by friends.
7. Wanted to make more money so I could go into business; couldn't do it in the South.
8. To earn more money.
9. For better wages.
10. Wanted to change and come to the North.
11. Came to get more money for work.
12. To better my conditions.
13. Better conditions.
14. Better conditions.
15. Better living.
16. More work; came on visit and stayed.

17. Wife persuaded me.
18. To establish a church.
19. Tired of the South.
20. To get away from the South, and to earn more money.

Question: Do you feel greater freedom and independence in Chicago? In what ways?

Answers:
 1. Yes.   Working conditions and the places of amusement.
 2. Yes.   The chance to make a living; conditions on the street cars and in movies.
 3. Going into places of amusement and living in good neighborhoods.
 4. Yes.   Educationally, and in the home conditions.
 5. Yes.   Go anywhere you want to go; voting; don't have to look up to the white man, get off the street for him, and go to the buzzard roost at shows.
 6. Yes.   Just seem to feel a general feeling of good-fellowship.
 7. On the street cars and the way you are treated where you work.
 8. Yes.   Can go any place I like here. At home I was segregated and not treated like I had any rights.
 9. Yes.   Privilege to mingle with people; can go to the parks and places of amusement, not being segregated.
10. Yes.   Feel free to do anything I please. Not dictated to by white people.
11. Yes.   Had to take any treatment white people offered me there, compelled to say "yes ma'am" or "yes sir" to white people, whether you desired to or not. If you went to an ice cream parlor for anything you came outside to eat it. Got off sidewalk for white people.
12. Yes.   Can vote; feel free; haven't any fear; make more money.
13. Yes.   Voting; better opportunity for work; more respect from white people.
14. Yes.   Can vote; no lynching; no fear of mobs; can express my opinion and defend myself.
15. Yes.   Voting, more privileges; white people treat me better, not as much prejudice.
16. Yes.   Feel more like a man. Same as slavery, in a way, at home. I don't have to give up the sidewalk here for white people as in my former home.
17. Yes.   No restrictions as to shows, schools, etc. More protection of law.

18. Yes. Have more privileges and more money.
19. Yes. More able to express views on all questions. No segregation or discrimination.
20. Sure. Feel more freedom. Was not counted in the South; colored people allowed no freedom at all in the South.
21. Find things quite different to what they are at home. Haven't become accustomed to the place yet.

Question: In what respects is life harder or easier here than in the South?

Answers:
1. Easier. I don't have to work so hard and get more money.
2. Easier in that here my wife doesn't have to work. I just couldn't make it by myself in the South.
3. Living is much easier; chance to learn a trade. I make and save more money.
4. Easier, you can make more money and it means more to you.
5. Easier to make a living here.
6. Easier, I get more money for my work and have some spare time.
7. Have better home, but have to work harder. I make more money, but spend it all to live.
8. Have more time to rest here and don't work as hard.
9. Find it easier to live because I have more to live on.
10. Earn more money; the strain is not so great wondering from day to day how to make a little money do.
11. Work harder here than at home.
12. Easier. Work is hard, but hours are short. I make more money and can live better.
13. More money for work, though work is harder. Better able to buy the necessities of life.
14. Easier; more work and more money and shorter hours.
15. Living higher, but would rather be here than in South. I have shorter hours here.
16. Don't have to work as hard here as at home. Have more time for rest and to spend with family.
17. Easier to live in St. Louis. More work here and better wages. Living higher here. Saved more there.
18. Must work very hard here, much harder than at home.
19. Harder because of increased cost of living.
20. The entire family feels that life is much easier here than at home. Do not find work as hard anywhere.

Question: Are you advising friends to come to Chicago?

Answers:
1. Yes.   People down there don't really believe the things we write back, I didn't believe myself until I got here.
2. No.   I am not going to encourage them to come, for they might not make it, then I would be blamed.
3. Yes.   If I think they will work.
4. Some of them, those who I think would appreciate the advantages here.
5. No.   Not right now, come here and get to work, strikes come along, they're out of work. Come if they want to, though.
6. Yes.   I have two sisters still in Lexington. I am trying to get them to come up here. They can't understand why I stay here, but they'll see if they come.
7. Yes.   People here don't realize how some parts of the South treat colored folks; poor white trash were awful mean where we came from; wish all the colored folks would come up here where you ain't afraid to breathe.
8. Yes.   Want friend and husband to come; also sister and family who want her to come back that they may see how she looks before they break up and come. Youngest son begs mother never to think of going back South. Oldest son not so well satisfied when first came, but since he is working, likes it a little better.

Only a few migrants were found who came on free transportation, and many of these had friends in Chicago before they came. Few expressed a desire to return.

The opinions of migrants and their feeling toward the community were solicited. It appeared that above all they prized the social and political freedom of the North. Satisfaction was expressed over the escape from "Jim Crow" treatment in the South. They valued the independence possible in the North, and sometimes spoke of having come North "out of bondage." They recalled frequently the "shameful treatment received by the Negroes from the white people in the South," the "intimidation and discrimination," and they were surprised and sometimes amazed at the fact that they could go and come at will in Chicago, that they could ride in the front of a street car and sit in any seat. Satisfaction was also expressed over the fact that they could get a job at good wages and did not have to buy groceries at plantation stores where they felt they had been exploited.

Thus, while they may have to work harder and may find it difficult for a long time to adjust themselves to the environment, few indicated any intention of returning to the South. In some instances, where adjustments have not been made, some discouragement was evidenced, and they sometimes expressed the feeling that they were no better off in Chicago than in their former homes. The prevailing sentiment, however, was in favor of remaining in spite of some greater difficulties.

A GROUP OF FAMILY HISTORIES

Mr. J—, forty-nine years old, his wife, thirty-eight years, and their daughter twenty-one years, were born in Henry County, Georgia. The husband never went to school, but reads a little. The wife finished the seventh grade and the daughter the fifth grade in the rural school near their home.

They worked on a farm for shares, the man earning one dollar and the women from fifty to seventy-five cents a day for ten hours' work. Their home was a four-room cottage with a garden, and rented for five dollars a month. They owned pigs, poultry, and a cow, which with their household furniture, were worth about $800. The food that they did not raise and their clothing had to be bought from the commissary at any price the owner cared to charge.

They were members of the Missionary Baptist Church and the wife belonged to the missionary society of the church and the Household of Ruth, a secret order. Their sole recreation was attending church, except for the occasional hunting expeditions made by the husband.

Motives for coming to Chicago.   Reading in the *Atlanta Journal,* a Negro newspaper, of the wonderful industrial opportunities offered Negroes, the husband came to Chicago in February, 1917. Finding conditions satisfactory, he had his wife sell the stock and household goods and join him here in April of the same year. He secured work at the Stock Yards, working eight hours at $3 a day. Later, he was employed by a casting company, working ten hours a day and earning $30 a week. This is his present employment and is about forty minutes' ride from his home. Both jobs were secured by his own efforts.

The family stayed in a rooming-house on East Thirtieth Street. This place catered to such an undesirable element that the wife remained in her room with their daughter all day. She thought the city too was cold, dirty, and noisy to live in. Having nothing to do and not knowing anyone, she was so lonely that she cried daily and begged her husband to put her in three rooms of their own or go back home. Because of the high cost of living, they were compelled to wait some time before they had saved enough to begin housekeeping.

Housing experience.   Their first home was on South Park Avenue. They bought about $500 worth of furniture, on which they are still paying. The wife then worked for a time at the Pullman Yards, cleaning cars at $1.50 a day for ten hours' work. Their house leaked and was damp and cold, so the family moved to another house on South Park Avenue, where they now live. The house is an old, three-story brick containing, three flats. This family occupies the first flat, which has six rooms and bath. Stoves are used for heating, and gas for light and cooking. The house is warm, but dark and poorly ventilated. Lights are used in two of the rooms during the day. The rooms open one into the other, and the interior, as well as the exterior, needs cleaning. There are a living-room, dining-room, and three bedrooms. The living-room is neatly and plainly furnished.

The daughter has married a man twenty-three years old, who migrated first to Pittsburgh, Pennsylvania, then to Chicago. He works at the Stock Yards. They occupy a room and use the other part of the house, paying half the rent and boarding themselves. A nephew, who was a glazier in Georgia, but who has been unable to secure work here, also boards with Mr. and Mrs. J—, paying $8 a week. He is now unemployed, but has been doing foundry work. Mrs. J— occasionally does laundry work at $4 a day.

How they live.   The cost of living includes rent $25; gas $5.40 a month; coal $18 a year; insurance $9.60 a month; clothing $500 a year; transportation $3.12 a month; church and club dues $3 a month; hairdresser $1.50 a month. Little is spent for recreation and the care of the health. The family carries insurance to the amount of $1,700, of which $1,200, is on the husband.

The meals are prepared by the wife, who also does the cleaning. Greens, potatoes, and cabbage are the chief articles of diet. Milk, eggs, cereals, and meat are also used. Meat is eaten about four times a week. Hot bread is made daily, and the dinners are usually boiled.

Relation to the community.   The whole family belongs to the Salem Baptist Church and attends twice a week. The wife is a member of the Pastor's Aid and the Willing Workers Club, also the Elk's Lodge. The husband is a member of the Knights of Pythias. He goes to the parks, bathing-beaches, and baseball games for amusement. The family spends much of its time in church and helped to establish the "Come and See" Baptist Mission at East Thirty-first Street and Cottage Grove Avenue. They have gone to a show only once or twice since they came to the city. During the summer they spend Sunday afternoons at the East Twenty-ninth Street Beach.

Heavier clothes were necessary because of the change of climate, and more fresh meat is used because of the lack of garden space and the high cost of green vegetables.

The wife thinks that northern Negroes have better manners, but are not as friendly as the colored people in the South. She says people do not visit each other, and one is never invited to dine at a friend's house. She thinks they cannot afford it with food so high. She thinks people were better in the South than they are here and says they had to be good there for they had nothing else to do but go to church.

She feels a greater freedom here because of the right to vote, the better treatment accorded by white people, the lack of "Jim Crow" laws. She likes the North because of the protection afforded by the law and the better working conditions. "You don't have an overseer always standing over you," she remarked.

Life here is harder, however, because one has to work all the time. "In the South you could rest occasionally, but here, where food is so high and one must pay cash, it is hard to come out even." The climate is colder, making it necessary to buy more clothes and coal. Rent also is very much higher here. They had to sell their two $50 Liberty bonds.

Economic sufficiency.   With all this, Mrs. J— gets more pleasure from her income because the necessities of life here were luxuries in Georgia, and though such things are dear here there is money to pay for them. Houses are more modern, but not good enough for the rent paid. They had to pay $2 more than the white family that moved out when they moved in.

Sentiments on the migration.   Mrs. J— says "some colored people have come up here and forgotten to stay close to God," hence they have "gone to destruction." She hopes that an equal chance in industry will be given to all; that more houses will be provided for the people and rent will be charged for the worth of the house; and the cost of living generally will be reduced. She does not expect to return to Georgia and is advising friends to come to Chicago.

A FACTORY HAND

In his home town in Kentucky, Mr. M— was a preacher with a small charge. Now, at the age of forty-nine, in Chicago, he works in a factory and is paid $130 a month. He has an adopted son, twenty-three years of age, who is an automobile mechanic in business for himself, drawing an income of $300 a month.

Mr. M— might still be a preacher on small salary but for the intervention of his wife. He came to Chicago about 1900. His wife came from Nashville, Tennessee, in 1902, and they were married in 1904. Mrs. M— felt that she was too independent to "live off the people" and persuaded her husband to give up the ministry. He got a job as foreman at a packing-house, where he earned $25 a week for a ten-hour day. Next he worked for the Chicago Telephone Company, and finally secured the position with a box-manufacturing company which he now holds.

Family life. The M—s have adopted three children, having had none of their own—the adopted son already mentioned, an adopted daughter now twenty years of age, and another foster son of thirteen. The latter is in a North Side school. The girl is in a normal school in Alabama. Both Mr. and Mrs. M— completed high school. All speak good English.

Wife and husband have separate banking accounts. Living expenses for such a large family are, of course, heavy. For example, the bills for food aggregate from $42 to $45 a week, and more than $200 a year is paid in insurance premiums. Frequently a woman is hired to come in and help with the housework. Food in good variety is used. Illness prevented adding to the bank accounts during the year of 1920. An operation performed on Mrs. M— cost $650 and the illness of Mr. M— and the daughter consumed between $900 and $1,000.

Housing experience. The M—s' first home in Chicago was a cottage in the "Black Belt." They wanted a large house and found one on South State Street. The neighborhood, however, was displeasing to them, and they moved to the North Side to be near a brother's children. The house was too small, and they moved again to another North Side address. Again the neighborhood proved distasteful, so they bought the three-story dwelling on the North Side where they now live. It is in good sanitary condition and is supplied with gas. As lodgers they have the wife's sister and brother, who are actually members of the family.

Community participation. They belong to the Baptist church. Affiliations of a secular nature include the Masons, the Household of Ruth, the

Court of Calanthe, the Eastern Star, the Heroines of Jericho, the North Side Men's Progressive Club, the Twentieth Century and Golden Leaf clubs, and the Young Matrons and Volunteer Workers. Mrs. M— is president of a settlement club and a member of the Urban League. After coming to Chicago three years passed before she mingled much with people. She had always done community work in her southern home and feels that her reluctance here was due to the fact that she did not know what the northern people were like. She found them friendly enough when at last she did associate with them.

Sentiments on community problems.   They came to Chicago because they had visited here and liked it well enough to come back and settle. Conditions are not all that they would like. They would like to see Negroes allowed to live anywhere they choose without hindrance, they would suppress moving pictures that reveal murder, drinking, and similar acts that lead young people to commit crimes. They would also like to see newspapers abandon their habit of printing articles that are derogatory to the Negro, thus creating prejudice, and of printing items unfit for children. Also they would like to see better homes for Negroes.

For the Negroes, they feel, life in the North is considerably easier than in the South, since they can always get plenty of work and do not have to work so hard as in the South. The mixed schools in the North are especially appreciated because no discrimination can creep in. The general lack of segregation on street cars, in parks, and in similar public places also pleases them. Still they see difficulties for southern Negroes who come North to live and are easily led astray. Southern Negroes are not accustomed to the new kinds of work and are inclined to slight it. This is, of course, unsatisfactory to their employers and accounts in some measure for the frequency with which they change jobs. This may also account for the fact that white people are averse to paying migrants well.

17

Social Service in the 1920's:
Administering the aid-to-mothers program

Although the widow's pension bill promised to keep substantial numbers of the poor out of orphan asylums and almshouses, the actual administration of the program in the 1920's demonstrated all too clearly that bureaucratic demands could be almost as insulting and degrading as life in a custodial institution. Moreover, the selection processes and relief procedures in giving pensions were often so cumbersome and so demanding that the program could not expand to assist all the eligibles, even among widows with dependent children. Two prominent social workers of the period, Edith Abbott and Sophonisba Breckinridge, examined the operation of Aid to Mothers in Illinois, and their findings provide a sharp picture of the state of relief giving.

The first Illinois statute providing for mothers' pensions was enacted June 5, 1911, as an amendment to section 7 of the Illinois juvenile-court law. The new statute was entitled the "funds-to-parents act" and became operative July 1 of the same year. Its purpose was to keep dependent children under 14 years of age with their own parents, when the parents were unable to provide for them, instead of providing out of public funds for their support in institutions. The administration of the law was placed with the juvenile courts, which were already caring for children declared dependent and delinquent, instead of with the county agents or supervisors of the poor, who were in charge of the public outdoor relief.

No provision was made by any of these statutes for boarding children in private homes. No authority existed for the payment of public money either to enable a parent, such as a widowed mother, to keep her children in her own home; or if the child's own home was unfit but the child capable of being dealt with under home conditions, to board the child in another home carefully selected and supervised. If, in any individual case, either of these forms of treatment approved itself to the court, that treatment was possible only to the extent to which private charitable aid might be obtained.

Edith Abbott and Sophonisba Breckinridge, *The Administration of the Aid-to-Mothers Law in Illinois.* United States Department of Labor, Children's Bureau publication No. 82 (Washington, 1921), excerpts from 7-8, 19-21, 34-36, 39-41.

Thus, if a mother were left destitute because of the death or incapacity of her husband, the law offered provision for her children if she wished to place them in institutions. If she refused to part with them the State made no provision except for outdoor relief under the pauper law. In Illinois, as in many other American States, outdoor relief consists for the most part of spasmodic and inadequate doles, and a widow with a family of small children can not maintain her home with such irregular assistance. In Chicago outdoor relief is given only in kind, and no rents are paid, so that, even if regularly given, the relief consists only of baskets of groceries with occasional allowances of coal and of shoes for school children.

METHODS OF MAKING PENSION GRANTS

After a mother has filed an application for a pension the application is referred to the probation officer in the aid-to-mothers department, who has charge of the investigations for the district in which the applicant lives.

The first step in the investigation is to clear the name of the family in the confidential exchange, which is known in Chicago as the social service registration bureau. In this bureau all the standardized social agencies in Chicago, both public and private, register the names of the families or individuals with whom or for whom they have been working. It is, therefore, a preliminary inquiry to learn what agencies are already acquainted with the applicant. If the family is found to be already on the books of other social agencies, those agencies are asked to submit a written report summarizing their knowledge of the family before a court officer undertakes any further investigation. The officer may or may not visit the agencies later to consult their records.

This work of clearing with the social agencies by the officer to whom the applicant is assigned is followed by visits to the applicant's home, to relatives, and to other persons to whom the family may be known. When relatives are found able to help and liable for the support of the applicant under the pauper act, they are visited and asked to contribute. If they refuse, the applicant is asked if she is willing to have the relatives who are legally liable for her support prosecuted in the county court. If she refuses, her application for a pension is dismissed and she is left to her own resources. If she is willing that a prosecution should be undertaken, the information that has been obtained is sent to the division of nonsupport of the bureau of social service of Cook County.

Relatives who are not liable under the pauper act are also asked to help, and if the relatives do not live in Cook County and can not be visited by the officer, letters are written asking them to contribute to the support of the family.

Verification of all facts relating to the receipt of insurance money and its expenditure is required. If the applicant refuses to make a reasonably exact accounting as to the expenditure of the insurance money, the investigation halts until such an accounting is furnished. Many of the women feel that it is a great hardship to be obliged to tell a public officer how they have spent their money, and they complain that asking for such an accounting is a needless prying into their private affairs. It is not easy for any one who has spent money foolishly to tell about it, and it must be very hard to give an account of unwise expenditures to be presented to an official committee. To the court, however, such an accounting seems necessary, not only because the court must determine whether or not the woman possesses property that would render her ineligible for a pension, but also because the committee must form a judgment concerning her ability to spend money wisely. If the woman is obdurate, however, and to the end refuses any statement, the final decision of the court will not necessarily be adverse, but will be determined by all the circumstances of the particular case. If there is no money left and if there has been no attempt to deceive the court, a pension will not be withheld solely because an accounting is impossible or because the insurance money is shown to have been unwisely spent.

A thorough investigation, such as the court requires, necessarily takes a good deal of time. During this period the court gives no emergency relief, and the family is left to its own resources or to the assistance of charitable agencies. If the family needs appear to be very pressing a letter may be given to the mother introducing her to the county agent or to the united charities, and the mother is always told by the interviewer that relief can be obtained from these sources while the investigation is pending.

Summary of Record of the B Family

The father, who was American born, had been a teamster, earning $48 a month. The court's investigation brought out the fact that the family had previously been known to the Cook County agent, the visiting nurse association, the adult probation department of the municipal court, and to the united charities. The united charities record showed that the family had been first reported to them in November, 1904, when the father was ill and the children were begging from house to house; and again in 1908 this complaint was made about the children. The family at this time were living in a house owned by Mr. B's mother and were not paying rent. When the application for pension was made, however, the family were living in four rooms in a basement, described on the record as "filthy, damp, and dark." Mrs. B, a woman of 35 years, complained of ill health and looked frail, slovenly, and discouraged.

The Teamsters' Union raised a purse of $100 for the family which just covered funeral expenses, as Mr. B had carried no insurance. During the investigation by the court, which lasted a month and a half, the family was dependent upon county supplies and the irregular help of relatives. At the end of this time a pension of $40 a month was granted. This seems to have constituted the family's only income until the two older girls were old enough to become wage earners.

For nearly three years Mrs. B was sick practically all the time. It was difficult to improve her housekeeping, which was very slatternly, and to get the children properly cared for.

In all there were eight probation officers on this case, but each one seems to have given herself to the problems in hand with energy and determination, and gradually the standards of living were raised, and the mother's health began to show a decided improvement. The family was moved from time to time to more desirable rooms. Medical treatment for Mrs. B was secured, and regular dispensary treatment was insisted upon. The diet and buying of the family was carefully supervised, and Mrs. B instructed in the art of keeping a clean home.

The pension for this family has been gradually reduced from $40 to only $24, as the children have become old enough to go to work. Both girls have good positions, one as a stenographer, and the other working for the telephone company. In another year one of the boys will be able to go to work.

In the words of the present probation officer: "This family will soon be self-supporting, has greatly improved in health and standard of living, will probably move into better quarters." This family illustrates the effect that constant, intelligent supervision may have upon the most careless housekeeping habits. The record shows a woman who, when the court began its work with the family, had a miserable home and neglected children, and whose own physical resistance was so low that the slightest ailment incapacitated her. Gradually she has become a woman who washes and scrubs her house, launders her curtains, paints the walls, keeps the children clean and fairly well dressed, and is herself practically discharged from the doctor's care.

Summary of Record of the C Family

In June, 1913, Mrs. C, a Polish woman, applied for a pension for her two children aged 8 and 5 years because she found it impossible to earn enough to support them. Her husband had died of heart disease in 1909, leaving some insurance; but the money had been used for paying funeral bills, debts, and living expenses. The family had been compelled to ask help from the county agent and the united charities a number of times during the four years following the death of the father. A stepson had gone to work at the age of 14, but Mrs. C found him so unmanageable that in 1911 she sent him to his uncle in Tennessee. Mrs. C had been earning only $10 a month by sweeping in a school.

The family budget was estimated at $34, and in October, 1913, the court granted a pension of $10 for each of the two children. With the mother's earnings of about $10 a month, the income of the family was brought up to within $4 of their estimated needs. It was found that the dust raised by sweeping in the school was very bad for the mother, as it caused her to cough so much that she could not sleep. Her work was changed to cleaning in a bank, where she earned $3 a week instead of $10 a month.

The probation officer found that Stephania, the older child, had never gone to school because she was extremely anemic and had very bad teeth. The officer had the mother go with both children, neither of whom were strong, to the municipal tuberclosis dispensary for examination, saw to it that the mother's teeth and eyes received attention, and watched the weights of the children. During the pension period the children had whooping cough, and in 1914 the doctor said that they were likely to become tubercular if they were not very well nourished. However, the fact that in 1916 all of the family were in good health indicated close attention by the officer to the health of the family as well as competent oversight by the mother. Both children are in school, their attendance is regular, and their scholarship and deportment good.

The officer has also secured gifts of clothing and food from the church and parochial school, given the family tickets to settlement parties, and interested Mrs. C in the mothers' club at the Northwestern University settlement. Continuous effort during the past two years has been made by the officer to secure from Mrs. C's mother and brother more generous help for the family. In this the officer has been very successful, since both relatives continued to increase the aid given to the family.

The mother provides a good variety of food and has learned to do her buying in large amounts. The home is reported as being always spotless, the children are well cared for, and a recent comment of the officer is, "Family very happy and comfortable; children exceptionally attractive."

PENSION "STAYS" OR WITHDRAWALS OF PENSION GRANTS

The standard of supervision maintained demands the withdrawal of the pension grants whenever a change in family circumstances has occurred that makes a pension no longer necessary or its continuance undesirable for the good of the children. If the supervision of the pensioned family is adequate the court will be promptly informed of such changes in family circumstances or home conditions. The important questions to be asked concerning the families who are dropped from the pension lists may be summarized as follows: Were they dropped because they were no longer in need of assistance? Were they dropped because the homes failed to come up to the standards set by the court? Were they dropped because the pension had been granted on the basis of an inadequate investigation, and the court discovered facts that would have prevented the grant had those facts been known at the time of the grant? Unfortunately the reasons given in the records for the "stay" of funds are often expressed in a small number of set phrases that are frequently ambiguous. An attempt was made by a careful study of each record, to relate the reason for the stay to the work of the court and in this way to answer the questions suggested above. Further explanation of the reasons for stays given in the table is, therefore, possible. In the first class of families —those in which the reasons given is "pension no longer needed"—are included 39 families who were said to be dropped because their income was "sufficient," 32 who "should be self-supporting," 12 who had money that they had received after the pension grant, 12 in which the mother remarried, 5 in which the mother died, 2 in which the mother withdrew voluntarily, and 4 in which the family had left the city. These 106 families, 62 percent of the total number "stayed," were dropped from the pension roll because the family circumstances had changed; and the fact that this change of circumstances was known to the court and was acted upon by the court is evidence of the fact that the families were being carefully supervised.

The most important fact is, of course, that 62 percent of the stays were ordered because the circumstances in the families had changed, that only 14 percent were dropped because the mother could not be brought up to a proper standard, and only 9 percent because the family had been found to be ineligible. It is also important to note that of the families whose circumstances had changed, the majority—78 out of 106—had been pensioned for a year or longer.

Most of the mothers who did not come up to the standards required of them had also had pensions for a year or more. This may be interpreted either as showing the patience of the court in dealing with the families whose care it assumes; or it may be taken as an indication of the rising standard set by the court and the gradual weeding out of the unfit.

18

Poverty and the Aged:
Abraham Epstein's argument for social security

Although the 1920's did not witness many advances in social legislation, they were years in which many social thinkers planned and elaborated programs that would be enacted during the New Deal. One of the most important of these efforts was made by Abraham Epstein, who investigated the problem of old age dependency. Epstein, who immigrated to the United States in 1910 at the age of 18, was director of the Pennsylvania Commission to Investigate Old Age Pensions in 1918–1919, and he organized the American Association for Old Age Security in 1927 to press for reform. The Challenge of the Aged, *which he published in 1928, persuasively detailed the problems facing the aged and advanced the solution of social security pensions to combat them.*

It is not surprising that a great many recipients of relief are advanced in years. Old age and dependency are indeed inter-related and too closely associated. The reports of the State Commissions delegated to study this subject make this so clear that no additional comments are necessary.

In 1910 the Massachusetts Commission on Pensions and Annuities found in the case of almshouse inmates that:

Reprinted by permission of the publisher, The Vanguard Press, from *The Challenge of the Aged* by Abraham Epstein. Copyright 1928, 1957, by Mrs. Henrietta Epstein. Excerpts from pp. 35-36, 45-48, 52-53, 58-59, 144-148, 258-259, 291-292.

Less than one percent of those for whom the age at entrance was stated in the returns became inmates before the age of 40; only eight percent entered before the age of 60; thus 92 percent had passed the sixtieth year before they took up residence in the Almshouse.

Commenting on this, the Commission added:

The strikingly high proportion of persons entering pauper institutions late in life points to the close connections between old age and institutional pauperism. It is clear that such pauperism is in most cases the result of the infirmity of advancing years, rather than of the misfortunes of earlier years.

The 1919 Pennsylvania Commission on Pensions concluded:

It appears that only about 13 percent of the inmates in almshouses were admitted under 50 years of age; 24.8 percent were admitted between the ages of 50 and 60; 31.9 percent between 60 and 70, while 24.7 percent were admitted after they had reached their seventieth years.

It is obvious that the great majority of the aged inmates enter the institution late in life. This would indicate a close relationship between institutional pauperism and old age. The combination of advanced years and infirmity, when coupled with the fact that in most cases these people have no one to depend or fall back upon is—as will be seen later—the chief cause compelling an aged person to go to the poorhouse.

An examination of the economic classes from which the overwhelming proportion of paupers are recruited illustrates the relation between low wages, and dependency in old age. Of the 57,888 male paupers admitted to the different county almshouses in 1910, 37.5 percent were designated as common laborers. The other occupations showed very small percentages. The Massachusetts investigation in 1910 disclosed that 33.7 percent of the almshouse paupers were previously employed in manufacturing and mechanical pursuits, 22.6 percent in housekeeping and domestic service, and 14.5 percent were recorded as common laborers. In Pennsylvania, of 1,939 paupers stating their last occupation, 47.6 percent were common and unskilled workers; 29 percent were previously occupied in housekeeping and domestic service, and less than 18 percent had jobs in the skilled or semi-skilled trades.

The study of the Pennsylvania Department of Public Welfare also found that:

The male almshouse population is recruited largely from the ranks of unskilled labor. About 20 percent were classed as common laborers and almost 23 percent as farmers and agricultural laborers. The bulk of the female inmates were in domestic or personal service before admission to the almshouse.

The abundant facts cited above strikingly concur to present a complete picture of the forces which make for dependency in old age, forces which are beyond the control of the individual. The investigations failed to show that any considerable amount of poverty was due merely to personal negligence or inadvertence. On the contrary, the great majority of these paupers were merely victims of the social conditions and circumstances which they could not surmount. With laborers' wages all through their lives, with health undermined, children gone or dead, and their economical usefulness a thing of the past, poverty in old age could hardly be avoided!

The estimates of the Massachusetts Commission, being based upon the most thorough investigation ever undertaken by a State Commission, may probably serve as fair indications of the conditions prevailing in the entire country. Granting, however, that possibly better conditions may exist in our less industrial states, it would seem rather conservative to state that approximately one-third of the aged population in the United States is definitely dependent in part or entirely upon children, relatives or organized charity for their support. Accordingly, of the approximately 5,500,000 persons 65 years of age and over in the United States at the present, from 1,800,000 to 2,000,000 are supported in one way or another. Only a small proportion of these are under the care of organized philanthropy.

While many of these aged, it is true, will hesitate for a long while before applying for relief to the existing charitable agencies, most of them are facing a pitiful struggle for subsistence. Obviously when one person out of three faces a helpless old age, the roots of poverty must lie deep in the economic and social forces which are beyond individual control.

Since even an annuity of approximately $1.00 a day beginning at 65 requires an initial outlay of from $3,500 to $4,000 per person, it is obvious that only a few aged wage-earners may hope to remain economically independent upon attaining three-score and five years. Only their ability to hold on to their jobs till their last days would make that possible. But, as already noted, the opportunities for old persons in industrial establishments are growing rarer. Thus after a lifetime of toil in a modern factory, with physical vigor gone, children and relatives either scattered or dead, the aged wage-earner or his widow can hardly escape falling dependent in old age.

Both the nature and extent of old age dependency in the United States would indicate that the problems facing the old are as real and difficult of solution by mere individual effort in this country as they have been found abroad. Old age dependency, whether of one form or another, is with us and has come to stay since it is largely a result of our industrial development. Once a wage-earner has passed the half-century mark the question of how to escape the poorhouse in old age and a pauper's grave at the end, does not altogether depend upon his own desires and ambitions. Conditions which lie outside his own control will decide this for him.

Our present system of aged relief is not only inadequate, incompetently administered, and destructive of industrial efficiency, but it must be called to account even more because of its injurious effect upon the future. The present methods necessitate a reconsideration and a readjustment, chiefly because of their evil results upon the coming generation and upon society as a whole. For of more far-reaching importance and greater social significance than either the money spent on the decrepit aged or the treatment received by the old whose hopes of rehabilitation or restoration to society are slight, and more sinister even than industrial inefficiency, are the effects of our present methods of aged relief upon great numbers of the younger wage-earners.

We now generally recognize that society ultimately pays the price for all its unconcern and resultant maladjustments. Superficially it seems that the price in the case of the neglected aged would be reduced to a minimum. For the great majority of the old folks are rarely restored to active social participation, and their influence upon society, whether for good or evil, would seem to be nil. However, a closer observation reveals an intimate relationship between the superannuated worker and the younger generations.

The preceding data showed that, while old age dependency is widespread in this country, most persons, despite their poverty, succeed in avoiding either public or private charitable agencies. Obviously, all these persons do not commit suicide upon reaching old age; nor are many found actually starving on the streets. Most of them are taken care of by their children or relatives. Indeed, this is generally the chief difference between those who remain "non-dependent" and those who must seek shelter of the poorhouse. Few children, able to do so, are unwilling to aid their parents. On the other hand, how very often are children supporting their aged parents against great odds, either because of deep attachment or because of pride, who would rather suffer in silence than accept charity. This may seem a very meritorious act to those who value family solidarity above everything else and consider children bound to support their parents. Under present conditions, however, it is hardly desirable that the older generation should be supported by the younger. This is especially deplorable when the choice lies between supporting aged parents or giving a better education to young children.

The younger generation must be considered in any discussion of the aged problem, especially if we accept that the aged should fall back upon their children. The proverbial "mother-in-law" is undoubtedly blamed for many more things than she is actually guilty of. Nevertheless, we all know among our acquaintances some people whose young lives have been made pitiably wretched, and in some instances totally ruined, by the constant "pestering" of an old father-in-law or mother-in-law. Such conflicts are almost inevitable and are especially irritating at the present time when the pace and mode of life change so rapidly.

As a rule, the elders hate to feel dependent upon their children. They suffer greatly from not being "able to make their own dollar." They, who for years have been accustomed to be looked up to as the superiors and masters of the household, can hardly adjust themselves to a position of "added burdens." They find it difficult to give up their authority. On the other hand, even loyal children begin to lose their respect for parents who have become feeble, irritable, and burdensome. As a result there is frequently great suffering on the part of both generations, which some-times ends disastrously for the younger. It is also a well known fact that the support of parents frequently means the postponement or complete denial of marriage or parenthood for the children.

In addition to this, the third generation must also be considered. It seems cruel to force any father or mother in this twentieth century to decide between supporting old parents and contenting themselves with a little less food, less room, less clothing, and the curtailment of their children's education, or sending their parents to the poorhouse or to charitable agencies to accept the stigma of pauperism, and thus assure themselves of more food, more room, more clothing and a better educa-tion for their children which would help them to become somewhat more proficient workers. This is a difficult alternative, yet it is certain that thousands of parents in the United States are annually faced with it.

The hateful odium of charity and pauperism is so repugnant to self-respecting laboring men and women that the decision, in the majority of such cases, is made in favor of the passing generation. Thus the lack of provisions for the old is often responsible for the stunted and thwarted growth of the children. Because of the necessity of supporting the aged, the children are frequently compelled to leave school early in life and to join the ranks of the unskilled; to add further to the already over-crowded industries and thus lower the wages of their own fathers and other workers. They are doomed to physical deterioration early in life, and later to aged dependency in order that they may keep up the vicious cycle!

The movement for a definite and constructive social policy towards the superannuated workers of the United States is comparatively recent. Government insurance or pensions for the needy aged citizens aside from military and civil pensions were until recently unknown in this country. Indeed, while in England legislative committees were seeking a solution to the problem early in the nineteenth century, and on the European continent adequate provision for the aged was a dominant issue throughout the latter half of the last century, there were hardly any demands for such a movement in the United States until a few days ago.

Our backwardness in humane provisions for the aged is not surprising in view of the comparatively recent development of our industries, our wealth, and our ample supply of free and fertile land. As long as our population remained largely rural and when our country was predominantly agricultural there was no serious problem of old age dependency. For a few dependent aged who represented the flotsam and jetsam of society, the poor law provisions were adequate. But the expansion of our industries, the migration from rural into urban centers, the disappearance of free land, and the shortened working period have made old age dependency no longer a question purely of good and thrifty habits but rather one depending mainly upon vast social and economic forces which lie beyond the control of the individual. The poor law, originated in 1601 by Queen Elizabeth, cannot, of course, provide for the increasingly large number of dependent old folks. Because of the changed industrial conditions there has finally come a realization even in the United States that the present methods of treating the aged poor are thoroughly out of step and insufficient. Agitation for some system of old age pensions or insurance to provide effectively and humanely for the worthy aged who have become dependent has therefore followed the successful operation of these plans abroad. Although, at this writing, little actual achievement has as yet been made, the subject of old age dependency and its solution has at last become a national issue. Legislation has been urged not only in almost all states in the union, but for many years bills seeking to establish an old age pension system have been proposed in the United States Congress.

The movement for old age security in the United States, although hardly a decade old, has made enormous strides during the past few years. It has, like all other progressive legislation, aroused the bitter animosity of the same groups who fought workmen's compensation laws, child labor regulations and all the social legislation which today is on the statute books of practically all states. By misrepresentations and by spreading falsehoods these persons have in some states, in Pennsylvania for instance, succeeded in delaying the justice due our old fathers and mothers. But the movement for the protection of the aged is daily arousing new enthusiasm and is gaining in vigor. The time is not far off when the United States will desert its present companions—China and India —and like all industrial nations will permit its old toilers to retain their self-respect during their sunset days instead of branding them with the stigma of pauperism.

Part Four

ONE-THIRD OF THE NATION

1930–1940

19

The New Deal Response to the Great Depression: Lewis Meriam's evaluation

One of the most useful summaries of the New Deal's relief program appears in Lewis Meriam's Relief and Social Security. *Meriam's careful research sets out in clear detail the major legislation treating poverty in the 1930's. He explains some of the administrative problems inherent in pre-1932 procedures and shows through an analysis of eligibility requirements both the contributions and limits of WPA and the Social Security plan. This outline is a useful beginning point for evaluating the national effort to mitigate the effects of the Great Depression.*

When the depression came in 1929, thousands of workers who had previously supported themselves and their dependents, and who had none of the characteristics of the people customarily cared for under general public assistance, required public relief because of mass unemployment. Legally in many states they fell into this category. The general property tax—already overburdened—was a poor producer in bad times. It could not be expanded to yield additional revenue; generally it failed even to produce normal revenue. The existing provisions for relief were totally inadequate to meet the situation caused by the depression. Local governments, state governments, and finally the national government had to improvise, with little or no time to consider theory, principles, or sound administration.

Under American law and practice, at the onset of the depression the primary responsibility rested on the states or their subordinate units, but

Lewis Meriam, *Relief and Social Security* (Washington: Brookings Institution, 1946), excerpts from pp. 10-19.

many of them were entirely unprepared to meet the situation. For the purposes of the present book it is essential to ask: Why? Among the most important reasons were:

1. Many of the states had never modernized their tax systems. They still placed great reliance on the general property tax, which broke down under the strain. Often it was not so much that the states and local governments did not have the resources, the capacity to pay, as that they did not have tax devices for tapping their resources. In many states new laws and new administrations were required and in some constitutional amendments.

2. Many states and local governments could not borrow to meet the emergency because: (a) They were already in debt practically up to statutory or constitutional debt limits. (b) Relief was in the main an operating expense of government and not an outlay for capital improvements; and laws restricted borrowing for expenses. (c) Some state constitutions gave the state government no powers with respect to relief and prohibited them from borrowing for an object over which they had no power. (d) The states and local governments had no power over the currency and no real influence over the banking system. They had to go to the banks or other financial institutions to borrow much as a private individual would go. (e) The banks frequently could not safely lend to the state or local government, because they could not collect on a loan unless it complied with all the requirements of the constitution and the laws.

Under these circumstances the states and the politically powerful municipalities turned to the national government, supported by the mass of voters, not only those who were in need and their dependents, but others who saw the suffering or feared a complete breakdown of our economic, social, and political system. Not only was disorder prevalent in many sections of the country, but it was often apparent that the government officials responsible for maintaining law and order were in sympathy with the objectives of the disturbers if not with their methods. Public sentiment would not sustain the officers who took drastic action. The new political philosophies that had developed in Europe after the first World War added to the fears of many persons.

The first national action was in the form of loans and later grants to the states to enable them to meet the situation. In so far as there was division into categories, it was at the outset primarily the work of the states. The national government first made loans to the states through the Reconstruction Finance Corporation, established under the Hoover administration. Early in the Roosevelt administration it was succeeded by the Federal Emergency Relief Administration. These organizations generally worked with a temporary emergency relief administration, which had been quickly improvised by the states to meet the emergency, for few of them had any permanent coordinated public welfare department to assume the heavy responsibility. Experienced welfare workers from state, local, and private agencies often played a large part in organizing and operating the temporary state and local government emergency relief administrations, but these administrations were created almost overnight.

Differentiation was introduced in the early days of the Roosevelt administration, however, apparently primarily on the initiative of the national government. The national government was in the relief business operating on an emergency basis making grants to the states. Thousands of able-bodied, competent citizens were existing on doles or on wages earned on relief projects operated by state or local governments. The administration decided that the national government should get out of the relief business by furnishing employment to the employables on local projects, mainly at the expense of the national government.

The first general national experiment in furnishing relief employment, the Civil Works Administration, under the same direction as FERA, was almost immediately swamped and was soon abandoned. It offered work on federally financed projects, without any real use of a test of need. A person did not have to be on relief to be eligible. Thousands of workers who were being supported, perhaps more or less unsatisfactorily by primary breadwinners, got CWA jobs, and other workers who had some available resources conserved them by earning CWA wages. Thousands had to be turned away, although the actual need of some of them was far greater than that of persons who were given employment. The impracticability of the program and its political inexpediency were soon obvious, and the government fell back on the Federal Emergency Relief Administration working in co-operation with the states.

THE WPA

The national administration soon returned to the idea of substituting in the case of unemployed employables, work on relief projects mainly at the expense of the national government. Under the new plan which came to be the Works Progress Administration, an evolution from FERA, two of the major difficulties of the earlier CWA were avoided in that:

1. To be eligible for employment, a person had to be receiving relief or be eligible to receive it. In other words, a means test was used. In most states the means test was administered by the state or local public welfare agency, which certified the applicants found in need to the national WPA agency in the locality.

2. Not more than one member of a family, ordinarily the principal breadwinner, was eligible for employment on WPA.

Persons who were not certified as being in need could not get WPA work unless they were hired as regular employees of the organization for administrative and supervisory positions or for required skilled work that could not be done by persons available from the relief rolls.

In the official pronouncements of the period, the position taken was that the national government would assume responsibility for meeting the needs of the unemployed employables through the national work program. The responsibility for persons in need from causes other than unemployment would be returned to the states. The idea was apparently that the states, relieved of responsibility for unemployment relief, would have sufficient funds to meet the need from other causes.

As a matter of fact the program never worked out entirely in accordance with this theory. Whether the unemployed employables secured work on a WPA project depended on many factors, among the most important of which were:

1. The total amount the Congress, acting upon the recommendations of the President, made available for work relief.

2. The amount of the aggregate appropriation allocated to a particular state by the administration, which had wide discretion in making the allocations.

3. Whether there was an approved project with available funds that had openings or positions for the needy unemployed employables in the area.

4. Whether the needy unemployable had qualifications which would permit of his employment in the available positions. Projects were generally selected largely on the basis of furnishing the kind of work that could be done by the type of persons who were available, but in many instances, especially in smaller communities, there were no projects available for workers who did not fit the particular pattern.

In most communities there were unemployed employables on relief or certified as eligible for relief who could not secure positions on WPA. The national government did not provide for them but left them to be cared for by the state or the local government. In other words they were generally dependent on the old general public assistance.

Two factors added to the difficulties in some communities:

1. Under the WPA system, the state, the local government, or some other public or quasi-public agency had to put up a sponsor's contribution toward the costs of the WPA project. In communities hard hit by the depression, a sponsor's contribution had a priority over many other demands for public funds. If the community were to get the benefits from WPA, it had to have an approved project. Thus in many localities little was appropriated for general public assistance.

2. Although no person could get a work relief job on WPA unless he was certified as being in need, the WPA did not adjust its wages or earnings to need. Wages and hours of employment were fixed on a basis that resembled in many ways ordinary employment. Skilled workers got more than semi-skilled and semi-skilled more than unskilled. The unskilled worker with a big family of dependents got less for working the standard number of hours than the skilled worker with no dependents. Thus more money went into WPA wages than was necessary for relief.

When the WPA earnings were insufficient to sustain a big family, the welfare agencies occasionally had to supplement them from general public assistance funds. These agencies could do nothing when WPA earnings paid by the national government carried a worker and his dependents above the standard being used by them to determine need and occasionally even above the prevailing local level. This situation was particularly embarrassing in rural areas where the customary payment for work had been in allowances plus some cash, whereas the WPA paid all cash. The cash went to some persons who had little experience in handling money. From the standpoint of many local people, the national government was paying far more than necessary to those who succeeded in getting on WPA, and it was leaving to the locality the responsibility of caring for others whose need was really greater. Some were unemployable, and others were employable but unable to get on a project within a reasonable distance of their homes.

The WPA was ultimately abolished, when the defense and war efforts absorbed most of the unemployed. Under present conditions the unemployed employables who have no benefits coming to them from the unemployment insurance system are now back in the miscellaneous general public assistance category unless they can qualify for some of the other special categories established under the Social Security Act.

SOCIAL SECURITY AND OTHER PROGRAMS

The Social Security Act, passed in 1935, resulted in the differentiation of five additional categories, three in the field of means test relief and two in the field of no-means test social insurance.

By federal grants-in-aid to the states, the national government offered great inducements to the states to set up special relief categories for (1) the needy aged, 65 years of age or over, (2) dependent children living with relatives within the degrees specified by the national law, and (3) the needy blind.

By the exercise of the power to tax, the national government established and operated a system of old-age insurance applicable to persons who were in the status of employee to employer in industries and occupations, but with certain fairly large and important exceptions. By the same power the national government virtually forced the states to adopt systems of unemployment insurance, again applicable to persons in the employee status, but with important exceptions.

This broad outline traces the evolution of the major programs of relief, old-age insurance, and unemployment insurance in the social insurance field and the work program of the thirties, now abolished, for the unemployed employables.

There are other programs that require mention, two in the insurance field and four that stemmed from relief. The two in the insurance field apply to the steam railway industry, one providing for old-age retirement and the other for unemployment compensation. They are both national programs, nationally administered, and came into existence in the thirties. The four in the field of relief and work relief were:

1. The Civilian Conservation Corps, which was originated by the national government in the early days of the Roosevelt administration as a special work program for unemployed boys from families in need. Gradually the requirement that the boys be from needy families and allot most of their money earnings to their respective families was relaxed, and the program became more of a kind of governmental work conducted by the national government in the interest of a special class of youth.

2. The National Youth Administration grew out of the activities of the Federal Emergency Relief Administration. It engaged in two types of activities: (a) work projects in co-operation with educational institutions to enable needy students to earn money so that they could continue their schooling, and (b) independent NYA projects to train and educate youth whose formal schooling was completed or interrupted and who did not find normal jobs. Originally conceived as a relief agency, the NYA

gradually shifted its emphasis from relief as such and tended to become an educational agency. It was a national organization, and at least so far as its special work projects were concerned, it was not integrated with the public educational system of the state and its subordinate units.

3. The Farm Security Administration which developed out of the Federal Emergency Relief Administration and the Subsistence Home-stead Division of the Department of the Interior, authorized by the National Industrial Recovery Act. The activities of the FERA that related to rural relief, rural rehabilitation, and drought relief were merged with those of the Subsistence Homestead Division to form the Resettlement Administration. It, in turn, was transferred to the Depart-ment of Agriculture, where with some modifications it became the Farm Security Administration. Still later the FSA was relieved of the nonagri-cultural projects originally undertaken by its predecessor agencies and became an agricultural agency concerned entirely with farm families who were in need of special assistance.

Perhaps the most significant fact brought out by this outline of the several programs is the subdivision and the dispersion of responsibility and authority that has taken place. Despite the inherent interrelation-ships among the several programs, some are administered solely and exclusively by the national government, others by the state governments in co-operation with the national government through conditional grants-in-aid, one—unemployment insurance—by the states under the compulsion of a federal tax law, and one—the residual general public assistance—exclusively by the states or their subdivisions without any national participation.

20

Making a Living Without a Job: E. W. Bakke questions the unemployed

One of the most brilliant studies of the reaction of the unemployed to the Depression is E. Wight Bakke's The Unemployed Worker. *Through extensive and sensitive interviews conducted during the 1930's, Bakke*

E. Wight Bakke, *The Unemployed Worker* (New Haven, 1940), excerpts from pp. 315-327, 363-367, 371-377. Copyright © 1940 by Yale University Press.

was able to learn about the daily experiences of the unemployed and grasp their social outlook. Their very ambivalent sentiments toward relief emerge vividly in the pages below, and so do their incredible efforts to keep body and spirit together during that catastrophe.

If no job is offered him as a result of his search, if unemployment compensation is too long delayed or inadequate, if no amount of economic ingenuity can make available resources cover all the needs of his family, the unemployed man must seek other sources of maintenance. In an urban society this means one thing—relief. We view the application for relief merely as an additional step in his attempts to maintain himself and his family.

Several general conclusions, grounded in our observations of the adjustments of the unemployed who were not on relief, have a bearing on this particular problem when we consider the situation of relief clients. The first conclusion is that the goals present in the life of the employed worker are not suddenly forgotten and eliminated when he becomes unemployed. They may be modified but not destroyed.

What forces impinge upon the worker's desire to play a socially respected role when he turns his steps toward the relief office? "Being on relief" is definitely an obstacle to that desire for any worker who, previously, has been successful in finding a self-supporting place in contemporary society. The anxiety, despair, and desperation attendant upon the first application for relief are evidence of that fact. The long struggle to stay off relief which we shall describe later corroborates such a conclusion. The rationalizations which men and women develop when at last they are forced to make application for public assistance are further testimony, perhaps the best testimony, that self-respect requires that the new status shall be squared with the old and that it be justified in the light of rights earned by the worker during the years when he was a producer, a good provider, an "X" man, an important fellow among his workmates.

The most frequent rationalization made by the man who has paid taxes (and all citizens have presumably paid poll taxes) is that such payments have been used for community services for others, now it is his turn to receive service from the funds to which he has contributed.

That such rationalizations were not satisfactory solutions is evident from the fact that only those on relief were observed to make use of such self-justification, that even in the case of relief clients the attitude was frequently ascribed to someone else, and that if the worker talked long enough he would eventually end with some such comment as, "But you can say what you will, it is still charity." A satisfactory social role is premised upon the holding of a job and the spending of income from it. No rationalization could produce even the limited sense of progress toward that goal which the worker can make while employed. This is particularly true if the material evidence of one's social status—home furnishings, residence in a good neighborhood, ownership of one's own home, a car, decent clothes, superior education for the children, insurance policies, and the like—have been curtailed. The worker finds it difficult to believe that he occupies a social status the symbolic evidence of which does not exist.

In spite of this fact, however, events have conspired to reduce to a degree the loss of status involved in being a "reliefer." The social status implicit in becoming a "reliefer" may be measured against several standards. A worker and his family may be concerned with "public opinion" voiced in the newspapers, public addresses, and other representations of what the community as a whole thinks about the unemployed and relief clients. They may be concerned about the contrast of such status with that labeled in their family tradition as "proper." They are, of course, aware of the standards set by the working group and their customary associates within that group, by which standards a relief client is at least a partial failure. Such standards are not invariably the same, but all place independence and self-support on a plane superior to public assistance. Forced to accept a relief role, however, the worker may find his present status made somewhat bearable by modifications apparent in the standards to which it is compared.

The onset of the depression in 1929 found the attitude of the community toward the unemployed on relief, as revealed in the evidences of it mentioned above, fully consistent with the belief that any willing worker could find a job, and that any who did not were inferior individuals. Only the "ill, the lame, and the lazy" found their way to charitable societies or public relief. We have no comparable data on the predepression point of view of the workers themselves, but judging from the resistance displayed in applying for relief we are not unwarranted in concluding that family and group tradition among the workers approximated to this attitude. Self-respect defined as living up to the expectancies of the groups of which one is a member would have received a blow, varying in severity for different groups no doubt, but in any case destructive of the assurance that one "belonged" when a worker was forced to apply for relief. No development of group attitude during the succeeding

Unemployment line, San Francisco, 1939. The isolated, almost resigned quality of those in need of relief or a job in the Depression is conveyed well in this photograph. The men look ahead, they do not mingle, there is no conversation among them. Photograph by Dorothea Lange, Library of Congress.

decade has reversed this situatiôn, although several developments have modified it.

The clue to those developments lies in the fact that the unemployed have gradually been distinguished in the public eye and in their own eyes from the general relief group. The steps by which this has been accomplished can be traced in the types of relief provision and their underlying assumptions.

For the first two years of the depression no definite change in the status of the unemployed among relief recipients could be noticed. Public opinion still labeled them as paupers and incompetents. They went through the same procedure as all applicants for relief. They were to be found standing in line, getting city milk, being investigated at home, signing the pauper's oath, carrying food orders to designated grocers.

From 1930 to 1932, to judge from published comments and our own observations in the field, there was little change in the public's picture of the unemployed. The organization of the Citizens Committee on unemployment as an emergency relief agency, however, prepared the way in action for a system of relief for the unemployed distinguishable from that designed for ordinary paupers. Similarly the agitation for bond issues to support the unemployed on public works called attention to the fact that men without work were not the normal type of relief applicants. Work-finding efforts having disclosed a small demand for labor relative to the supply, however, the unemployed man forced to apply for relief found his position even more degrading if possible than in the preceding period. The creaking of the relief arrangements under the tremendous pressure of an unpredicted and unprepared for volume of applicants was obvious.

Coupled with the impact of local experiments in "unemployment relief," however, was an increasing amount of reporting and analysis available to those who read the daily papers emphasizing the universality of the unemployment problem. The unemployed became the symbol of a national catastrophe. They were not merely unfortunate individuals; they were the visible evidence of a national crisis, the unwilling victims of an economic storm the rumblings and damage of which were felt throughout the land. They stood before the bar of public opinion increasingly as "the unemployed" and not as normal "reliefers." The shift in public identification was not yet clear-cut, but it was making progress.

By 1933 the layoff notices had been widely enough distributed so that it was no longer possible for any rational citizen to charge the unemployed with laziness, or to lump them with all "reliefers." Too many obviously competent workers came within the casual contacts of everyone. In many cases they were members of "the best" families.

In 1933 and 1934 the division of responsibility between the private and public agencies, in which straight relief cases were taken over by the latter and the "problem" families requiring case-work service retained by the former, further emphasized the fact that the primary need of the unemployed was lack of money, not lack of character, employability, or adequate adjustment to community life.

Increasingly during the next two years the "unemployed" were cared for through federally supported agencies. For the most part, save in case of employment on PWA projects, relief investigations still preceded his qualifications for assistance. CCC, FERA, Department of Public Charities direct relief, transient aid, all made use of the investigating techniques developed for giving assistance to paupers. Frequently the transfer from one agency to another involved duplication of question answering. But in the midst of it all the unemployed man was aware that public opinion with respect to his status had changed. He was looked upon as a respectable citizen caught by factors beyond his control and deserving of aid without disgrace.

The introduction of WPA carried on still further the special assistance for the unemployed. Much publicity was given to the basic formula upon which the federal and local governments based their division of responsibility. WPA, the federal agency, was to take care of all "employables" on useful work projects. The local governments were to care for the unemployables. The blurring of this distinction in practice had not yet become evident.

It is unlikely however that the cycle of community attitude and its accompanying development of the unemployed man's conception of his status will become complete. The agencies for the relief of the unemployed have made great strides in their techniques and basic philosophy. Whatever citizens in the community may think, the institutions of welfare have undergone an evolution toward provision for the unemployed as a particular group of dependents whose problems are distinguishable from "reliefers" in general. The enactment of unemployment compensation took place in an atmosphere of public discussion which emphasized this fact. Although unemployment compensation was available only to those who during and after 1937 could show a record of employment in private industry and although its benefits were anomalous in some respects, its enactment marked another milestone in the realistic analysis of the nature of unemployment and the acceptance by the community of the separate status of the unemployed among those unable to support themselves.

Our observations of the adjustments and reactions of the unemployed over this period lead us to assess the primary result of this shift in public attitude upon the unemployed as a welcome release from unwarranted degradation in status rather than as a release from efforts to return to the normal status of workers. In the face of the natural tendency for unemployment to cut men off from community relations, this tendency to separate them from chronic dependents was at least a temporary barrier to complete separation from participation in the processes of community life. We offer no moral judgment upon the stimulating effect of the fear of becoming a pauper, nor upon the justice of such release from desperate effort to maintain an impossible standard of self-respect. The fact remains that such a release was effected in a measure by the separation in the public mind between the unemployed and chronic dependents.

Another modification of standards unconsciously used by the unemployed may be effected by virtue of the fact that his neighbors are facing problems similar to his, and that in adjustment to the hard knocks of circumstance they are holding less strictly to the *mores* developed in times of greater economic security. Other things being equal, it is less painful to "go on relief" if one has neighbors in the same circumstances. The community, family, and friends may have altered their standards very little. That is a barrier to rationalization too high to surmount satisfactorily in any neighborhood, and particularly so if one has been forced to move into a section inhabited by many who are on relief. Yet in the absence of complete consolation, one may legitimately shift some of the responsibility for a reduced status from his own shoulders in view of the apparently large number of people associated with him in his own difficulty.

The neighborhood contacts in certain areas were therefore on an increasing scale with those forced to derive what comfort to wounded pride they could from the facts of relief receiving. This contact with "others in the same boat" was emphasized for many forced to move to cheaper rents. Certain tenement houses where cheap rents might be had became the inevitable magnet drawing the unfortunate.

Thinking of this individual about to go on relief, not as "a poor person," but as a person who is a member of a number of groups which are also poor and many of whom need relief, helps to explain the instances where public aid is sought with less humiliation than the majority of citizens would feel.

In general, then, the unemployed could not possibly maintain the social status customary to them as workers while in receipt of relief. Of this, they gave ample evidence in their anxieties, in their efforts to stay off relief, as we shall see presently, and in their rationalizations. The blow to prestige, however, was somewhat softened by the separation in the public mind of "unemployed" from ordinary reliefers, and by association with companions in distress whose standards of self-respect must needs be modified in adjustment to realistic possibilities for the maintenance of those standards.

The unemployed man who asks for assistance from a relief agency has obviously admitted failure in his attempt to be independent and self-supporting. To the extent that that attempt is considered a "mark" of the normal citizen and the "proper" endeavor of all men he has been forced beyond the bounds of socially acceptable behavior. No rationalization and no modification of relief procedures enable him to escape the fact that this new relationship to the community has separated him in this respect from his fellows. Since satisfactory living is inhibited by that separation we should expect great resistance to it.

This is not a judgment based on "faith in human nature." The actual records of the unemployed justify the conclusion that relief was for the great majority a last resort in the losing battle to remain "normal." In 1933 a sample study involving 2,000 representative New Haven families revealed 988 individuals to be unemployed. In 1935, two years later, these 988 were revisited to learn how many had sought relief. Less than one fourth (24%) had done so, the majority of these asking for only partial support. Half of this 24% had had contacts with relief agencies prior to this period of unemployment. How long did the other half wait after the layoff before crossing the threshold of the relief office for the first time? Ten percent applied in less than three months, 17% in less than six months, 30% in less than one year after unemployment. Even after two years of unemployment 40% of this applying-for-the-first-time group were "getting by" somehow without public assistance. Remember that these figures apply to 1935 after the full force had been felt of relief policies declared by some at the time to have killed self-reliance!

The indication of the survival of self-reliance is even more apparent when one realizes that the three fourths of 988 workers unemployed in 1933 who had not by 1935 applied for relief had already, when first visited, been out of work approximately as long on the average as the one fourth who eventually did apply for relief. Sixty-eight percent of both groups had been out of work for over a year, 44% of both groups for over two years, 22% of the nonrelief and 18% of the relief group for over three years.

Lack of knowledge of relief resources in the community may have prevented some from applying. Certainly ignorance of relief agencies, their practices and requirements, characterized most workers in 1933.

Such information as they did possess came in a roundabout fashion from "a friend of a friend." The "indignities suffered" by this friend's friend, the complete dependence required before eligibility for relief was established, the "red tape and forms," the control over where and how one spent his money, "the investigator that thinks she's got as much rights as your mother-in-law," the discrimination involved when "a fellow who owns a brick house got help from two places, while a poor widow couldn't get a penny," "the widow who had to get permission before she could visit her children in Naugatuck and it's like keeping her in prison," "the humiliating and personal questions they ask you"—such bits of detail, however, indicate a source of information somewhat more definite than those which usually are back of rumors. They have the authentic ring of reported experience in them. Their character also indicates the unpleasantness of the circumstances with which relief receiving is associated. Emphasized particularly and frequently was the necessity for surrender of independent management of one's affairs when one became dependent upon others for financial assistance.

One fact, however, cannot be denied. Those who had no personal contact with such agencies wished to steer clear of them. Such phrases as "rather be dead and buried," "would hide my face in the ground and pound the earth" were common. Life on the margin of economic independence had not produced a degree of willingness to accept relief proportional to the nearness of the possibility. If anything, the proximity of the necessity had pulled it into the center of consciousness where contemplation of it had furnished a determination to avoid it.

Once that fight for independence, as normally defined, had ended in defeat, however, the actual experience of relief receiving did not hold all its expected horrors. It was notable that the few families who had relief records prior to 1933 had much less dread of the disgrace of getting community help than did those who had never applied for relief. Actual experience is an excellent corrective of a cultural standard which excludes that experience from the list of "proper" alternatives.

The socially "proper" thing for a relief client is to get off relief as quickly as possible and back into private employment. That definition of propriety he has shared with other employed workers. Once he has become a relief client, however, he must be guided as every human being is guided—by the adjustment expedient in his present circumstances. His culture defines what is expected of him. But the definitions are premised on the normal operation of societal arrangements in which work for wages plays a dominant and all but exclusive part. They are "right" because it is customary for people to buy a living with wages. Practically, for the time being, they are inconsistent with his action possibilities. We have seen the sort of experience men face in job hunting. "What the unemployed need is jobs" is only half a truth. What they need is maintenance, economic security for themselves and their families. Normally that maintenance is secured through jobs and wages. But the job is a means to an end, not the end itself. Even when the means has become a relief allowance, it is only natural, therefore, that the end shall be given primary attention and the acceptability of the means be judged in terms of its usefulness in accomplishing that end.

I have neither seen nor heard of any evidence in my contacts with the unemployed either in England or in America that would lead me to suspect that when a job which promised a degree of security comparable to relief was offered, it would not find more applicants than could be taken. Indeed, as I have indicated elsewhere, reaching even noneconomic goals depends upon job holding. This fact will stimulate a man to accept normal work even at the sacrifice of a degree of economic security. To expect, however, that any available job regardless of its reward in economic or social security should be accepted in preference to relief is to expect that workers shall renounce all of that foresight and economic intelligence, the decay of which is popularly supposed to be indicated by the single fact of job refusal.

21

A Farmer's Story:
The WPA reports

Some of the most intimate and revealing studies of the effects of poverty emerged from research sponsored by the WPA. In part, that New Deal agency wanted to give intellectuals, writers, photographers, and others an opportunity to practice their skills. But it also wished to sensitize the country to the plight of the poor. The WPA's educational effort may not have been altogether successful in that the stigma of poverty survived the New Deal. But such case studies as appeared in the WPA publication The Personal Side *offer some of the most accurate and persuasive pictures of how Americans confronted the Depression.*

Mr. Crumbaugh, with his shaggy snow-white hair, looks older than his 58 years; a network of little broken veins shows through the skin of his cheeks and nose; the pupil of one eye, its vision lost when Mr. Crumbaugh was only 7 years old, is slightly smaller than the other, and the eyelid droops. He is a broad and heavy-set man, who moves and talks with a heavy slowness.

Jessie A. Bloodworth and Elizabeth J. Greenwood, *The Personal Side* (Washington, 1939), excerpts from pp. 317-327.

In 1930 after he had been forced to sell the last 114 acres of his farm–a mortgage on 100 acres had been foreclosed in 1926—Mr. Crumbaugh came to Dubuque with his wife and the seven children then living at home. Two daughters were married and away from home, and Antony stayed behind to work for a while on a neighbor's farm.

When he came to town, Mr. Crumbaugh had about $1200, the amount realized from the sale of the farm beyond what was necessary to pay off the mortgage; he hoped that this fund would tide him over until he could find work in Dubuque. But he has had no private employment except a few odd jobs, none lasting so long as a week. When this sum and amounts secured by cashing in insurance policies had been exhausted, Mr. Crumbaugh applied for relief. Since 1933 the family has been at least partially dependent on direct relief grants, work relief, and Mr. Crumbaugh's CWA and WPA employment. For more than 2 years he has been steadily employed on WPA projects.

His acceptance of the present situation has in it something of defeatism; he is not wholly satisfied with his present job or with his present earnings, but he "wouldn't know where to look" for other work. In fact, he has never applied for factory work in Dubuque; it has been his feeling that there were no jobs available. He is handicapped by his age and by his lack of any sort of experience as an industrial wage earner. Perhaps he is still more handicapped by his feeling of helplessness; he does not know how to look for a job, or where. Though he feels that his one sightless eye never lessened his effectiveness as a farmer and does not think of it in terms of a physical handicap, Mrs. Crumbaugh and the oldest son, Antony, believe that it would preclude the possibility of his being employed in any local factory; the factories can find plenty of unhandicapped and experienced men to take over what few jobs are open.

Mrs. Crumbaugh's fatalistic outlook somewhat resembles her husband's, though she is not quite so resigned as he, for her resignation is tinged with bitterness. She is a pleasant, friendly woman, too stout, a little nervous and fidgety, and not very well. Since she has never been satisfied with living in town, she would like now to take the younger children to a farm. Mrs. Crumbaugh is somewhat irritated by her husband's failure even to express any interest in planning to go back to farming, though she states that unless he had some money to invest, Mr. Crumbaugh could not go to a farm except as a hand, in which case no provision could be made for the family to be with him.

Tenant purchase applicants, Stockton, California, 1938. Poverty was no less disheartening and depressing in rural than in urban settings. The resignation and fright of these applicants makes clear how much of a last resort was the turn to any form of government aid. Photograph by Dorothea Lange, Library of Congress.

No one of the three children of employable age now at home has full-time work. All of the older children have evidently made considerable effort to find jobs, and, for the most part, have not been entirely unemployed. But they have shifted from job to job with some frequency, and their earnings have been consistently meager.

It was in 1909, the year of his marriage, that Mr. Crumbaugh purchased his first farm land—114 acres. Until the early twenties his farming was profitable, especially during the war years, and from time to time he made a number of new investments: in additional acreage; in livestock, farm equipment, and buildings; in stocks, bank accounts, and insurance policies. He purchased 100 more acres of land at $135 an acre, built a $1000 house and a $3000 barn. He explains jestingly that since the first two children "unfortunately were girls" he regularly employed farm hands before the boys were old enough to help with the work. His chief crops were corn and oats. He estimated that the value of the farm, including livestock and equipment, was at one time $50,000. Once he was offered $250 an acre for the entire farm. Perhaps he should have sold then, but he did not even consider giving up farming; besides, in those days when land values were high, he, like other farmers, anticipated that values would rise even higher.

By 1920 Mr. Crumbaugh was carrying a mortgage of $25,000, the first loan having been secured when he planned the building of the new house. From 1920 on, he had ever increasing difficulties. That year a tornado caused losses involving about a thousand dollars. One or two summers later all but three of the hogs died of cholera. Meanwhile, during the depression of the early twenties land values were steadily declining and prices of farm produce going lower and lower. Within this same period, the bank in which he had a savings account failed and paid out only 15 percent of the total deposits. This bank had loaned as much as $200 an acre on farm lands.

In 1926, Mr. Crumbaugh thinks it was, a mortgage was foreclosed on 100 acres of his farm. At the same time, he sold a part of his personal property in order to settle all of his debts except the mortgage on the remainder of the farm. Thus, for a while, the family was relatively secure, but much too heavy a mortgage was now being carried on the 114 acres. In 1930, burdened with debts and threatened with foreclosure, Mr. Crumbaugh sold his farm; he realized enough to pay off the mortgage and other debts, and he had remaining about $1200. The family then moved to Dubuque; there was "nothing else to do." Looking back on his farm experience, Mr. Crumbaugh is not certain that he had any greater feeling of security on the farm than he has had during the past 7 years, for "farming was always a gamble."

Mr. Crumbaugh does think that he "might have held on a little longer" if he had not bought stocks which were later valueless. He had 50 shares of stock, valued at $3000, in a Dubuque packing company when it failed in 1921. A dividend for the first half of 1920 netted him about $173; he believes this was the last dividend declared. He also lost money invested in stock in a Rockford packing company. Mrs. Crumbaugh calls sinking money in stocks "foolish stuff"; city stock promoters sold shares to farmers who "didn't know enough" about investments to evaluate the worth of stocks. For her husband's "foolishness," the whole family now "has to pay."

From the spring of 1930 until the spring of 1933 the Crumbaughs lived on the amounts secured from the sale of the farm and from the cashing in of insurance policies, plus earnings from odd jobs.

When the Crumbaughs applied for relief in 1933, they had exhausted available resources, and run up grocery and doctor bills. Two of the children were working: Antony had managed to go from one farm job to another, keeping rather steadily employed, and sometimes contributing a little to the family; Marlene, who had gone to country school until she was 16 but had never attended school in Dubuque, was earning $3 a week at housework. The younger children were still in school. Mr. and Mrs. Crumbaugh are both anxious to make it clear that they did not apply for relief until it was absolutely necessary to do so. But, having come to this necessity, they applied for assistance without any special reluctance—"there was nothing else to do."

Though Mrs. Crumbaugh found it difficult to manage on the meager food allowance with the seven children in the home, she "didn't complain" about the relief grants. Mr. Crumbaugh inclines to the belief that there was a good deal of "partiality" and "preference" in the distributing of relief; persons with "the most guts" got most in the way of relief; others who were "a little bashful" did not fare so well. Being among the bashful ones, the Crumbaughs made few requests.

Before the inauguration of the CWA program Mr. Crumbaugh had some work relief, for which he was paid only in grocery orders. Then for several months he worked on the CWA airport project, earning $15 a week. The Crumbaughs consider this work the first "real help" they were given. On completion of the CWA project the family received direct relief until Mr. Crumbaugh was assigned to a WPA project in November or December 1935. Mr. Crumbaugh is rather proud of his record of having missed only 1 day of work in almost 3 years of CWA and WPA employment.

During the past 2 years he has worked on various WPA projects—in a county stone quarry, on park clearing projects, and "out in the sticks" clearing brush. Working 3 days a week, he earns $48 a month. Out of his wages he must pay $2.50 a month for transportation to and from work. Mr. Crumbaugh much prefers WPA work to direct relief; as he says, "I like working for what I get, but I would like to get more." Mrs. Crumbaugh believes that "there's nothing like private work," and that the family could manage much better if Mr. Crumbaugh had one of the factory jobs, some of which, she understands, pay as much as $100 a month. The Crumbaughs would consider even $80 a month a reasonably adequate income.

Mr. Crumbaugh thinks that he could not have managed so well during the past few years if he had not had "good kids." But he is sorry that none of his children have done very well, or been much interested, in school. He feels that young people nowadays need good educations in order to find jobs. However, the four oldest unmarried children have all helped the family to some extent.

Though the Crumbaughs as a family group do not share in many activities (for they have little recreation of any kind), the children apparently get along well with each other and with the parents. Marlene and Antony are sympathetic with their father in his inability to find work. Marlene thinks that he is discouraged, as "any man would be" when he can't earn enough to support his family. She understands, too, her mother's wish to return to a farm, though Marlene herself would prefer to remain in town.

The Crumbaughs go regularly to church, but Mrs. Crumbaugh says despondently that "people won't even be able to go to church" now that the pastor has asked every adult to contribute 10c each Sunday. Mrs. Crumbaugh seems to be more discouraged than her husband. If Marlene had only kept her work at Hall's, the family could probably have managed to get along during the winter months; Mr. Crumbaugh's and Patience's earnings combined are not enough to meet minimum expenses. Now the Crumbaughs are getting farther and farther behind with rent and water bills. The water bill, Mr. Crumbaugh may be able to work out, as he has done several times in the past, but no arrangement can be made about the rent.

Mr. Crumbaugh, though not very articulate at any time, shows more interest in a discussion of his farm experience and in the problems of farmers than in any consideration of industrial situations or his own chances of finding private employment. He approves of the present administration because it has "at least tried to help the farmers." He believes that the AAA accomplished its purpose of increasing farm incomes, but does not approve of having lands "lay idle" or "taken out of production." Though he has heard many people "hollering about over-production," Mr. Crumbaugh thinks that if all employable men had jobs paying reasonably good wages, they would be able to buy everything that could be produced. He speaks of the "new depression" which has already seriously affected Dubuque. As far as he can see, times are no better than they were in 1930, when he first came to town. Certainly he has no greater hope now than then of finding a job in Dubuque.

22

Getting Relief:
A firsthand account

Despite the investment of federal funds in relief operations, those who needed help in the 1930's did not face an easy time obtaining it. Their own sense of personal shame in going to a relief office was more than equaled by the bureaucratic red tape and even hostility that they often met there. Some of this response may well have been a calculated strategy by social workers to spread the limited sums at their disposal to as many families as possible. Instead of informing the poor and giving them all the benefits they were entitled to, social workers were tight-fisted, whenever possible withholding funds. But some of the response also revealed that the social workers themselves had not escaped the American suspicion of the poor—their hostility to the clients reflected a real distrust. The description below, written by a woman who had to apply for relief, demonstrates that it was not an easy task to claim one's rights.

When I went to college I studied sociology. I was taught that hunger, squalor, dirt, and ignorance are the results of environment. Charity, therefore, is no solution. We must change the environment. In order to do this we have settlement houses, playgrounds, and social workers in the slums.

In the past year and a half I have again revised my opinion. I am no longer one of *us.* For all my education, my training in thrift and cleanliness, I am become one of *them.* My condition is shared by a large sector of the population. From my new place in society I regard the problems and misery of the poor with new eyes.

Two years ago I was living in comfort and apparent security. My husband had a good position in a well-known orchestra and I was teaching a large and promising class of piano pupils. When the orchestra was disbanded we started on a rapid down-hill path. My husband was unable to secure another position. My class gradually dwindled away. We were forced to live on our savings.

In the early summer of 1933 I was eight months pregnant and we had just spent our last twelve dollars on one month's rent for an apart-

---

Ann Rivington, "We Live on Relief," *Scribner's Magazine,* **95** (1934), excerpts from pp. 282–285.

ment. We found that such apartments really exist. They lack the most elementary comforts. They usually are infested with mice and bedbugs. Ours was. Quite often the ceilings leak.

What, then, did we do for food when our last money was spent on rent? In vain we tried to borrow more. So strong was the influence of our training that my husband kept looking feverishly for work when there was no work, and blaming himself because he was unable to find it. An application to the Emergency Home Relief Bureau was the last act of our desperation.

We were so completely uninformed about the workings of charitable organizations that we thought all we need do was to make clear to the authorities our grave situation in order to receive immediate attention.

My husband came home with an application blank in his pocket. We filled out the application with great care.

The next morning my husband started early for the bureau. He returned at about two o'clock, very hungry and weak from the heat. But he was encouraged.

"Well, I got to talk to somebody this time," he said. "She asked me over again all the questions on that paper and more besides. Then she said to go home and wait. An investigator should be around tomorrow or day after. On account of your condition she marked the paper urgent." The next day we waited, and all of two days more. The fourth day, which was Saturday, my husband went back to the bureau. It was closed until Monday.

On Sunday morning the Italian grocer reminded me of our bill. "It get too big," he said. We cut down to one meal a day, and toast.

Monday brought no investigator. Tuesday my husband was at the bureau again. This time he came home angry.

"They said the investigator was here Friday and we were out. I got sore and told them somebody was lying."

"But you shouldn't. Now they won't help us."

"Now they will help us. She'll be here tomorrow."

Late Wednesday afternoon the investigator arrived. She questioned us closely for more than half an hour on our previous and present situation, our personal lives, our relatives. This time we certainly expected the check. But we were told to wait.

"I'm a special investigator. The regular one will be around Friday with the check."

My husband was in a torment of anxiety. "But we can't wait till Friday. We have to eat something."

The investigator looked tired. "I must make my report. And there are other cases ahead of yours."

By Monday morning we had nothing for breakfast but oatmeal, without sugar or milk. We decided we must go together to the bureau and find out what was wrong. Therefore, as soon as we had finished breakfast, we borrowed carfare from our kind neighbors and started out.

We reached the relief station a good fifteen minutes before nine, but the sidewalk was crowded with people. My husband explained to me that they were waiting to waylay the investigators on their way to work, to pour complaints and problems in their ears.

At last the doors were opened. The line crept forward. Three guards stood at the entrance, and every person in the crowd had to tell his business before he was admitted. Many were turned away. For the insistent there was the inevitable answer, "I got my orders," and the policeman within ready call.

By half-past nine we had made our way up to the door.

"Room two," the guard said, handing us each a slip of paper.

The place was filled with long brown benches, crowded with our drab companions in hunger. Others were standing along the walls. The air was stifling and rank with the smell of poverty. We sat down at the end of the rear bench. Gradually we were able to slide to the end of our bench, then back along the next bench.

I watched the people around us. There they sat waiting, my fellow indigents. Bodies were gaunt or flabby, faces—some stoical, some sullen—all care-worn like my husband's. What had they done, or left undone, to inherit hunger? What was this relief we were asking for? Certainly it was not *charity.* It was dispensed too grudgingly, too harshly, to be that.

When our turn came to talk to one of the women behind the desks we were told that the checks had been held up for lack of funds and that we should go home and wait for an investigator "some time this week." We were not going to be put off in this manner. My husband told her, "We have to have something more than promises. There's no food in the house, and my wife can't live on air."

"Well, that's all I can tell you," said the woman.

"If that's all you can tell me, who knows more than you? We're not leaving without a better answer. I want the supervisor." At last the supervisor was called.

"The checks will be out tomorrow night. You will get yours Thursday."

Sure enough, early Thursday afternoon the regular investigator arrived. He gave us a check for eight-fifty to cover two weeks' food. We had already spent two dollars at the grocer's and this amount, of course, was counted off the check. But Pete was not satisfied.

"Gotta take off more. I poor too."

I shook my head. "Wait," I said. "We'll pay you, but not this time."

I looked around the little shop hungrily. I was tortured by a great longing for fresh fruit.

"How much are the grapes?" I asked.

"No grapes," said Pete. "No grapes for you."

"But why not, Pete?"

"Grapes are luxury. You get beans, potatoes, onions. Poor people no eat grapes."

I was bewildered. But Pete meant what he said. He showed me a bulletin he had received from the Relief Bureau, listing the things allowed on the food checks of the jobless. I cannot remember all the regulations. But I do remember that only dried fruit was listed. The quantities of eggs, butter, milk, were strictly limited. No meat except salt pork, unsliced bacon, pig's liver and other entrails. Rice, beans, potatoes, bread, onions were the main items to be sold. I saw no mention of fresh vegetables. I was highly indignant.

"Listen, Pete, my stomach isn't leather even if I have no money." I picked up a nice juicy cantaloupe and two bunches of carrots.

"These are onions and potatoes," I said, and marched out the door trailing carrot tops.

My baby was born one week later in a public ward where I was taken as an emergency case. The nine days' hospital experience is no part of this history, which deals with my adventures, as one of the city's unemployed, in obtaining food and shelter. But it is necessary to state in this place that I came home after nine days, ill and weak from inadequate care, bad food, and far too short a rest in bed. I came home with a dawning consciousness of my position, not as a unique sufferer, but as one of the mighty and growing mass who had somehow come to be cast aside as useless in the present scheme of things, cast aside in spite of the various skills and talents they may have possessed.

Gradually the more and more deficient diet began to tell on us. We did not lose much weight—the very poor usually eat plenty of starch—but we began to suffer from general debility, colds, minor infections.

We began to have other serious worries. Now the landlord was becoming a frequent and insistent visitor.

We admitted that we were on relief, and promised to ask for a rent check. He explained that such a thing was impossible. The relief was not giving out rent checks except after eviction. It would cost him fifteen dollars to evict us, and the check would be for only twelve. He would lose three dollars.

"Try to borrow," he said.

The city elections were approaching. We did not suppose that they would affect us in the least. What, then, was our surprise when the investigator brought us a rent check. It might or might not have been intended as a bribe for our vote. We were too cynical, at that time, to see any connection between economics and politics, and we refrained from voting. However, the check helped us for the time being to stave off the fear of eviction.

The problem of insufficient food was becoming daily more serious. My husband decided to complain once more at the bureau. He was told in so many words, "You can't expect to eat well. All we're trying to do is to keep you alive."

A few days later, when the investigator came on his regular visit, we found that by complaining we had done the best thing possible. Our food check was for nine dollars and a half.

We had dinner with our friend.

"How much relief did you say you're getting," our host wanted to know. We told him.

"Is that all? It seems pretty small. We have a neighbor over here who's working as an investigator. I'll ask her to come in and give us the dope."

The neighbor was called. She took a pencil and did some figuring.

"You should be getting ten dollars," she said, "ever since early fall." She showed us how the amount was determined: "$1.65 a week for a man, $1.55 for a woman, $1.00 for a baby, add 15 percent, then add 15 cents for soap; multiply by two. That should be the check."

"But why don't they give us that, then?"

She laughed. "Either your investigator was too lazy to figure, or, well, he may have been trying to make sure of his job. You see, the investigators are terribly overworked, and always afraid of being fired and having to go back to the relief allowance themselves. We're under pressure to give as little help as possible, to refuse relief on the slightest excuse, to miss some families with the checks occasionally. At the same time, if cases complain, the whole blame is thrown on us. So if we lie to people, or 'put the fear of God into them,' it's all in self-defense. The only ones who get what they're entitled to are those who know what is their quota and demand it, especially if they make their demands in an organized way."

We got our rent check, our ten-dollar food check, letters to turn on our light and gas, a weekly order for salt pork, butter, bread, and eggs, by demanding these things and demanding them fearlessly. My husband applied for work under a musicians' project of the Civil Works Service. As yet he has not been notified of any work, though he takes the long hike across town several times a week, to be sure he is not being forgotten.

Meanwhile we are still living on the relief. We keep wondering, questioning. What if our check does not come next week? What when the relief bureau stops paying rents for the summer? Will we be evicted? Will our family be broken up, our little girl taken away from us? After a time these questions reach out beyond our burning personal needs. What is the cause of our suffering? Whither is it leading us, and the increasing millions like us? What is wrong with the system, the civilization that brings with it such wholesale misery? My own voice is one of many that are asking, more and more insistently.

23

Boy and Girl Tramps:
Thomas Minehan tells their story

While the Great Depression had an obviously injurious effect on unemployed husbands and wives, it also took its toll on the young. Thousands of children left home, eager to relieve their parents of the burden of another mouth to feed and demoralized by the bleak future that awaited them. Restless, bewildered, and without a clear sense of alternatives, many of them wandered through the country, subsisting from day to day on the food they could beg or occasionally pilfer. They were a very different sort from the hobos that Josiah Flynt had described earlier. They were not so much the deviant as the unfortunate. Some New Deal programs, especially the Civilian Conservation Corps, tried to support the young in work camps. But many of them took to the road anyway.

Thomas Minehan, in the Flynt tradition, took up with them and in Boy and Girl Tramps of America *told their story.*

"It wasn't so bad at home," says Texas to me in the early weeks of our wandering, "before the big trouble came." The other boys have gone to sleep. Texas and I are sitting on a log near a jungle campfire and talk of other days.

"Before the big trouble came," he goes on and his eyes are somber in the firelight. "We got along pretty good. Dad, of course, never was very well. He was in the war and he got some kind of sickness, I guess, but he couldn't get a pension. He was always sick for about a month every year, and that meant that he had to look for a new job each time he got well. If he had been husky it might have been easy to get a good job, but he was kinda small and then sick you know.

"But we got along swell before the big trouble came even if there were seven of us kids. I shined shoes in a barber shop. Jim carried papers. And Marie took care of Mrs. Rolph's kids. Mother always did some sewing for the neighbors. We had a Chevvie and a radio and a piano. I even started to high school mornings, the year the big trouble came.

"Dad got sick as usual but we never thought anything of it. When he comes to go back to work he can't get a job, and everybody all of a sudden-like seems to be hard up. I cut the price of shines to a nickel but it didn't help much. I even used to go around and collect shoes and shine them at the houses or take them away, shine and return them, but even then some weeks I couldn't make a dime.

"Mrs. Rolph's husband got a cut and she cans Marie. Jim had to quit the paper route because he lost all his cash customers, and the others never paid. Nobody wanted Mother to sew anything. And there we were, seven of us kids and Dad and Mother, and we couldn't make a cent like we could before the big trouble came." "But the big trouble came," he continues, caressing his chin with warm palms, "and there we were. Oh, we tried hard enough, and everybody did their best. Marie made the swellest wax flowers. The kids peddled ironing cloths. Mother tried to sell some homemade bakery, and Dad did everything. We did our best, I guess, but it wasn't good enough, for the big trouble had come and nobody had any money.

"Dad gave up pipe smoking in the fall. All last winter we never had a fire except about once a day when Mother used to cook some mush or something. When the kids were cold they went to bed. I quit high school of course, but the kids kept going because it didn't cost anything and it was warm there.

"In February I went to Fort Worth. Mother used to know a man there, and she thought maybe he could help me get a job. But he was as hard up as anybody else. I didn't want to return home and pick bread off the kids' plate so I tried to work for a farmer for my board. Instead, I got a ride to California. Near Salinas I worked in the lettuce fields, cutting and washing lettuce. I made $32 and I sent $10 home. But that was my first and last pay check. I got chased out of California in June."

The fire flickers and ebbs. We pull a night log into the embers and prepare to join our companions in sleep. I turn my back to the fire and face the eternal stars.

"Since then," concludes Texas and his voice sounds far away and distant as Arcturus blinking unconcernedly down on me, "I just been traveling."

Practically all the families were hit by the economic whirlwind. "Else," as Texas explained, "why on the road?"

Yet even in the days of the boom before the big trouble came, many homes of the boy tramps were extremely tenuous. Death had taken the father, divorce the mother; separation divided the family and many never had had a home at all.

The older youths have been away from home longer than the younger. For all ages and all sexes, the young tramps were on the road about fourteen months, when this study was made. Boys and girls under sixteen had been away from home about eight months; boys and girls over sixteen (but under twenty-one) about eighteen.

Fall draws the young tramps south, particularly the first cold days in October and November. Later, in December, many return north, with tales of hostile police, hungry missions, and a work relief policy in Southern cities, in which there is much work and no relief. Transients in the North hole up in jungles or bed down in the missions. Southland trips taper off until spring.

Whether in the North or in the South, the large metropolises call the boys in winter and the smaller towns and rural villages in summer. The reasons for this seasonal variation are simple enough. In winter the boys must live upon relief or what they can beg on the city streets. They need the shelter of a mission or police station to protect them from storm and cold. In summer every farmer's garden, every henyard, offers a meal of mulligan, and every haystack or grove is a sleeping place.

Yet even in summer the young migrants prefer the rural districts near large cities.

"You never can tell," said Slim Jim to me one day, as we planned a route out of Chicago, "what may happen when you get too far away from a main drag. You may even have to go to work."

"Sure," agreed Bill, "if you are near a main drag and things get tough in the small burgs, you can always return and hit the missions for a meal."

The young tramps seek the cities because cities are their natural habitat. Few farmer boys and girls are on the bum. It is the city youths who have been forced into vagrancy, and they wait around cities for a job. And while waiting in cities they are assured of a minimum amount of relief, and consoled and comforted by the presence of many of their own kind, deriving a pleasant feeling of strength and solidarity from mere numbers, like birds and sheep.

For some reasons unknown, city relief stations as a rule are much more stringent in their attitude toward youthful vagrants than toward older transients. Where an adult is given six meals and two nights' lodging, a boy tramp is given one meal and one night's lodging; a girl tramp is sent to jail. By forcing the youngster out of town, the relief men say they are forcing them to return home. In reality, because the young tramps have no homes, they are forcing them into begging and thieving.

This policy, too, forces them into the smaller cities and semi-rural towns. Here are no tax-supported relief stations, no shower baths, no soup kitchens, but thousands of sympathetic housewives, mothers willing to give handouts and clothes, and farmers who can always spare a few pecks of vegetables. Rural jails are always open for any tramp to find shelter without the formality of registration or the necessity of fumigation.

Some become tired of the same climate and scenery and take a long jump across the continent. The majority remain within five hundred miles of the place they once called home. Within a circle, after several experiments, they lay out a route. From city to city they move, making the rounds of different relief stations and returning to different shops and houses, and panhandling the same towns and streets. Occasionally they fly or are pushed off on a tangent into a new hunting ground and a new series of towns and relief stations. If the new series is equal or superior to the old, the youths will follow it; if not, they will return to the towns and places that once fed them.

On their own, toward Los Angeles, 1937. Photograph by Dorothea Lange, Library of Congress.

In the first years of the depression the child tramps hitch-hiked more than they do today. Then they were not pests on the highways. Motorists were sympathetic, the stem was not so tough, and boys and girls had not acquired the habit of traveling in railroad gangs.

Since they began traveling in small groups, the boys and girls have abandoned the highways and motors for box cars. On the highways the hitch-hikers were separated. Relatively speaking, they were on highways at the mercy of police and tourists. In box cars and jungles, boys and girls are able to associate in large gangs and to protect themselves. Girls in box cars are not entirely at the mercy of any man on the road whatever their relations with the boys may be. In event of loneliness or illness, the boys and girls have friends to comfort and care for them. Fear of being alone, fear of being spied on and seized by the first cop who comes along is absent.

And here is one fertile source of accidents which daily cripple boy and girl tramps for life. The train is in motion. Scores of boys and girls crowd, boost and shove one another. Youths in the car reach down and lift others. Boys on the ground boost friends or try to leap up themselves, and all the time the speed of the train is accelerating. First you walk, but soon you must trot to keep up with it. The ones near the door are trying to get in. The ones away from the door are pushing forward, fearing they may be left. And in the jumble and confusion, the stumbling over cinders and tripping over ties, someone may fall. Fortunately the train is moving so slowly that in most cases the youth has time to recover and slide out of the way. But not always—and another homeless girl is crippled for life, another boy killed.

Communities differ in their systems of caring for all transients. Almost all, however, give one free meal, work for the second meal, a bed on the floor, and eviction before a second or third day.

A boy tramp arriving in any large city walks from the railroad yards to the bread line. The bread line may be a mission, a Salvation Army flop house, or a municipal welfare station, or, literally, a bread line. Some cities have two bread lines; others, only one. The more bread lines, the better for the boy tramp. Rivalry between them forces each to give better service. Meals are varied, privileges and accommodations greater, and sometimes on lucky days it it possible to get food in both. All agencies follow more or less the same procedure. Generally there is some form of confidential exchange, so that the agencies can compare records and information, keep from being imposed upon, and force the young tramps out of the city in two or three days.

As soon as he arrives at the station the boy registers, receiving a slip of identification. Generally the registration is a mere formality to keep a record of the number of transients accommodated. After the registration, the youth is usually entitled to something. Some agencies give him a card for the next meal; others, a bowl of soup immediately; still others, merely an opportunity to work for a meal. Before a second meal is served, however, the young tramp must work two to four hours. The work is not onerous, but for a tired boy laboring on a bowl of beans or soup it is difficult enough. The soup is invariably—I write from experience—thin, watery, lukewarm, tasteless, and served without even stale bread, and never with soda crackers. A portion equals about a small cupful. No second bowl is ever given, no matter how tired and hungry the boy.

Begging is by far the most common occupation of the young tramps. Even in the country where it is easy to raid a farmer's garden or henyard, begging is more common than stealing. It is easy for a young tramp to beg food. Few back doors refuse a hungry boy bread. If then at a butcher shop he can get a hunk of bologna or a few wieners, he has a meal. Storekeepers, too, are solicited and less frequently restaurateurs. Housewives, especially in the smaller towns, are "hit" regularly and successfully. Bakeries always have some stale returns.

But when a boy is hungry and unable to obtain food by begging or working he must steal or starve.

To date, stealing has not developed many complicated techniques among the young tramps. In summer, the farmer's gardens and orchards are raided regularly. Chickens, turkeys, ducks, and even small pigs are picked up when they stray from the farmyard into a grove. They are run down, snared, or caught in any convenient fashion with as little noise and fuss as possible. Seldom, I suspect, do farmers miss the fowl. If they are missed, the farmer most likely blames a skunk or a fox.

The [following] diary is Blink's, the one-eyed Dutch boy from Pennsylvania. He had been on the road a year when I met him. He had two good eyes when he left his father's farm. Now he has but one. A bloody socket forms a small and ever-weeping cave on the left side of his face. Tears streak his cheek, furrowing the dirt and coal soot, leaving a strange moist scar alongside his nose. He lost his eye when a live cinder blew into it on the Santa Fé. All night he suffered while companions probed for the cinder with dirty-handkerchief covered sticks. In the morning a special agent took him to a physician, but the eye was already gone.

From his diary I copied the first month's entries of the days when he had two glims and the world, he believed, was an oyster.

Aug. 24, 1932. Fight with the old man. He can't boss me. Packed clothes and left. Got a ride on truck full of furniture going to Louisville. Two men driving. Good guys, bought me my meals. Slept in truck. Men took turns driving. We stole some melons and apples from a farmer.

Aug. 27. Truck burned out bearing near Covington. Picked ride to Cinci. Man gave me a quarter and bought me a good meal. Paid 10¢ for bed and 15¢ for breakfast. Met Frank. Took me to soup kitchen. Two meals for three hours work washing walls.

Aug. 30. Chicago. Picked ride with salesman. Let me drive car. Bought meals. Four days in Chicago. Good town. Everything free. Met Al. Showed me how to get seven free meals a day.

Sept. 1. Me and Al got caught raiding fruit store. Cop let us go if we'd scram. Separated from Al. Grant Park. Lots of big houses. Plenty to eat. Every house wanted to feed me. Got 14¢ cash and made 80¢ cutting grass and cleaning basement. Old lady gave me a pair of shoes and sweater. Good town but small.

Sept. 2. Momence. Slept in farmer's barn last night. Helped with chores for breakfast. Swell apple jelly. Man wanted me to stay and work all winter. No money. Nothing doing I tells him, but I helps out with chores just the same. Lady makes me a pick lunch. Hit a man in front of hotel for dime. Caught by cop. Two hours to get out of town.

Sept. 6. St. Anne. Lots of Catholics, but all tight. Plenty of handouts but you have to eat outside on porch. No money. Dog bit me. Little fuzzy white dog as I was talking to big fat lady. Went to convent and hit sisters for pair of pants. Told them my mother was sick. Got pants from priest and 10¢. Slept in corn crib.

Sept. 7. Walked Papineau, hitting farmers on way. Plenty to eat. Swell chicken at one house and all I want. Offered job. Help farmer shingle barn. Ask him for 50¢. Offer only 25¢. Nothing to it. Didn't like him anyway. Made 10¢ helping truck driver shift load. Going wrong way or I'd rode with him. Papineau small burg. N. G.

Sept. 8. Woodland. Tough town. Marshall boots me soon as I hits the main drag. Picked ride with farmer to Goodwine. Wanted me to dig potatoes. 35¢ a day. Look place over. Have to sleep with cows and maybe don't get any money, too. Nothing in it. Met Slim. Says no good down the line. We killed four chickens and made stew. I got a loaf of bread from a girl.

Sept. 9. Walked part way from Cessna. Took freight Hooperton. Good town. Picked 40¢ from doorsteps and swell meals. Stayed down in jungles near river with four other guys for four days. Nothing to do and all we want to eat from farmer's field. Chicken every day and roast corn and potatoes. We even had can ice cream, from church picnic.

Sept. 10. Slept in paper box. Bummed swell breakfast three eggs and four pieces meat. Hit guy in big car in front of garage. A cop told me to scram. Rode freight Roessville. Small burg, but got dinner. Walked Bronson. N. G. Couple a houses. Rode to Sidell. N. G. Hit homes for meals and turned down. Had to buy supper 20¢. Raining.

Sept. 11. Villa Grove. Rode with truck. Good town. Raining when I hit first house. Woman gave me three eggs, two big pieces of meat. Cream and corn flakes, cookies, jell and all the coffee I want. Ask lots of questions. Man in house too. He gives me a dime when I go. Made thirty cents hitting stem. A junction. Took train. Friendly. Good for supper and that's all.

Sept. 12. Shelbyville. Cop picked me up. Sent to jail, had to work two hours for dinner and supper. Stayed in jail all night. Six guys of us. N. G. Got out before breakfast. Walked with Shorty to Baxter. Small burg. N. G. Rode with farmer to Clarksburg. N. G. Got handout from farm girl, bacon and bread. Me and Shorty came back to ask for drink of water and she says, "Sic 'em," to big gray

Martial law on the Colorado border, 1936. In the effort to stop the intrusions of migrants, states patrolled their borders with all the vigilance that one expects on an international frontier. The spirit of localism in America, so characteristic of the eighteenth century, was still alive in the twentieth. Photograph by Arthur Rothstein, Library of Congress.

dog. Dog jumped at Shorty, but Shorty socks it. I gets a club. Dog chases us a mile until we get to gravel and a lot of bricks. Boy did we give it to him then.

Sept. 15. Slept out with Shorty and girl for three nights. Two in farmer's barn, one in parked truck. We got all we want to eat from farmers for helping the work. Shorty got a pair of overalls. Went to Mode. N. G. Small.

Sept. 16. St. Elmo. Good. 20¢ and a new pair of socks. Shoemaker fixed shoe for nothing.

Sept. 20. Granite City. Swell guy give me a ride from St. Elmo. Bought lunch. Good town. Made 80¢ helping guy build fence. Spent 5¢ for ice cream cone. 10¢ movie. Swell show. All about gangsters and true to life. Swell girl in picture. Slept under loading platform. Rain. Got wet. Hit woman for breakfast and dry shirt. Got sweater.

Sept. 22. Cop caught me with pockets full of apples. One hour to scram. Took freight. Going East St. Louis.

24

The Fate of the Migrant Worker:
The LaFollette committee gathers testimony

Under the chairmanship of Robert LaFollette, the Senate conducted one of the most enlightening, if disheartening, investigations of conditions of migrant workers and tenant farmers during the 1930's. They interviewed countless union organizers, employer-farmers, and the workers themselves. What emerged was a clear sense of the limits of the New Deal farm program, the misery in which many of the rural poor subsisted, and the hostility they met in such states as California. The report added up to a sorry picture. In many ways, the rural poor were the most neglected group in the nation; and even today migrant workers do not receive substantially greater protection than did their counterparts of thirty years ago. In this sense, the findings of the LaFollette Committee remain all too relevant.

During July, 1937, wide publicity was given the living conditions of migratory agricultural workers in the San Joaquin Valley. Seventy thousand families were said to be living there in temporary abodes. It was stated that deaths had occurred from exposure and lack of food. The press also referred to "the losses occasioned in communities where hundreds of thousands of persons congregate without incomes and are forced to live by foraging." The homes of thousands of persons were said to be "a piece of canvas stretched from a truck."

The impression created in the minds of those not intimately familiar with the problem was that there were vast numbers of starving people in California's central valleys.

An investigation was made in the San Joaquin Valley by a few special SRA interviewers. Likewise, it was thought valuable to obtain expressions of opinion from farmers and health officers.

The results of the investigation and of the opinions obtained are presented in the following report.

Violation of Free Speech and Rights of Labor. Hearings before a Subcommittee of the Committee on Education and Labor, U.S. Senate, 76th Congress, 3rd session (Washington, 1940), Part 62, excerpts from pp. 22643, 22651-22655, 22662-22666.

1. Four hundred seven interviews were taken in 59 agricultural labor camps in the San Joaquin Valley during the last part of July and the first part of August, 1937.

2. Six percent of those interviewed had no funds, and an additional six percent had enough to buy food for 1 to 3 days at an allowance equivalent to the daily pro-rata of the SRA food budget.

3. Median annual earnings for the year ending June 30, 1937 were $574 for migratory families engaged primarily in California agricultural work.

4. Of those families not receiving relief, almost one out of three earned enough in a year to meet the requirements of a subsistence budget including allowances for food, rent, clothing, incidentals and transportation between jobs.

5. Seventy-five percent of the families interviewed came from five states: Arizona, Arkansas, Missouri, Oklahoma and Texas.

6. Seventy-nine percent of the families interviewed plan to remain in California. Sixteen percent plan to return to the state of origin.

7. Six percent of the population in the camps visited was without shelter in the form of tents, trailers or cabins. Thirty percent had poor shelter, and twenty percent had good shelter. The remainder were living in fair surroundings.

8. The majority of farmers expressing opinions agreed that a great many migratory laborers live under extremely undesirable conditions.

Migratory labor camps fall into three principal classes when grouped according to type of management. These classifications are:

1. Those operated by a rancher on his own premises for his own help.

2. Those operated privately for profit, either as a separate undertaking or in conjunction with a store or service station.

3. Squatters' camps that spring up in shady spots usually near a canal or a service station from which water can be carried.

The squatters' camps are often in out of the way places, off the well-traveled roads and therefore are not as evident to the traveler or field interviewer. For this reason the following statements of the number of camps visited, according to ownership, does not necessarily indicate the actual proportional distribution of migratory labor camps in the San Joaquin Valley.

Population. The 59 camps surveyed contained 1,366 household groups, representing approximately 6,147 persons, an average of 4.5 persons per household group. These figures indicate an increase of 14 percent in the population of the camps during the month immediately prior to the date of interview, when it is estimated there were about 5,380 persons living on these sites.

Living quarters.   The camp sites visited contained 1,408 cabins, trailers or tents. In eight camps families were found with no provision of any kind for shelter. There were 87 of these families, with more than 390 persons, or 6 percent of the total population of the 59 camps.

In the counties where there has been a large increase in cotton acreage in the last two years, many new camps were under construction. Frame cabins were in the majority, although adobe was found in Kern County. It was noted that all of the newer camps represented great improvements over average camps already in operation.

In the instances where the camp was operated by a rancher, most of the buildings were of the frame type. In most instances where the camp was privately operated for profit, the operator merely rented space for tents.

Rental charges.   Six of the 24 ranchers charged for their facilities. Three of these offered exceptionally good facilities (for which a charge was made to insure proper care) and in the other three instances the conveniences was considered fair.

Five of the private camp operators made no charge. In all of these cases the camp was simply an open space for camping offered by a storekeeper or service station operator. These camps were almost invariably of the worst type from the standpoint of health and sanitation, and had little or no supervision.

Utilities.   In most camps cooking was done on a coal-oil or wood stove. Five of the better camps furnished natural gas.

Electric light in the cabins was available in 24 of the camps. Seven of these charged for this accommodation at rates which ranged from 25¢ to 40¢ per week.

On the average, there was one toilet unit for every 24 persons. The same facilities were used by both men and women in 9 camps. In the 6 camps where there were no toilet facilities, there were about 270 persons.

Bathing facilities.   In 30 camps, containing 61 percent of the total population of the 59 camps, there were bathing facilities. There was one unit for every 24 persons. Twenty-five of these camps had showers with

A Missouri family escaping the drought, 1937. The victims of dust and drought went on the road, hoping to find work and food. With their life possessions piled on top of rickety vehicles, they moved from section to section, the most hard-hit victims of the Great Depression. Photograph by Dorothea Lange, Library of Congress.

concrete floor. In two camps the same bath-house was used by both men and women.

The most bitter and persistent complaints against State relief and WPA policies came from the Southern California counties.

The number of persons who took time to add comments to the general problem of migratory agricultural labor was surprising. In reading them one gets the impression that those making the replies are definitely concerned about the problem and are anxious for remedial action of some kind. Many of these comments are sufficiently interesting and suggestive to warrant inclusion in this report. In no other way can one better judge the feeling of these people who are in daily contact with the migratory workers.

The following actual quotations are classified roughly. Most persons took the opportunity to voice their opinion of relief policies—Federal and State. Of more interest perhaps are the suggestions for remedial action.

GENERAL COMMENTS

"The state should discourage these families from migrating to California; it only increases the relief problem to communities without adding anything to the state. We do not want them!" (Stanislaus County)

"The burden of providing for the families coming from other states is becoming intolerable. These people cannot qualify to any degree except in the harvest season and then they only can be used for short periods." (Kings County)

"I have a dry yard, and have almost every day since June 20 from five to ten cars a day out of the state looking for work, and every one has from three to five children. When we hire them they stay from three to five days and then move to seek for better wages, never satisfied. Thank God that most of our hired labor are local people or else the fruit would stay in the field. Once in a great while we find a good worker." (Stanislaus County)

"I went to the camps, owners, and foremen of the orchards and talked with them. I must say the outlook is anything but encouraging. I find some hire mostly Jap labor; others nothing but local, and some both. It is hard to tell the number of migrants as they are on the move if they don't get work. Our man told me he had turned away over 500 wanting work and over fifty percent were men who had their families with them. How many are in the camp at Marysville I don't know. At Gridley I am informed there are over 600 where usually there were a dozen. I talked to the campers and tried to find out what they would like to do and the amount of their earnings. I found all ages there, from babies born in the camp and young married couples to old gray-haired men and women. I found children who didn't even know what a home was. They told me that they got as much as $75 or $80 ahead but by the time they bought clothes and food it was all gone. The older ones would like to have a place where they could have a few cows and chickens and raise

Hungry children, 1936. Commissioned by the Farm Security Administration to photograph the rural poor, Dorothea Lange brought great compassion and sensitivity to her task. The meaning of poverty to the migrant worker is only too apparent in portraits such as this. Library of Congress.

beans or cotton, according to what they have been accustomed to doing. These people are not the riffraff of society; they are mostly good honorable citizens and are not here by choice but by force of circumstances, believing it to be their only way to make a living. I am thoroughly convinced the job of caring for them is too large for the state. They are citizens of the United States and I think it to be the duty of the Federal Government to help meet the situation.

"First: The food situation. The county where they will spend the winter will bankrupt itself and send some of the taxpayers from their homes to join them on relief. Second: The school situation. The teachers are already hired and when these children come in it will tax the capacity of our schools and necessitate the hiring of more teachers which will naturally increase our taxes. Third: What effect will these conditions have on our government? A citizenship raised on relief with nothing to hold them in one place, with no responsibilities as citizens. It means a fruitful soil for communism to grow. We need not fear the present generation but the generation reared under such conditions with the 250,000 child tramps of America under nineteen years of age, with one in every nineteen a girl—they are the ones that will bring it to pass. They will say 'We have nothing to lose and all to gain.' Then we can write 'finis' to our present form of government.

"What would I do? I would take the price of a few battleships and a few subsidies and invest it in homes and give all an opportunity to settle down and become settled citizens and develop a patriotism that will save our country. I am inclined to believe that helping them to homes might help keep our $15,000,000,000 crime bill down." (Yuba County)

"The migratory agricultural worker is not as ambitious; he is inclined more along the lines of radicalism, is more likely to cause labor disturbances. He comes to this territory usually because he has not been successful elsewhere. His credit is poor. As a rule, they run a credit account among local merchants and then 'skip out' of the county. They then become excellent subjects for county hospitals and WPA." (Health Officer)

"Migration from other states, due probably to failure of crops in those areas and the ever fond hope of Easterners to come to California, the state of 'golden opportunities.' From personal experience, Mexican and Filipino labor is much more satisfactory and make far better citizens than the riffraff and agricultural aristocrats from the East. The old theory that one calls two is evident. The Bowl Weevil arrives, finds enough to eat, makes enough money to get back to Oklahoma, and brings out the family for the taxpayers of California to support. Of course, parts of Texas and Arkansas are also the chief offenders in our district. The only solution to this problem is sterilization, which is a long ways off in the future." (Health Officer)

"I would say that the State Relief policy has lured many to our state. I have talked to many and they say that they get as much here in one week as they did back home in a month." (Stanislaus County)

"I think the most significant factor affecting the quality and quantity of agricultural labor is the policy of our government paying 50c per hour for WPA workers who stick up their noses at farm wages, then spend their money easily and say the government will feed us when we need it." (Stanislaus County)

"SRA and WPA have been a serious handicap to agriculture, as in the raisin-grape harvest of 1935. Better cooperation now." (Fresno County)

"The only trouble I have had with my ranch labor has been due to relief received by them and labor they have been able to obtain from WPA and other sources provided by the government. Mexicans who are good ranch hands and have worked for me for many years I recently have been unable to obtain their services due to the fact that they were on relief (not entitled to it) or working a few days per month on WPA, etc., for more money than I can afford to pay, yet enough for them to get by on." (Kern County)

"Relief has spoiled ninety percent of agricultural workers. It has made them lazy, bold and communistic. They now feel the world owes them a comfortable living without any effort on their part. Feed the needy but make them do an honest day's work for a day's pay. The taxpayer has to, so why shouldn't the people who are receiving work or aid from his tax money?" (San Joaquin County)

"As long as the wage earner knows that he can receive help from the government when he needs it, he will not try for anything else. I do not believe in giving aid to able bodied people unless they work for it, although that work may seem unnecessary. If the WPA wage scale is as high or higher than prevailing wages, they will never look for anything better." (San Joaquin County)

"SRA and WPA have made lots of surly 'lazy bones' lazier. An employer can no longer drive this poor help so that it is economically possible to use them. The Mexican people seem to be the only people that we can rely on to harvest grapes. All the others would rather not do this work and are quite generally unsatisfactory; especially so, our own people, the whites." (Fresno County)

"State relief is absolutely necessary if we are not all to be sunk by the forces of unrest and discontent. But to those without pride, ambition, or incentive, it offers the easy way to get something for nothing. State relief has NOT made loafers and social misfits. It has merely listed their names, along with the other 50 percent who are really deserving. But relief is a temporary measure and really solves nothing. We farmers believe that there should be a permanent State Planning Program that will lift the non-producing consumer class from the relief and indigent rolls and transform them into community assets, instead of permanent liabilities. God only knows how it is to be done. I don't." (Contra Costa County)

LIVING CONDITIONS

"The migratory workers in this county who are fortunate enough to locate on large holdings generally have fair shelter and sanitary living conditions. However, there are many families who are forced to live under trees near streams with no toilet facilities. My observation has been that most migratory workers are very inefficient in the handling of the money which they earn." (Fresno County)

"Much publicity in the press has been given Kern County. I think the true impression of conditions is not given. Many of these people are living in camps established from their own choice. Some of them wouldn't return to their own homes if fare was furnished. Many of them are not used to living in camps of the standard required by California, and many of them if interviewed by reporters like to give the impression they are now living under worse conditions than those to which they are accustomed. I know because some of them interviewed have much better incomes and living conditions than the reporters quoted them as saying they had; these are individuals I know about." (Kern County)

"I am positive that there have been a great many misstatements and exaggerations made about the 'horrible conditions under which the agricultural workers live in California.' Many of the people making these statements do so with the intention of smearing agriculture. We all admit that the living conditions of the migratory worker are seldom satisfactory; neither are they as bad as many times represented. Camp facilities and housing conditions for this class of laborer are being constantly improved, but the burden imposed on agriculture by the large influx of new people is great." (Stanislaus County)

SUGGESTIONS FOR REMEDIAL ACTION

"I believe a thorough survey of transient migrants in this state should be made by a recognized competent authority in order to determine both the amount of migratory labor needed in the state, and the total number of transients in the state. Then the problem could be divided into the following phases:

1. Caring for migratory labor needed: (a) in agriculture; (b) in industry.

2. Caring for destitute migrants from other states and sending them back, as many as possible.

3. Placing on agriculture and industry a large amount of the responsibility of supplying adequate and proper housing conditions for the labor it requires and employs. Supplement this with a program extending over *3 or 4 years* whereby both farmers and industrial operators *must* make adequate housing provision for labor by erecting each year a certain number of dwellings in proportion to the amount of labor employed.

4. Stopping of further influx of not-needed destitute families.

5. Stop building by state or government public camps for migratory labor. Compel and assist employers to make individual adequate and decent camps on their own farms or properties.

6. Stop criticism of farmers for conditions of the new destitute migrants for the farmers neither asked or encouraged these people to come into the state." (Kern County)

"I think that the best solution to housing of migratory workers is camp permanently situated on farms. Anything that would tend to work that way would help matters. I do not like large Federal or community-owned camps as it leads to more labor unrest and poorer living conditions than well kept farm camps, similar to many we have. Many people might be helped to own homes in small towns in agricultural communities where they may be employed for nine or ten months of the year. Some plan to help farmers to establish camps to house most of their labor on their own places might be worked out." (Kern County)

"Migration from other states perhaps is one of the greatest factors, which in time should not give us any trouble provided the government handles it rightly. They should be made to take care of themselves and be informed where to go for work by officials. Also, officials should see that decent camps are maintained. Perhaps also see that decent livable wages are paid." (Alameda County)

"People have come here from the central states faster than we can absorb them. A high percentage of these folks are the finest kind of people and will re-establish themselves in this state and become self-supporting. Relief should be given only in cases of absolute necessity and people given to understand that they must rely on themselves. Send the Mexicans home and exclude Filipinos." (San Luis Obispo County)

"This is a matter of Federal Government concern. When farmers starve out in one section and must migrate they should be fed until they can in some way rehabilitate themselves. Professional migrants have learned to care for themselves in a way satisfactory to themselves." (Santa Clara County)

"I feel that state and federal relief has affected agricultural labor much more than any other factor, as this type of labor has a changed feeling of more or less of independence, not to be interested only in certain classes of work. If this type of present relief were abolished and in its stead a system of transportation furnished from one locality to another, would be of a greater assistance to our present problems. See to it they receive the proper information on the seasonal harvests, that is, the time, place and wages throughout the year all throughout the state. My experience has been as an individual employing 600 in my seasonal harvest to hire a contact man to round up and arrange transportation, gas, tires, etc. at my expense in order to get my quota of harvest hands in and settled. Most of this hauling is at least 200 miles distance. In the past we never had this condition because labor was strictly on its own and they would rustle and keep informed on all types and classes of work by writing ahead and personal contacts. But this all has stopped because they feel sure of food, shelter and care and that is about all they give a damn for, as their ambitions are for just that and no more—never were and never will be." (Sonoma County)

SUMMARY

A careful reading of the comments asked for in the ninth question leads one to believe that the typical California farmers would probably agree that:

1. California is experiencing an abnormally high immigration of refugees from the Dust Bowl who are not wanted (at least not in the winter).

2. They are forced to leave home because of terrible conditions and are attracted to California by high agricultural wages.

3. They are generally of a low mentality and are not particularly good workers. They are for the most part restive, non-dependable, and do not make good use of the little they have.

4. Their independence makes them less desirable than Mexicans; the latter have been well-nigh ruined by high WPA wages.

5. What is needed is (1) "something" to stop the immigration at the source, (2) cut down on WPA and SRA relief, (3) extend help by better housing, opinion differing as to who should sponsor such a program.

6. While the poor conditions among migratory workers have often been exaggerated in the public press, there exists, nevertheless, a serious problem which calls for a much deeper study and more coordinated attack by all agencies concerned than is now being given or even contemplated.

Part Five
POVERTY IN AN AFFLUENT SOCIETY
1940–

25

Rediscovering the Other Americans: Michael Harrington's contribution

To Michael Harrington must go the credit for sparking the rediscovery of poverty in the 1960's. His best-selling volume, The Other America, *helped arouse the nation to the dimensions of the problem. Born in St. Louis in 1928 to parents who were, as he later described them, "Irish New Dealers," Harrington attended Holy Cross College and then went on to a career in social work. Soon he was an associate editor of a New York social-action newspaper, the* Catholic Worker, *and a member of the Young Socialist League. Determined to publicize the contemporary plight of the poor, he researched the statistical records and also traveled widely to see at first hand conditions in New York's ghettos, in Appalachia, and in California's migrant camps. The result was a very effective and telling tract on poverty in America today.*

There is a familiar America. It is celebrated in speeches and advertised on television and in the magazines. It has the highest mass standard of living the world has ever known.

In the 1950's this America worried about itself, yet even its anxieties were products of abundance. The title of a brilliant book was widely misinterpreted, and the familiar America began to call itself "the affluent society." There was introspection about Madison Avenue and tail fins; there was discussion of the emotional suffering taking place in the suburbs. In all this, there was an implicit assumption that the basic grinding economic problems had been solved in the United States. In this

Reprinted with permission of The Macmillan Company from *The Other America: Poverty in the United States* by Michael Harrington; © Michael Harrington 1962. Excerpts from pp. 9-16, 26.

theory the nation's problems were no longer a matter of basic human needs, of food, shelter, and clothing. Now they were seen as qualitative, a question of learning to live decently amid luxury.

While this discussion was carried on, there existed another America. In it dwelt somewhere between 40,000,000 and 50,000,000 citizens of this land. They were poor. They still are.

To be sure, the other America is not impoverished in the same sense as those poor nations where millions cling to hunger as a defense against starvation. This country has escaped such extremes. That does not change the fact that tens of millions of Americans are, at this very moment, maimed in body and spirit, existing at levels beneath those necessary for human decency. If these people are not starving, they are hungry, and sometimes fat with hunger, for that is what cheap foods do. They are without adequate housing and education and medical care.

The Government has documented what this means to the bodies of the poor, and the figures will be cited throughout this book. But even more basic, this poverty twists and deforms the spirit. The American poor are pessimistic and defeated, and they are victimized by mental suffering to a degree unknown in Suburbia.

This book is a description of the world in which these people live; it is about the other America. Here are the unskilled workers, the migrant farm workers, the aged, the minorities, and all the others who live in the economic underworld of American life.

The millions who are poor in the United States tend to become increasingly invisible. Here is a great mass of people, yet it takes an effort of the intellect and will even to see them.

I discovered this personally in a curious way. After I wrote my first article on poverty in America, I had all the statistics down on paper. I had proved to my satisfaction that there were around 50,000,000 poor in this country. Yet, I realized I did not believe my own figures. The poor existed in the Government reports; they were percentages and numbers in long, close columns, but they were not part of my experience. I could prove that the other America existed, but I had never been there.

My response was not accidental. It was typical of what is happening to an entire society, and it reflects profound social changes in this nation. The other America, the America of poverty, is hidden today in a way that it never was before. Its millions are socially invisible to the rest of us. No wonder that so many misinterpreted Galbraith's title and assumed that "the affluent society" meant that everyone had a decent standard of life. The misinterpretation was true as far as the actual day-to-day lives of two-thirds of the nation were concerned. Thus, one must begin a description of the other America by understanding why we do not see it.

There are perennial reasons that make the other America an invisible land.

Poverty is often off the beaten track. It always has been. The ordinary tourist never left the main highway, and today he rides interstate turnpikes. He does not go into the valleys of Pennsylvania where the towns look like movie sets of Wales in the thirties. He does not see the company houses in rows, the rutted roads (the poor always have bad roads whether they live in the city, in towns, or on farms), and everything is black and dirty. And even if he were to pass through such a place by accident, the tourist would not meet the unemployed men in the bar or the women coming home from a runaway sweatshop.

These are normal and obvious causes of the invisibility of the poor. They operated a generation ago; they will be functioning a generation hence. It is more important to understand that the very development of American society is creating a new kind of blindness about poverty. The poor are increasingly slipping out of the very experience and consciousness of the nation.

If the middle class never did like ugliness and poverty, it was at least aware of them. "Across the tracks" was not a very long way to go. There were forays into the slums at Christmas time; there were charitable organizations that brought contact with the poor. Occasionally, almost everyone passed through the Negro ghetto or the blocks of tenements, if only to get downtown to work or to entertainment.

Now the American city has been transformed. The poor still inhabit the miserable housing in the central area, but they are increasingly isolated from contact with, or sight of, anybody else. Middle-class women coming in from Suburbia on a rare trip may catch the merest glimpse of the other America on the way to an evening at the theater, but their children are segregated in suburban schools. The business or professional man may drive along the fringes of slums in a car or bus, but it is not an important experience to him. The failures, the unskilled, the disabled, the aged, and the minorities are right there, across the tracks, where they have always been. But hardly anyone else is.

In short, the very development of the American city has removed poverty from the living, emotional experience of millions upon millions of middle-class Americans. Living out in the suburbs, it is easy to assume that ours is, indeed, an affluent society.

This new segregation of poverty is compounded by a well-meaning ignorance. A good many concerned and sympathetic Americans are aware that there is much discussion of urban renewal. Suddenly, driving through the city, they notice that a familiar slum has been torn down and that there are towering, modern buildings where once there had been tenements or hovels. There is a warm feeling of satisfaction, of pride in the way things are working out: the poor, it is obvious, are being taken care of.

Clothes make the poor invisible too: America has the best-dressed poverty the world has ever known. For a variety of reasons, the benefits of mass production have been spread much more evenly in this area than in many others. It is much easier in the United States to be decently dressed than it is to be decently housed, fed, or doctored. Even people with terribly depressed incomes can look prosperous.

This is an extremely important factor in defining our emotional and existential ignorance of poverty. In Detroit the existence of social classes became much more difficult to discern the day the companies put lockers in the plants. From that moment on, one did not see men in work clothes on the way to the factory, but citizens in slacks and white shirts. This process has been magnified with the poor throughout the country. There are tens of thousands of Americans in the big cities who are wearing shoes, perhaps even a stylishly cut suit or dress, and yet are hungry. It is not a matter of planning, though it almost seems as if the affluent society had given out costumes to the poor so that they would not offend the rest of society with the sight of rags.

Then, many of the poor are the wrong age to be seen. A good number of them (over 8,000,000) are sixty-five years of age or better; an even larger number are under eighteen. The aged members of the other America are often sick, and they cannot move. Another group of them live out their lives in loneliness and frustration: they sit in rented rooms, or else they stay close to a house in a neighborhood that has completely changed from the old days. Indeed, one of the worst aspects of poverty among the aged is that these people are out of sight and out of mind, and alone.

The young are somewhat more visible, yet they too stay close to their neighborhoods. Sometimes they advertise their poverty through a lurid tabloid story about a gang killing. But generally they do not disturb the quiet streets of the middle class.

And finally, the poor are politically invisible. It is one of the cruelest ironies of social life in advanced countries that the dispossessed at the bottom of society are unable to speak for themselves. The people of the other America do not, by far and large, belong to unions, to fraternal organizations, or to political parties. They are without lobbies of their own; they put forward no legislative program. As a group, they are atomized. They have no face; they have no voice.

Thus, there is not even a cynical political motive for caring about the poor, as in the old days. Because the slums are no longer centers of powerful political organizations, the politicians need not really care about their inhabitants. The slums are no longer visible to the middle class, so much of the idealistic urge to fight for those who need help is gone. Only the social agencies have a really direct involvement with the other America, and they are without any great political power.

To the extent that the poor have a spokesman in American life, that role is played by the labor movement. The unions have their own particular idealism, an ideology of concern. More than that, they realize that the existence of a reservoir of cheap, unorganized labor is a menace to wages and working conditions throughout the entire economy. Thus, many union legislative proposals—to extend the coverage of minimum wage and social security, to organize migrant farm laborers—articulate the needs of the poor.

That the poor are invisible is one of the most important things about them. They are not simply neglected and forgotten as in the old rhetoric of reform; what is much worse, they are not seen.

Out of the thirties came the welfare state. Its creation had been stimulated by mass impoverishment and misery, yet it helped the poor least of all. Laws like unemployment compensation, the Wagner Act, the various farm programs, all these were designed for the middle third in the cities, for the organized workers, and for the upper third in the country, for the big market farmers. If a man works in an extremely low-paying job, he may not even be covered by social security or other welfare programs. If he receives unemployment compensation, the payment is scaled down according to his low earnings.

One of the major laws that was designed to cover everyone, rich and poor, was social security. But even here the other Americans suffered discrimination. Over the years social security payments have not even provided a subsistence level of life. The middle third have been able to supplement the Federal pension through private plans negotiated by unions, through joining medical insurance schemes like Blue Cross, and so on. The poor have not been able to do so. They lead a bitter life, and then have to pay for that fact in old age.

Indeed, the paradox that the welfare state benefits those least who need help most is but a single instance of a persistent irony in the other America. Even when the money finally trickles down, even when a school is built in a poor neighborhood, for instance, the poor are still deprived. Their entire environment, their life, their values, do not prepare them to take advantage of the new opportunity. The parents are anxious for the children to go to work; the pupils are pent up, waiting for the moment when their education has complied with the law.

Today's poor, in short, missed the political and social gains of the thirties. They are, as Galbraith rightly points out, the first minority poor in history, the first poor not to be seen, the first poor whom the politicians could leave alone.

The first step toward the new poverty was taken when millions of people proved immune to progress. When that happened, the failure was not individual and personal, but a social product. But once the historic accident takes place, it begins to become a personal fate.

The new poor of the other America saw the rest of society move ahead. They went on living in depressed areas, and often they tended to become depressed human beings. In some of the West Virginia towns, for instance, an entire community will become shabby and defeated. The young and the adventurous go to the city, leaving behind those who cannot move and those who lack the will to do so. The entire area becomes permeated with failure, and that is one more reason the big corporations shy away.

Indeed, one of the most important things about the new poverty is that it cannot be defined in simple, statistical terms. Throughout this book a crucial term is used: aspiration. If a group has internal vitality, a will—if it has aspiration—it may live in dilapidated housing, it may eat an inadequate diet, and it may suffer poverty, but it is not impoverished. So it was in those ethnic slums of the immigrants that played such a dramatic role in the unfolding of the American dream. The people found themselves in slums, but they were not slum dwellers.

But the new poverty is constructed so as to destroy aspiration; it is a system designed to be impervious to hope. The other America does not contain the adventurous seeking a new life and land. It is populated by the failures, by those driven from the land and bewildered by the city, by old people suddenly confronted with the torments of loneliness and poverty, and by minorities facing a wall of prejudice.

In the past, when poverty was general in the unskilled and semi-skilled work force, the poor were all mixed together. The bright and the dull, those who were going to escape into the great society and those who were to stay behind, all of them lived on the same street. When the middle third rose, this community was destroyed. And the entire invisible land of the other Americans became a ghetto, a modern poor farm for the rejects of society and of the economy.

It is a blow to reform and the political hopes of the poor that the middle class no longer understand that poverty exists. But, perhaps more important, the poor are losing their links with the great world. If statistics and sociology can measure a feeling as delicate as loneliness (and some of the attempts to do so will be cited later on), the other America is becoming increasingly populated by those who do not belong to anybody or anything. They are no longer participants in an ethnic culture from the old country; they are less and less religious; they do not belong to unions or clubs. They are not seen, and because of that they themselves cannot see. Their horizon has become more and more restricted; they see one another, and that means they see little reason to hope.

What shall we tell the American poor, once we have seen them? Shall we say to them that they are better off than the Indian poor, the Italian poor, the Russian poor? That is one answer, but it is heartless. I should put it another way. I want to tell every well-fed and optimistic American that it is intolerable that so many millions should be maimed in body and in spirit when it is not necessary that they should be. My standard of comparison is not how much worse things used to be. It is how much better they could be if only we were stirred.

26

Hunger, USA:
A Senate committee learns about poverty

The rediscovery of poverty in the 1960's alerted Americans to the plight of the rural poor. As unlikely as it might appear, starvation did exist in this country, and physicians reported the facts to a Senate investigation committee. It was not the kind that plagues India—people were not

Hunger and Malnutrition in America. Hearings before the Subcommittee on Employment and Manpower and Poverty of the Committee on Labor and Public Welfare. U.S. Senate, 90th Congress, 1st session, (Washington, 1967), excerpts from pp. 24-30, 109-111, 113-115.

dying on the streets from hunger. It was more hidden and insidious— health and well-being were being slowly undermined by too meager a diet, day after day. Many Americans were prepared to admit to "relative poverty" in this country; some people lived far worse than others and felt deprived by comparison with their more prosperous and fortunate neighbors. But that the nation allowed the existence of "absolute poverty," need in the most ordinary nonpsychological sense, came as a shock to many citizens.

Statement of Robert Coles, M.D., University Health Services, Harvard University

I am a child psychiatrist and I have been working with rural families in the South and in Appalachia for nearly 10 years now.

I followed migrant farm children from Florida up to the New England area and back, and worked in a mobile public health clinic that went into the fields and tried to provide medical services for migrant farmworkers.

I wish to emphasize how national their problems turn out to be. When a sick, chronically malnourished child leaves a plantation or mountain hollow for Chicago or Detroit, rural poverty becomes urban poverty. Internal migration in this country has recently been enormous. Had the same dislocated people come from outside we should no doubt have had all kinds of emergency plans made to help them and also help the area in which they settled.

I am describing in detail what it means to a child when his or her parents are sick more or less all the time, and hungry more or less regularly. That the children can adjust to such a state of affairs goes without saying. They become tired, petulant, suspicious, and finally apathetic.

One will talk with them and play with them and observe their behavior and ask them to draw or paint pictures. From all that one can learn how the aches and sores of the body become for a child of 4 or 5 more than a concrete physical fact of life, brings in the child's mind a reflection of his worth, and judgment upon him and his family of the outside world by which he not only feels but judges himself.

They ask themselves and others what they have done to be kept from the food they want or what they have done to deserve the pain they seem to feel.

When the rest of us miss a meal or two or experience a stomach ache or injury we are moved to do something about it and succeed in evading the irritability and ignorance and anger we quite naturally feel. Consider what it means for a child to grow up without doctors for his complaints and without the dependable and balanced diet we take for granted.

In my experience with families in the Delta, their kind of life can produce a chronic state of mind, a form of withdrawn, sullen behavior. I have seen some of the families I know in the South go North and carry with them that state of mind and I am now working with them in Boston. They have more food, more welfare money, and in the public hospitals of the northern city certain medical services.

But as one tape records their expressed feelings and attitudes month after month, as I am now doing, one sees how persistently sickness and hunger in children live on into adults who doubt any offer, mistrust any goodness or favorable turn of events as temporary and ultimately unreliable.

I fear that we have among us now in this country hundreds of thousands of people who have literally grown up to be and learned to be tired, fearful, anxious, and suspicious and in some basic and tragic sense simply unbelieving.

All one has to do is ask some of these children in Appalachia who have gone north to Chicago and Detroit to draw pictures and see the way they will sometimes put food in the pictures or draw pictures of trees which they then explain are ailing with branches in some way falling. All one has to do is ask them what they want, to confirm the desires for food and for some kind of medical care for the illnesses that plague them.

Now we have been discussing this morning the condition of not only the people of Mississippi but the rural people throughout this country, and we have been discussing the condition of urban people because the people who are now causing so much difficulty for us in the cities of the North, be it reminded, are people who in the last few years came from the rural areas.

I don't know what we are going to call the condition that we have seen, but I will submit that they are certainly disastrous conditions for the people who are experiencing them. They are certainly emergencies so far as these children and parents are concerned, and I would imagine for a country like this we are in that sense facing a constant disaster, a constant state of emergency.

We are dealing with urban problems, with problems of migration, and also dealing with special problems of those who are still isolated not only from the mainstream American life but even from the money economy.

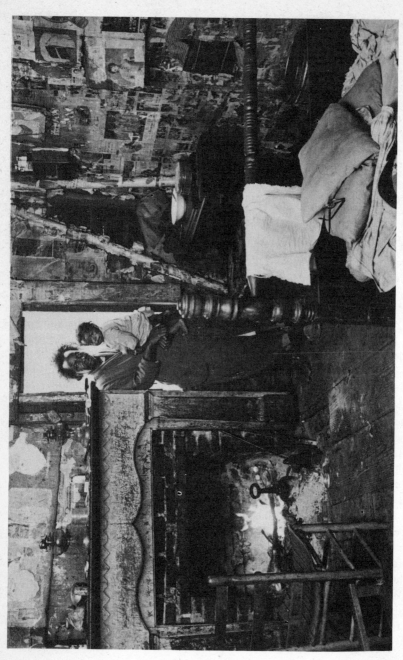

Poverty in Selma, Alabama. This photograph by Bruce Davidson of a black southern household should make it clear that hunger and malnutrition continue to plague America today. Magnum Photos.

Let me now summarize what we have seen: Evidence of vitamin and mineral deficiencies; serious untreated skin infections and ulcerations: eye and ear diseases; unattended bone diseases, secondary to poor food intake; prevalence of bacteria and parasitic disease; the chronic anemias that we have discussed; diseases of the heart and lungs requiring surgery which has gone undiagnosed, untreated; epileptic and neurological disorders receiving no care; kidney ailments that in other children would warrant immediate hospitalization.

Finally, in boys and girls in every county we visited, evidence of severe malnutrition with injuries to the body tissues, muscles, bones, and skin. Diarrheas, sores, untreated leg and arm injuries and deformities have again been brought to your attention.

What do we have to say and what do we have to recommend? Well, medically, physical examination of every child to include all of the various laboratory tests that our children take for granted from the first year of life when they go see a doctor; followup treatment: vitamin supplements to these children who urgently need them; an immunization program. These children are not getting immunization that all American children deserve and need and do get outside of these areas. Birth control information should be provided where wanted, and medicines as they are needed.

Finally, the children need food, the kind of food that will enable their bones to grow, their blood to function as it should, their vital organs to remain healthy, and their minds to stay alert.

Senator Prouty. Dr. Wheeler, you are engaged in private practice in North Carolina?

Dr. Wheeler. That is correct, sir.

Senator Prouty. Do any of the conditions which you have found in Mississippi exist in your State or in other areas of the South?

Dr. Wheeler. As Dr. Coles just pointed out, all of us are convinced that these conditions exist not only in Mississippi, but in almost every State in the South, in areas of the Southwest, and, as pointed out, have been carried into the urban centers of the North as well. I am certain that we could find situations as bad as I described this morning in parts of my own State, in South Carolina, in Georgia, and in perhaps every State in the South.

Senator Prouty. Are efforts being made to correct the situation in your State?

Dr. Wheeler. Poverty in North Carolina, as I have observed it, is quite different in most areas than the poverty I saw in Mississippi, and it is different in several ways. In my own home county of Mecklenburg there are ghettos, slums, and there is poverty. Some of it perhaps is bad as we have described it here, but the difference is that in Mecklenburg County there is compassion and concern for these people and there are agencies working as friends of these people to help them. No child in Mecklenburg County, for instance, ever need go without adequate medical care. We have charity hospitalization funds, we have clinics, we have every diagnostic service that a child could need. We have an excellent welfare department. We have an area fund funded by the poverty program. We have many organizations working not only to give emergency relief, but also to correct the causes.

Senator Prouty. Then there is not the malnutrition, which you and your associates found in other areas of the South, in your State?

Dr. Wheeler. There is, I am certain, but not to the degree, and there is more being done about it.

Senator Prouty. Do you believe that the U.S. Public Health Service could provide a vital service to the counties that you visited? I am now talking about Mississippi.

Dr. Wheeler. I certainly do. I think they can do a great deal more than they are doing in terms of health education, in terms of diagnostic facilities, in terms of immunization, in terms of both birth control information for those who desire it, in terms of establishing clinics where children could go to be examined and treated and referred to proper agencies that could correct their difficulties.

Senator Kennedy of New York. We have talked about the fact there is malnutrition and we have talked about the fact that there are diseases. Will you describe the conditions that you found in this area in Mississippi, will you describe the conditions of starvation?

Dr. Coles. Well, we get into the problem of language.

Senator Kennedy of New York. What do you consider starvation?

Dr. Coles. I think there are degrees and kinds of starvation. There is starvation in an epidemic form of a most malignant kind when, for instance, literally people are dropping like flies on the street. This is the more notorious kind that we know about in certain parts of the world which still goes on. Then there is—

Senator Clark. Doctor, that would ordinarily be called famine, would it not?

Dr. Coles. That would ordinarily be called famine, worldwide. Then there is a kind of starvation in which the body is slowly in a sense consuming itself. It is taking in carbohydrates, enough to keep the person going, and yet it is not adequately supplied with protein. In that sense, it has to consume its own protein. There is a constant buildup and accretion of tissues rather than a stability of tissues. And there is an associated acute vulnerability to all kinds of illnesses which hover over all of us all the time.

So what one finds is a severe kind of malnutrition with weakening of the body, diseases cropping up in various parts of the body, definite shortening of life that can be graphed and measured and that can be turned into statistics. In that sense, the loss of life more gradual, not acute, not dramatic, but yet specific, real, and prevalent. I guess we would call this severe malnutrition, hunger which is the feeling that the child or the adult has, and starvation in the sense that the body is slowly going downhill irredeemably, predictably, and to a clear end that is measurable and that spells out a shortening of life. That is the way I would answer it.

The children I have seen in Mississippi, in Kentucky, and in other parts of the South in Appalachia and among migrant families up and down the Atlantic seaboard, some of the children as you get to know the families and children and talk with them, you ask them what they are thinking. They say, "Nothing." After a while they tell you that they are dreaming of something that they would be eating, or they are dreaming of being able to leave the house and go and be healthy and active. Many of them will stay in bed large parts of the day, get up, move around on the floor, and then crawl back to bed as one kind of heaven that they feel safe in.

These are conditions that all one needs are eyes to see, it is a very marked psychological condition that differentiates these children from all other children who have all kinds of other problems and not this kind.

Statement of Elonzo Felton, Blytheville, Ark.

Senator Clark. You are from what part of Arkansas?

Mr. Felton. Blytheville, Ark. That is in Mississippi County.

Senator Clark. Are you married?

Mr. Felton. Yes.

Senator Clark. How many children do you have?

Mr. Felton. Thirteen.

Senator Clark. Is your wife still alive?

Mr. Felton. Yes, sir.

Senator Clark. And you only had one wife?

Mr. Felton. One wife.

Senator Clark. How old are your children?

Mr. Felton. One boy 21, one 19, one 17; I have a girl 20 and the rest are younger.

Senator Clark. How old is the youngest?

Mr. Felton. Two years old.

Senator Clark. What do you do for a living, Mr. Felton?

Mr. Felton. I works when I can.

Senator Clark. What kind of work?

Mr. Felton. I have been working disc bag. I worked 2 weeks on that and made enough to meet my needs and meet my bills.

Senator Clark. Do your children have enough to eat?

Mr. Felton. Right at present they do but they haven't been getting enough.

Senator Clark. There have been times when they didn't?

Mr. Felton. That is right.

Senator Clark. Do you have a food stamp plan in your county?

Mr. Felton. Yes, sir.

Senator Clark. Do you get the food stamps?

Mr. Felton. Yes, sir.

Senator Clark. How much do you have to pay for food stamps for your family for 13 children?

Mr. Felton. I pay $30 and get $116.

Senator Clark. Is that enough to keep you pretty well fed?

Mr. Felton. Not too well with all my kids and the wife. One hundred and sixteen food stamps with 13 heads to eat off, it don't last too long.

Senator Clark. How about your neighbors and friends?

Mr. Felton. I have lots of neighbors and friends but they can't get on the food stamps not even to buy them.

Senator Clark. They can't get get them because they can't pay for them?

Mr. Felton. That is right.

Senator Clark. Are a lot of people unemployed in your neighborhood?

Mr. Felton. That is right.

Senator Clark. A lot of people out of work?

Mr. Felton. That is right.

Senator Clark. What can you tell us about the hungry people in your county? Do you see a lot of people hungry around you?

Mr. Felton. Yes, sir; I have been going right along with them. Mr. Paul Kleckendall, he is a—people been around his place just like they run around here to get food and he gives them food, and he carried many man through a winter and he carries many of them now.

Senator Clark. Do you have welfare in your county now?

Mr. Felton. Yes, but it don't mean too much.

Senator Clark. Don't they pay some money to people so they can buy food?

Mr. Felton. No; I went to the welfare and asked them for aid and they said I had to go to the doctor to get an examination to find out if I was disabled or could work. I said you have to be dead in this community to get help.

Senator Clark. Is there anything else that you can tell us that you think would help this committee as to how we can see that you get enough food in your community?

Mr. Felton. No, sir; we don't get enough food down there. At the present I am doing pretty good now but others aren't.

Senator Clark. Do you think you are going to keep this job for quite a while?

Mr. Felton. Yes, sir; it is supposed to last 8 months.

Senator Clark. How much do you get paid?

Mr. Felton. $1.40 an hour.

Senator Clark. How much do you make in a month?

Mr. Felton. $1.40 an hour, and that would be for 8 hours, it would be about $11.20 a day.

Senator Clark. You can keep your family in food with that amount of money?

Mr. Felton. I do the best I can buying my stamps. I buy the stamps until the money is gone.

Senator Clark. Did you say right now your children are not hungry?

Mr. Felton. Right now they are not hungry because I have just bought my stamps last Thursday.

Senator Clark. How often are you allowed to buy the stamps?

Mr. Felton. Every month. I have a card—3 months—it lasts 3 months and you buy the stamps for 3 months and then you have to go back and sign up all over again.

Senator Clark. Do you rent your house or own?

Mr. Felton. No, sir; I don't rent no house.

Senator Clark. You own it?

Mr. Felton. No, sir; I live out on a farm. A man gives me a house to live in.

Senator Clark. A plantation owner?

Mr. Felton. I got no landlord. He gives me the house to take care of his equipment.

Statement of Ben Eagle, Sisseton, S. Dak.

Senator Clark. Mr. Eagle, you are from what part of South Dakota?

Mr. Eagle. I am from Day County in northeastern South Dakota. There are 13 of us in the family, nine children, two grandchildren.

Senator Clark. Is your wife still alive?

Mr. Eagle. Yes, my wife still lives.

Senator Clark. Mr. Eagle, are you an American Indian?

Mr. Eagle. Yes, I am.

Senator Clark. That is where the name Eagle comes from, I guess. You probably had a grandfather who was a chief?

Mr. Eagle. Yes, my great-grandfather was a chief. His name was Blue Dog.

Senator Clark. Have you always lived in South Dakota?

Mr. Eagle. All my life.

Senator Clark. Is there a reservation there?

Mr. Eagle. Yes.

Senator Clark. Do you live on it?

Mr. Eagle. Yes.

Senator Clark. What do you do to work?

Mr. Eagle. Back in 1934 through 1945 I worked on different constructions and in the year 1956 I worked with the BIA working as a maintenance man. Due to a heart ailment, high blood pressure, I was disabled from the BIA and I have been living on a retirement check which is $132.85 a month. [Bureau of Indian Affairs]

Senator Clark. Is that enough money to feed this big family?

Mr. Eagle. No.

Senator Clark. Are they hungry part of the time?

Mr. Eagle. Yes.

Senator Clark. Do you have the food stamp plan in your county?

Mr. Eagle. No, we haven't. We have the commodity.

Senator Clark. That commodity food is not very good to eat, is it?

Mr. Eagle. No.

Senator Clark. What do they give you, just dried beans?

Mr. Eagle. Corn grits, corn meal, barley, wheat, wheatflour, candy crock with not too much salt or fat, lard, peanut butter. Raisins are given, dried beans, dried split peas, and dried milk.

Senator Clark. If you had your choice you wouldn't eat that, would you?

Mr. Eagle. No.

Senator Clark. What can you tell us about the conditions of your neighbors and friends on the reservation? Do they have hungry children?

Mr. Eagle. Yes, farmwork is very scarce due to the drought that we are having now.

Since most of the teenagers now are able to work but due to the drought they just can't go out to work.

Senator Clark. The end result is that the children are hungry; is that right?

Mr. Eagle. Yes, sir.

Senator Clark. Do you want to add anything?

Mr. Eagle. Yes, I brought some complaints from other people

Senator Clark. Let's hear about them.

Mr. Eagle. This is on commodity and a small technicality such as there be a day when the commodity is to be distributed, regardless if you have transportation or not or troubles or snowbound and can't get out, if you are not there, you just lose out for the whole month.

Most people rely on the commodity and I have known one wife who had been getting commodities all the time and was told one day as she was going to get her commodity—she was to have her husband send it to her, although she had been previously getting them without his signature—they closed at 4:30 which meant that she had to drive in town 70 miles and back. She was not able to find him so she made the trip for nothing and still lost out for the whole month.

These are some of the things that could be looked into as wants and needs are established.

The community asks can you make exceptions as they are really needed.

Another complaint about an Indian woman who is married to a non-Indian: Somehow they were separated for 3 years. She is not helped through BIA distribution. She must go through the county where the non-Indians are helped.

And about welfare: Most people rely on welfare and somehow if they are living out in the country and if they want to be helped through the welfare, the assistants say you will have to move into town in order to get the help this month so likewise, naturally, the Indian would pack up his things and move into town.

The moving in town—houses are not in good conditions but the rent is very high. Somehow, the only income that Indians are getting has to keep up with the rent they put up. Due to the houses, some of these houses are not worth to live in or even a rat to occupy but still the Indian lives in this place.

When a BIA welfare gives an Indian a home to take care of foster children, Indian people receive less money for the care than if the child was placed in a non-Indian home.

As I say, something is wrong there. Again, welfare is not following up on all of the problems that need to be followed up on.

Until we improve on our welfare office and strengthen our policy—welfare is being abused. There is one person who is head of the welfare who should have been retired a long time ago. She is disabled, can just barely get around, especially to visit homes.

These homes would be something if some welfare workers would visit but only they come as far as the house but they wouldn't go inside to look in the cupboards to see what food they have and the welfare wouldn't go into a closet and look inside to see what clothing they have, the blankets they have.

Senator Clark. Thank you, very much, sir. I think that gives us a pretty good idea of the conditions in your community. We are very happy to have your statement.

27

The Black Ghetto: Claude Brown remembers his youth

After World War II, the black rather than the immigrant became the chief victim of ghetto poverty in America. Although most of the nation's poor were white, blacks suffered disproportionately from inequality of opportunity, deprivation, and the dangers of slum living. The ghetto was a world apart from the comfortable suburban communities of middle-class Americans. Novelist Claude Brown made clear in Manchild in the Promised Land, *an account of his upbringing in Harlem, that the ghetto was a trap that could rarely be escaped. Brown and his friend Arthur Dunmeyer became effective spokesmen for the black poor. In the document below, they described for a congressional committee the facts of modern ghetto life.*

Senator Ribicoff. I am just curious. Both of you, I assume, were born in Harlem.

Mr. Dunmeyer. No, I was born in Charleston, S.C.

Senator Ribicoff. You were born in Charleston, S.C.

The Federal Role in Urban Affairs. Hearings before the Subcommittee on Executive Reorganization of the Committee on Government Operations, U.S. Senate, 89th Congress, 2nd session, (Washington, 1966), Part 5, excerpts from pp. 1090-1092, 1109-1112.

Mr. Dunmeyer. That is right.

Senator Ribicoff. And how old were you when your parents moved to New York?

Mr. Dunmeyer. I was 6 months old when my mother came to New York.

Senator Ribicoff. You were 6 months old.

Mr. Dunmeyer. Yes.

Senator Ribicoff. How about you, Mr. Brown?

Mr. Brown. I was born and raised in Harlem.

Senator Ribicoff. And your parents, were they born in Harlem or did they come from the South?

Mr. Brown. They came from the South about 2 years before I was born in 1935, from South Carolina—not a large city, but the backwoods area of South Carolina.

Senator Ribicoff. And your respective parents then, they were married and had a family in South Carolina.

Mr. Brown. Yes.

Senator Ribicoff. Then they moved to New York. Did they ever tell you why they moved to New York? What did they expect to find in New York?

Mr. Brown. Yes. May I have a copy of "Manchild"? I think with it, I can answer it best. I could give a long dissertation. I have been told at times I am longwinded and this will shorten it.

I want to talk about the first Northern urban generation of Negroes. I want to talk about the experiences of a misplaced generation, of a misplaced people in an extremely complex, confused society. This is a story of their searching, their dreams, their sorrows, their small and futile rebellions, and their endless battle to establish their own place in America's greatest metropolis—and in America itself.

The characters are sons and daughters of former Southern sharecroppers. These were the poorest people of the South, who poured into New York City during the decade following the Great Depression. These migrants were told that unlimited opportunities for prosperity existed in New York and that there was no "color problem" there.

Perhaps now you can understand why the book was called ". . . The Promised Land."

They were told that Negroes lived in houses with bathrooms, electricity, running water, and indoor toilets. To them, this was the "promised land" that Mammy had been singing about in the cotton fields for many years.

Going to New York was good-bye to the cotton fields, good-bye to "Massa Charlie," good-bye to the chain gang, and, most of all, good-bye to those sunup-to-sundown working hours. One no longer had to wait to get to heaven to lay his burden down; burdens could be laid down in New York.

So, they came, from all parts of the South, like all the black chillun o'God following the sound of Gabriel's horn on that long-overdue judgment day. The Georgians came as soon as they were able to pick train fare off the peach trees. They came from South Carolina where the cotton stalks were bare. The North Carolinians came with tobacco tar beneath their fingernails.

They felt as the Pilgrims must have felt when they were coming to America. But these descendants of Ham must have been twice as happy as the Pilgrims, because they had been catching twice the hell. Even while planning the trip, they sang spirituals such as "Jesus Take My Hand" and "I'm On My Way" and chanted, "Hallelujah, I'm on my way to the promised land!"

It seems that Cousin Willie—

he is the one who had gone before and wrote back and told about the "promised land" and exaggerated it extensively.

Anyway—

It seems that Cousin Willie, in his lying haste, had neglected to tell the folks down home about one of the most important aspects of the promised land: it was a slum ghetto. There was a tremendous difference in the way life was lived up North. There were too many people full of hate and bitterness crowded into a dirty, stinky, uncared-for closet-size section of a great city.

Before the soreness of the cotton fields had left Mama's back, her knees were getting sore from scrubbing "Goldberg's" floor.

Goldberg is symbolic for the Jewish low or middle class, lower middle class who always has the colored girl—a term that Negroes resent very much, you know—come in to help his young wife. "The colored girl" is usually about 50 years old. The wife is about 25, this sort of thing. This is what I am talking about when I refer to "Goldberg."

Before the soreness of the cotton fields had left Mama's back, her knees were getting sore from scrubbing "Goldberg's" floor. Nevertheless, she was better off; she had gone from the fire into the frying pan.

The children of these disillusioned colored pioneers inherited the total lot of their parents—the disappointments, the anger. To add to their misery, they had little hope of deliverance. For where does one run to when he's already in the promised land?

That is why they came.

Senator Ribicoff. What is the impact on the Negro from the rural South who comes up to the slums of New York? What happens to them physically, emotionally, mentally, morally? What do you find happens when they have to make their change? Your parents came and you were born here, or you were just a child in arms, and now you are older and you observe this. What happens to them then?

Mr. Brown. Once they get there and become disillusioned, they can see the streets aren't paved with gold, and there exist no great economic opportunities for them, they become pressured. Many of the fathers who brought the families can't take the pressure any more, the economic pressure. How can you support a family of five kids on $65 a week? So he just leaves. He just ups one day and leaves: maybe becoming an alcoholic. Maybe he just goes out one night and he is so depressed because he missed a day's pay. During the week—he was sick. He couldn't help it. And he wasn't in the union, and this depression leads to a sort of touchiness, I will say—to become more mundane, where in a bar a person can step on his foot and he or the person gets his throat cut.

Somebody is dead. The other is in jail. He is going to the electric chair. It won't happen in New York today since they have abolished capital punishment. But this was one of the reactions.

Many of the physical reactions—they took out their frustrations on their kids—they beat the hell out of them. My father used to beat me nearly to death every day. Still they take it out on their wives. They beat their wives. It is just frustration that they feel.

The wives lose respect for their husbands. They can't really support their families. There are many affairs, you know, like when I use the term "Mama," I am using the term generally. Like, Mama is screwing the butcher for an extra piece of meat. Pardon the term. Mama is having sexual relationships with the butcher for an extra piece of pork chop for the kids. She wants to see them well fed—this sort of thing.

Or maybe the number runner on the corner digs Mama or something. She has got a couple of kids. He can give her $25 a week. All her husband can make is, say, $60 at most a week, and it isn't enough, and the $25 helps because she wants her kids to have the things that TV says that they should have.

Senator Kennedy. If you were in charge of the establishment, whether it is the economic or the political or whatever it might be, whether it is State, city, or Federal, if you had control over that, what would you do in the situation—whether it is Harlem, Bedford Stuyvesant, Watts, or whatever it might be?

Mr. Dunmeyer. First of all, I would find enough numbers runners in the neighborhood, all the dopepushers in the neighborhood who are doing this because, like I said, this is a way of life, but who have something more to offer in the way of intelligence. They know how to get around the police. These people I can use to my advantage. They might know how to get around another problem by using the same ideas, and I would use these people. And I wouldn't come out of this neighborhood until these people themselves felt that they were human, again, not until I felt it, because unless I was living there, unless I was a part of this thing, you see I couldn't sit behind a desk and do it. I would have to know it inside and out.

You can walk in Harlem or in the Bedford Stuyvesant section and walk three blocks in either direction and you will find a whole different world, a different class of people. In my block, for instance, I live in a block where the people are together and they don't even know it themselves. They have this gregarious thing going for them and they don't realize it, and yet in the next block the people all have big fine cars and they have their own homes; there is no noise. The police are always walking up and down the streets protecting them. These people don't even know each other. These people don't even know each other and they are the ones that are played up to by the politicians when it is time to vote.

These are the people that are considered people. But the people that really are people are the ones who are suffering together, and they have something already together. Just to suffer pulls them together, and this is what you have to look at. You have to go into a neighborhood or a block and look at it for that block, that neighborhood, those people. Not saying, well, all the black people all over the world, all the black people all over the country, all the ghettos. All the ghettos are different. This is a name you put on it. You call each ghetto by the same name if you want to, but they are not the same.

This is the way you have to look at it, because every problem creates a problem, and this is how you have to tackle it, problem by problem, individual by individual. There are no laws, and I defy anybody from now until doomsday to come up with a social mandate that is going to solve all the——

Senator Kennedy. Do you think that is being done now through the poverty program?

Mr. Brown. I would like to comment on that.

Mr. Dunmeyer. Not in the poverty program. In every—well, let's say the Welfare Department. On the books it is called the Welfare Department. In the eyes of the guy that can't get welfare it is called something else, see, and in the eyes of the guy that is running the welfare it is a slave to him. It is a job where he can't get enough people in his own thing to cooperate with him, enough people to go by his laws and do what he wants him to do.

In other words, to sum it up, it is a bureaucracy which I will never feel affiliated with, I can never see the intricate workings of this thing, because I could never be accepted, only as a recipient. It is the only way they see me. But I couldn't go in there and say, "Listen, you are doing this wrong when you come in my block, and knock on my door and say you are the Welfare Department, with a white face, and this woman has got her boyfriend in there. You don't expect her to open the door and say 'Oh, come on in. This is my boyfriend and he works so and so and he gives me $3 or $4 a week'."

You don't expect this. But everywhere you go that is what you get. You go to the telephone company. You are just a person who has got a telephone to them. You are not an individual. If you put a white tie on, you'll be put into maybe another class.

Mr. Brown. It is not just the white tie, baby. You have to put on a clean suit, clean up your diction and put on your best vocabulary.

Mr. Brown. And you can't take the psychologists and the sociologists who are at least 5 years behind in their theories to analyze these people and find out what kind of people they are, just what they are made of, and what is the best approach to them.

You have got to take the people from the neighborhood, with whom you can communicate.

Senator Kennedy. Do you think we are doing that at all now?

Mr. Brown. Pardon me?

Senator Kennedy. Do you think we are doing that at all now?

Mr. Brown. I don't know, Senator. I will tell you, I am certain you are familiar with the fiasco of Haryou-ACT last year. You see, implied in their approach, they were going to deal with the kids mainly, and ignore the parents, and this is ridiculous, you know. Like you can take the kid in school. A schoolteacher can only have so much influence. If the child went to school 8 hours a day, the greatest influence would still be in the home. He has been in the home 5 years—all of his ideas, all of his attitudes toward life have come from inside the home, and he spends more time there even if it is just sleeping.

You know he has to come home and eat with the parents, and in the approach of Haryou-ACT, that this "generation is gone but we are going to save the next one and work with the kids," you couldn't do it because if you don't get the cooperation of the parents, everything that Haryou-ACT could have accomplished with the children would have been undone immediately as soon as they got home that night.

Senator Ribicoff. In other words, perhaps the bureaucracy never gets down to talk to the people to find out just what is in their hearts.

Mr. Brown. Basically that is it.

Mr. Dunmeyer. They are caught up in their own troubles. They have troubles right within their own functioning. In other words, they do not get past—all they can do now is take the information: What is your name, your address? They can do this very well. This is as far as it goes. It has to go a little further than this. It has to go all the way up and come all the way back down maybe two or three times.

You know, you have to lubricate it with trouble. You have to run it all the way up and down until they can feel "Well, I know how to handle this. I know Miss Jones. I know this bloke."

Senator Ribicoff. As I listen to both of you, it seems that one of the great problems is that the overall white community sees the Negroes in a lump. They look at a Negro and they do not see Claude Brown, they do not see Arthur Dunmeyer. You look the same to all of them, instead of being treated as individuals. Arthur Dunmeyer is a different man than Claude Brown. Claude Brown has certain problems and has certain attributes, and Arthur Dunmeyer has certain problems and certain attributes. The time has come to look at everybody, no matter who they are, whether they are white or whether they are Negro or Puerto Rican or Mexican-Americans, or American Indians—let's look at each individual as an individual and treat him as an individual.

Mr. Dunmeyer. Instead of looking at it as a job, an 8-hour job, a 40-hour-week job, you have to look at it in this respect, you have to say this is a group of people who live like I live and if they are living wrong, I am going to feel the effects of this wrong, because I am going to walk through the streets and I am going to have my head knocked off for a couple of dollars. So they have to look at it and say well, if I can straighten this out with these people, they can live with me. We can live

together, and there is a difference. Those who have and those who have
not, you cannot just say it is this group, because on my block also I have
white people who are doing just as bad as I am doing, if not worse,
because they haven't anybody, there is nobody interested in their problems now, and as long as this goes on, it is not going to solve anything.
It is the same thing over and over again. All you are going to do is make
more trouble.

28

Poverty and the Negro Family: The Moynihan thesis

*One of the most controversial documents attempting to explain and
ameliorate black poverty is the Moynihan report, originally written for
President Johnson by Harvard University sociologist Daniel Moynihan.
Intended as the intellectual underpinning for Johnson's war on poverty,
the study sparked immediate controversy. To some it represented hard-
headed and wise thinking on a serious problem. To others it was one
more restatement of a general American tendency to blame the poor for
their poverty. Moynihan, who later became one of President Nixon's
major advisors, vigorously defended his analysis, insisting that his report
would have helped to increase federal aid to combat poverty. His critics
insisted that this type of thinking could never do much more than
reaffirm American stereotypes of the needy in general and the black in
particular. The debate continues today almost unabated, and reports on
the condition of the Negro family still make front-page news.*

At the heart of the deterioration of the fabric of Negro society is the
deterioration of the Negro family.

   It is the fundamental source of the weakness of the Negro community at the present time.

Daniel Moynihan, *The Negro Family: The Case for National Action,* reprinted
in Lee Rainwater and William Yancey, *The Moynihan Report and the Politics
of Controversy* (Cambridge, 1967), excerpts from pp. 51-52, 54-55, 58, 84-86,
93-94.

There is probably no single fact of Negro American life so little understood by whites. The Negro situation is commonly perceived by whites in terms of the visible manifestations of discrimination and poverty, in part because Negro protest is directed against such obstacles, and in part, no doubt, because these are facts which involve the actions and attitudes of the white community as well. It is more difficult, however, for whites to perceive the effect that three centuries of exploitation have had on the fabric of Negro society itself. Here the consequences of the historic injustices done to Negro Americans are silent and hidden from view. But here is where the true injury has occurred: unless this damage is repaired, all the effort to end discrimination and poverty and injustice will come to little.

It may be hazarded that the reason family structure does not loom larger in public discussion of social issues is that people tend to assume that the nature of family life is about the same throughout American society. The mass media and the development of suburbia have created an image of the American family as a highly standardized phenomenon. It is therefore easy to assume that whatever it is that makes for differences among individuals or groups of individuals, it is not a different family structure.

But there is one truly great discontinuity in family structure in the United States at the present time: that between the white world in general and that of the Negro American.

The white family has achieved a high degree of stability and is maintaining that stability.

By contrast, the family structure of lower class Negroes is highly unstable, and in many urban centers is approaching complete breakdown.

There are two points to be noted in this context.

First, the emergence and increasing visibility of a Negro middle-class may beguile the nation into supposing that the circumstances of the remainder of the Negro community are equally prosperous, whereas just the opposite is true at present, and is likely to continue so.

Second, the lumping of all Negroes together in one statistical measurement very probably conceals the extent of the disorganization among the lower-class group. If conditions are improving for one and deteriorating for the other, the resultant statistical averages might show no change. Further, the statistics on the Negro family and most other subjects treated in this paper refer only to a specific point in time. They are a vertical measure of the situation at a given moment. They do not measure the experience of individuals over time. Thus the average monthly unemployment rate for Negro males for 1964 is recorded as 9 percent. But *during* 1964, some 29 percent of Negro males were unemployed at one time or another. Similarly, for example, if 36 percent of Negro children are living in broken homes *at any specific moment,* it is likely that a far higher proportion of Negro children find themselves in that situation *at one time or another* in their lives.

Nearly a quarter of Negro women living in cities who have ever married are divorced, separated, or are living apart from their husbands.

The rates are highest in the urban Northeast where 26 percent of Negro women ever married are either divorced, separated, or have their husbands absent.

Both white and Negro illegitimacy rates have been increasing, although from dramatically different bases. The white rate was 2 percent in 1940; it was 3.07 percent in 1963. In that period, the Negro rate went from 16.8 percent to 23.6 percent.

The number of illegitimate children per 1,000 live births increased by 11 among whites in the period 1940–63, but by 68 among nonwhites. There are, of course, limits to the dependability of these statistics. There are almost certainly a considerable number of Negro children who, although technically illegitimate, are in fact the offspring of stable unions. On the other hand, it may be assumed that many births that are in fact illegitimate are recorded otherwise. Probably the two opposite effects cancel each other out.

A similar picture of disintegrating Negro marriages emerges from the divorce statistics. Divorces have increased of late for both whites and nonwhites, but at a much greater rate for the latter. In 1940 both groups had a divorce rate of 2.2 percent. By 1964 the white rate had risen to 3.6 percent, but the nonwhite rate had reached 5.1 percent—40 percent greater than the formerly equal white rate.

As a direct result of this high rate of divorce, separation, and desertion, a very large percent of Negro families are headed by females. While the percentage of such families among whites has been dropping since 1940, it has been rising among Negroes.

The percent of nonwhite families headed by a female is more than double the percent for whites. Fatherless nonwhite families increased by a sixth between 1950 and 1960, but held constant for white families.

It has been estimated that only a minority of Negro children reach the age of 18 having lived all their lives with both their parents.

Once again, this measure of family disorganization is found to be diminishing among white families and increasing among Negro families.

The majority of Negro children receive public assistance under the AFDC program at one point or another in their childhood.

At present, 14 percent of Negro children are receiving AFDC assistance, as against 2 percent of white children. Eight percent of white children receive such assistance at some time, as against 56 percent of nonwhites, according to an extrapolation based on HEW data. (Let it be noted, however, that out of a total of 1.8 million nonwhite illegitimate children in the nation in 1961, 1.3 million were *not* receiving aid under the AFDC program, although a substantial number have, or will, receive aid at some time in their lives.)

Again, the situation may be said to be worsening. The AFDC program, deriving from the long established Mothers' Aid programs, was established in 1935 principally to care for widows and orphans, although the legislation covered all children in homes deprived of parental support because one or both of their parents are absent or incapacitated.

In the beginning, the number of AFDC families in which the father was absent because of desertion was less than a third of the total. Today it is two-thirds. HEW estimates "that between two-thirds and three-fourths of the 50 percent increase from 1948 to 1955 in the number of absent-father families receiving ADC may be explained by an increase in broken homes in the population."

The combined impact of poverty, failure, and isolation among Negro youth has had the predictable outcome in a disastrous delinquency and crime rate.

In a typical pattern of discrimination, Negro children in all public and private orphanages are a smaller proportion of all children than their proportion of the population although their needs are clearly greater.

On the other hand Negroes represent a third of all youth in training schools for juvenile delinquents.

It is probable that at present, a majority of the crimes against the person, such as rape, murder, and aggravated assault are committed by Negroes. There is, of course, no absolute evidence; inference can only be made from arrest and prison population statistics. The data that follow unquestionably are baised against Negroes, who are arraigned much more casually than are whites, but it may be doubted that the bias is great enough to affect the general proportions.

Again on the urban frontier the ratio is worse: 3 out of every 5 arrests for these crimes were of Negroes.

The overwhelming number of offenses committed by Negroes are directed toward other Negroes: the cost of crime to the Negro community is a combination of that to the criminal and to the victim.

An examination of the family background of 44,448 delinquency cases in Philadelphia between 1949 and 1954 documents the frequency of broken homes among delinquents. Sixty-two percent of the Negro delinquents and 36 percent of white delinquents were not living with both parents. In 1950, 33 percent of nonwhite children and 7 percent of white children in Philadelphia were living in homes without both parents. Repeaters were even more likely to be from broken homes than first offenders.

The object of this study has been to define a problem, rather than propose solutions to it. We have kept within these confines for three reasons.

First, there are many persons, within and without the Government, who do not feel the problem exists, at least in any serious degree. These persons feel that, with the legal obstacles to assimilation out of the way, matters will take care of themselves in the normal course of events. This is a fundamental issue, and requires a decision within the Government.

Second, it is our view that the problem is so inter-related, one thing with another, that any list of program proposals would necessarily be incomplete, and would distract attention from the main point of inter-relatedness. We have shown a clear relation between male employment, for example, and the number of welfare dependent children. Employment in turn reflects educational achievement, which depends in large part on family stability, which reflects employment. Where we should break into this cycle, and how, are the most difficult domestic questions facing the United States. We must first reach agreement on what the problem is, then we will know what questions must be answered.

The argument of this paper does lead to one central conclusion: Whatever the specific elements of a national effort designed to resolve this problem, those elements must be coordinated in terms of one general strategy.

What then is that problem? We feel the answer is clear enough. Three centuries of injustice have brought about deep-seated structural distortions in the life of the Negro American. At this point, the present tangle of pathology is capable of perpetuating itself without assistance from the white world. The cycle can be broken only if these distortions are set right.

In a word, a national effort towards the problems of Negro Americans must be directed towards the question of family structure. The object should be to strengthen the Negro family so as to enable it to raise and support its members as do other families. After that, how this group of Americans chooses to run its affairs, take advantage of its opportunities, or fail to do so, is none of the nation's business.

Such a national effort could be stated thus:

The policy of the United States is to bring the Negro American to full and equal sharing in the responsibilities and rewards of citizenship. To this end, the programs of the Federal government bearing on this objective shall be designed to have the effect, directly or indirectly, of enhancing the stability and resources of the Negro American family.

29

One Strategy to End Poverty: The recommendations of Richard Cloward and Francis Piven

Dissatisfaction with the operations of the welfare bureaucracy is common to almost all contemporary students of the relief system—those who think it is too generous and those who insist that it does not meet the most elementary needs of the poor. There seems to be little doubt that current arrangements are inefficient, costly, and inadequate. Some critics, distrustful of the poor, argue for more punitive measures—tough residence requirements, compulsory-work provisions, and rigid investigations. Others, more structural in their approach, want to dismantle the bureaucracy and give the poor their due without an elaborate apparatus for checking, verifying, quizzing, and counseling them. One of the most important statements of the latter group was made by two Columbia University professors of social work, Richard Cloward and Francis Piven. Their perspectives on the relief system and their proposals to change it represent a radical and yet not unpopular response to the existing welfare crisis.

How can the poor be organized to press for relief from poverty? How can a broad-based movement be developed and the current disarray of

Richard A. Cloward and Francis Fox Piven, "The Weight of the Poor: A Strategy to End Poverty," *The Nation* (1966), excerpts from pp. 510-517.

activist forces be halted? These questions confront, and confound, activists today. It is our purpose to advance a strategy which affords the basis for a convergence of civil rights organizations, militant anti-poverty groups and the poor. If this strategy were implemented, a political crisis would result that could lead to legislation for a guaranteed annual income and thus an end to poverty.

The strategy is based on the fact that a vast discrepancy exists between the benefits to which people are entitled under public welfare programs and the sums which they actually receive. This gulf is not recognized in a society that is wholly and self-righteously oriented toward getting people *off* the welfare rolls. It is widely known, for example, that nearly 8 million persons (half of them white) now subsist on welfare, but it is not generally known that for every person on the rolls at least one more probably meets existing criteria of eligibility but is not obtaining assistance.

The discrepancy is not an accident stemming from bureaucratic inefficiency; rather, it is an integral feature of the welfare system which, if challenged, would precipitate a profound financial and political crisis. The force for that challenge, and the strategy we propose, is a massive drive to recruit the poor *onto* the welfare rolls.

The distribution of public assistance has been a local and state responsibility, and that accounts in large part for the abysmal character of welfare practices. Despite the growing involvement of federal agencies in supervisory and reimbursement arrangements, state and local community forces are still decisive. The poor are most visible and proximate in the local community; antagonism toward them (and toward the agencies which are implicated with them) has always, therefore, been more intense locally than at the federal level. In recent years, local communities have increasingly felt class and ethnic friction generated by competition for neighborhoods, schools, jobs and political power. Public welfare systems are under the constant stress of conflict and opposition, made only sharper by the rising costs to localities of public aid. And, to accommodate this pressure, welfare practice everywhere has become more restrictive than welfare statute; much of the time it verges on lawlessness. Thus, public welfare systems try to keep their budgets down and their rolls low by failing to inform people of the rights available to them; by intimidating and shaming them to the degree that they are reluctant either to apply or to press claims, and by arbitrarily denying benefits to those who are eligible.

A series of welfare drives in large cities would, we believe, impel action on a new federal program to distribute income, eliminating the present public welfare system and alleviating the abject poverty which it perpetrates. Widespread campaigns to register the eligible poor for welfare aid, and to help existing recipients obtain their full benefits, would produce bureaucratic disruption in welfare agencies and fiscal disruption in local and state governments. These disruptions would generate severe political strains, and deepen existing divisions among elements in the big-city Democratic coalition: the remaining white middle class, the white working-class ethnic groups and the growing minority poor. To avoid a further weakening of that historic coalition, a national Democratic administration would be constrained to advance a federal solution to poverty that would override local welfare failures, local class and racial conflicts and local revenue dilemmas. By the internal disruption of local bureaucratic practices, by the furor over public welfare poverty, and by the collapse of current financing arrangements, powerful forces can be generated for major economic reforms at the national level.

The ultimate objective of this strategy—to wipe out poverty by establishing a guaranteed annual income—will be questioned by some. Because the idea of individual social and economic mobility has deep roots, even activists seem reluctant to call for national programs to eliminate poverty by the outright redistribution of income. Instead, programs are demanded to enable people to become economically competitive. But such programs are of no use to millions of today's poor. For example, one-third of the 35 million poor Americans are in families headed by females; these heads of family cannot be aided appreciably by job retraining, higher minimum wages, accelerated rates of economic growth, or employment in public works projects. Nor can the 5 million aged who are poor, nor those whose poverty results from the ill health of the wage earner. Programs to enhance individual mobility will chiefly benefit the very young. Individual mobility is no answer to the question of how to abolish the massive problem of poverty now.

Several ways have been proposed for redistributing income through the federal government. It is not our purpose here to assess the relative merits of these plans, which are still undergoing debate and clarification. Whatever mechanism is eventually adopted, however, it must include certain features if it is not merely to perpetuate in a new guise the present evils of the public welfare system.

First, adequate levels of income must be assured. (Public welfare levels are astonishingly low; indeed, states typically define a "minimum" standard of living and then grant only a percentage of it, so that families

White migrants to Chicago. Can the welfare system manage to bring dignity and decency to needy families? This is the question that any discussion of reform must face. Photograph by Danny Lyon, Magnum Photos.

are held below what the government itself officially defines as the poverty level.) Furthermore, income should be distributed without requiring that recipients first divest themselves of their assets, as public welfare now does, thereby pauperizing families as a condition of sustenance.

Second, the right to income must be guaranteed, or the oppression of the welfare poor will not be eliminated. Because benefits are conditional under the present public welfare system, submission to arbitrary governmental power is regularly made the price of sustenance. People have been coerced into attending literacy classes or participating in medical or vocational rehabilitation regimes, on pain of having their benefits terminated. Men are forced into labor on virtually any terms lest they forfeit their welfare aid. One can prize literacy, health and work, while still vigorously opposing the right of government to compel compliance with these values.

Conditional benefits thus result in violations of civil liberties throughout the nation, and in a pervasive oppression of the poor. And these violations are not less real because the impulse leading to them is altruistic and the agency is professional. If new systems of income distribution continue to permit the professional bureaucracies to choose when to give and when to withhold financial relief, the poor will once again be surrendered to an arrangement in which their rights are diminished in the name of overcoming their vices. Those who lead an attack on the welfare system must therefore be alert to the pitfalls of inadequate but placating reforms which give the appearance of victory to what is in truth defeat.

How much economic force can be mobilized by this strategy? This question is not easy to answer because few studies have been conducted of people who are *not* receiving public assistance even though they may be eligible. For the purposes of this presentation, a few facts about New York City may be suggestive. Since practices elsewhere are generally acknowledged to be even more restrictive, the estimates of unused benefits which follow probably yield a conservative estimate of the potential force of the strategy set forth in this article.

Basic assistance for food and rent.   The most striking characteristic of public welfare practice is that a great many people who appear to be eligible for assistance are not on the welfare rolls. The average monthly total of New York City residents receiving assistance in 1959 was 325,-771, but according to the 1960 census, 716,000 persons (unrelated or in families) appeared to be subsisting on incomes at or below the prevailing welfare eligibility levels (e.g., $2,070 for a family of four). In that same year, 539,000 people subsisted on incomes reported to be *less than 80 percent* of the welfare minimums, and 200,000 lived alone or in families on the incomes reported to be *less than half* of eligibility levels. Thus it appears that for every person on welfare in 1959, at least one more was eligible.

The results of two surveys of selected areas in Manhattan support the contention that many people subsist on incomes below welfare eligibility levels. One of these, conducted by Greenleigh Associates in 1964 in an urban-renewal area on New York's upper West Side found 9 percent of those not on the rolls were in such acute need that they appeared to qualify for *emergency* assistance. The study showed, further, that a substantial number of families that were not in a "critical" condition would have qualified for supplemental assistance.

There is no reason to suppose that the discrepancy between those eligible for and those receiving assistance has narrowed much in the past few years. The welfare rolls have gone up, to be sure, but so have eligibility levels. Since the economic circumstances of impoverished groups in New York have not improved appreciably in the past few years, each such rise increases the number of people who are potentially eligible for some degree of assistance.

Even if one allows for the possibility that family-income figures are grossly underestimated by the census, the financial implications of the proposed strategy are still very great. In 1965, the monthly average of persons receiving cash assistance in New York was 490,000, at a total cost of $440 million; the rolls have now risen above 500,000, so that costs will exceed $500 million in 1966. An increase in the rolls of a mere 20 percent would cost an already overburdened municipality some $100 million.

In order to generate a crisis, the poor must obtain benefits which they have forfeited. Until now, they have been inhibited from asserting claims by self-protective devices within the welfare system: its capacity to limit information, to intimidate applicants, to demoralize recipients, and arbitrarily to deny lawful claims.

Ignorance of welfare rights can be attacked through a massive educational campaign. Brochures describing benefits in simple, clear language, and urging people to seek their full entitlements, should be distributed door to door in tenements and public housing projects, and deposited in stores, schools, churches and civic centers. Advertisements should be placed in newspapers; spot announcements should be made on radio. Leaders of social, religious, fraternal and political groups in the slums should also be enlisted to recruit the eligible to the rolls. The fact that the campaign is intended to inform people of their legal rights under a government program, that is a civic education drive, will lend it legitimacy.

But information alone will not suffice. Organizers will have to become advocates in order to deal effectively with improper rejections and terminations. The advocate's task is to appraise the circumstances of each case, to argue its merits before welfare, to threaten legal action if satisfaction is not given. In some cases, it will be necessary to contest decisions by requesting a "fair hearing" before the appropriate state supervisory agency; it may occasionally be necessary to sue for redress in the court.

Movements that depend on involving masses of poor people have generally failed in America. Why should the proposed strategy to engage the poor succeed?

First, this plan promises immediate economic benefits. This is a point of some importance because, whereas America's poor have not been moved in any number by radical political ideologies, they have sometimes been moved by their economic interests. Since radical movements in America have rarely been able to provide visible economic incentives, they have usually failed to secure mass participation of any kind. The conservative "business unionism" of organized labor is explained by this fact, for membership enlarged only as unionism paid off in material benefits. Union leaders have understood that their strength derives almost entirely from their capacity to provide economic rewards to members. Although leaders have increasingly acted in political spheres, their influence has been directed chiefly to matters of governmental policy affecting the well-being of organized workers. The same point is made by the experience of rent strikes in Northern cities. Their organizers were often motivated by radical ideologies, but tenants have been attracted by the promise that housing improvements would quickly be made if they withheld their rent.

Second, for this strategy to succeed, one need not ask more of most of the poor than that they claim lawful benefits. Thus the plan has the extraordinary capability of yielding mass influence *without* mass participation, at least as the term "participation" is ordinarily understood. Mass influence in this case stems from the consumption of benefits and does not require that large groups of people be involved in regular organizational roles.

Third, the prospects for mass influence are enhanced because this plan provides a practical basis for coalition between poor whites and poor Negroes. Advocates of low-income movements have not been able to suggest how poor whites and poor Negroes can be united in an expressly lower-class movement. Despite pleas of some Negro leaders for joint action on programs requiring integration, poor whites have steadfastly resisted making common cause with poor Negroes. By contrast, the benefits of the present plan are as great for whites as for Negroes. In the big cities, at least, it does not seem likely that poor whites, whatever their prejudices against either Negroes or public welfare, will refuse to participate when Negroes aggressively claim benefits that are unlawfully denied to them as well. One salutary consequence of public information campaigns to acquaint Negroes with their rights is that many whites will be made aware of theirs. Even if whites prefer to work through their own organizations and leaders, the consequences will be equivalent to joining with Negroes. For if the object is to focus attention on the need for new economic measures by producing a crisis over the dole, anyone who insists upon extracting maximum benefits from public welfare is in effect part of a coalition and is contributing to the cause.

The ultimate aim of this strategy is a new program for direct income distribution. What reason is there to expect that the Federal Government will enact such legislation in response to a crisis in the welfare system?

We ordinarily think of the major legislation as taking form only through established electoral processes. We tend to overlook the force of crisis in precipitating legislative reform, partly because we lack a theoretical framework by which to understand the impact of major disruptions.

By crisis, we mean a *publicly visible* disruption in some institutional sphere. Crisis can occur spontaneously (e.g., riots) or as the intended result of tactics of demonstration and protest which either generate institutional disruption or bring unrecognized disruption to public attention. Public trouble is a political liability; it calls for action by political leaders to stabilize the situation. Because crisis usually creates or exposes conflict, it threatens to produce cleavages in a political consensus which politicians will ordinarily act to avert.

Although crisis impels political action, it does not itself determine the selection of specific solutions. Political leaders will try to respond with proposals which work to their advantage in the electoral process. Unless group cleavages form around issues and demands, the politician has great latitude and tends to proffer only the minimum action required to quell disturbances without risking existing electoral support. Spontaneous disruptions, such as riots, rarely produce leaders who articulate demands; thus no terms are imposed, and political leaders are permitted to respond in ways that merely restore a semblance of stability without offending other groups in a coalition.

A welfare crisis would, of course, produce dramatic local political crisis, disrupting and exposing rifts among urban groups. Conservative Republicans are always ready to declaim the evils of public welfare, and they would probably be the first to raise a hue and cry. But deeper and politically more telling conflicts would take place within the Democratic coalition. Whites—both working-class ethnic groups and many in the middle class—would be aroused against the ghetto poor, while liberal groups, which until recently have been comforted by the notion that the poor are few and, in any event, receiving the beneficent assistance of public welfare, would probably support the movement. Group conflict, spelling political crisis for the local party apparatus, would thus become acute as welfare rolls mounted and the strains on local budgets became more severe. In New York City, where the Mayor is now facing desperate revenue shortages, welfare expenditures are already second only to those for public education.

If this strategy for crisis would intensify group cleavages, a federal income solution would not further exacerbate them. The demands put forward during recent civil rights drives in the Northern cities aroused the opposition of huge majorities. Indeed, such fierce resistance was evoked (e.g., school boycotts, followed by counter-boycotts), that accessions by political leaders would have provoked greater political turmoil than the protests themselves, for profound class and ethnic interests are at stake in the employment, educational and residential institutions of our society. By contrast, legislative measures to provide direct income to the poor would permit national Democratic leaders to cultivate ghetto constituencies without unduly antagonizing other urban groups, as is the case when the battle lines are drawn over schools, housing or jobs. Furthermore, a federal income program would not only redeem local governments from the immediate crisis but would permanently relieve them of the financially and politically onerous burdens of public welfare —a function which generates support from none and hostility from many, not least of all welfare recipients.

We suggest, in short, that if pervasive institutional reforms are not yet possible, requiring as they do expanded Negro political power and the development of new political alliances, crisis tactics can nevertheless be employed to secure particular reforms in the short run by exploiting weaknesses in current political alignments. Because the urban coalition stands weakened by group conflict today, disruption and threats of disaffection will count powerfully, provided that national leaders can respond with solutions which retain the support of ghetto constituencies while avoiding new group antagonisms and bolstering the urban party apparatus. These are the conditions, then, for an effective crisis strategy in the cities to secure an end to poverty.

No strategy, however confident its advocates may be, is foolproof. But if unforeseen contingencies thwart this plan to bring about new federal legislation in the field of poverty, it should also be noted that there would be gains even in defeat. For one thing, the plight of many poor people would be somewhat eased in the course of an assault upon public welfare. Existing recipients would come to know their rights and how to defend them, thus acquiring dignity where none now exists; and millions of dollars in withheld welfare benefits would become available to potential recipients now—not several generations from now. Such an attack should also be welcome to those currently concerned with programs designed to equip the young to rise out of poverty (e.g., Head Start), for surely children learn more readily when the oppressive burden of financial insecurity is lifted from the shoulders of their parents. And those seeking new ways to engage the Negro politically should remember that public resources have always been the fuel for low-income urban political organizations. If organizers can deliver millions of dollars in cash benefits to the ghetto masses, it seems reasonable to expect that the masses will deliver their loyalties to their benefactors. At least, they have always done so in the past.

30

The Debate on Income Maintenance: Arguments before a Senate committee

Despite public suspicion of the poor and a good deal of harsh rhetoric, the United States Congress in 1970 carefully considered legislation to

Income Maintenance Programs. Hearings before the Subcommittee on Fiscal Policy of the Joint Economic Committee of the United States Congress, 90th Congress, 2nd session (Washington, 1968), Vol. 1, excerpts from pp. 2-5, 58-63, 301-305.

guarantee a minimum income to all citizens. Advanced by a Republican President, Richard M. Nixon, this proposal does eliminate much of the bureaucratic tangle surrounding relief. It does not, however, provide a realistic income level for recipients (only about $3000), and contains compulsory-work provisions that border on the punitive. A curious combination of conservatives and liberals have attacked the measure—those on the right believe it goes too far toward a welfare state; those on the left are dissatisfied with the low sums it provides to the poor. The debate below captures the essence of these two positions. Nevertheless, it seems clear that no matter what the immediate fate of this particular bill, the principles behind income maintenance are certain to exert a major influence on all future welfare programs.

Statement of Lisle C. Carter, Jr., Commissioner of the New York State Department of Social Services, and Former Assistant Secretary of Health, Education, and Welfare for Individual Family Services

I want to commend you for holding these well-planned public hearings on welfare and income maintenance. This is a subject which is much discussed today but very little understood. There are an awful lot of myths and misinformation about existing welfare programs, and about the poor, which can only get in the way of serious efforts to examine the contribution which income maintenance programs can make to solve the problem of poverty. There needs to be informed and wide public debate. This is the only way in which significant changes in social policy requiring commitment of substantial resources are likely to be made and sustained.

There are four major federally supported public assistance programs generally grouped together as welfare aiding approximately 7-1/2 million persons. There are another 600,000 persons supported by local general assistance and relief programs. Of the Federal recipients, approximately 3 million are recipients under the three adult programs—aid to the blind, aid to the permanently and totally disabled, and old age assistance.

The rest—almost 5 million persons, of whom somewhat over 1 million are adult—receive aid to families with dependent children, or AFDC.

Trends in adult Federal assistance programs show a decline in recipient rates, with one exception. The declines in adult categories are largely attributable to the development of other sources of support and protection, specifically a broadening of social security benefits. The slight rise in aid to the disabled is generally attributed to the case-finding effects of medicaid. The number of AFDC recipients, however, has risen sharply. The increase in fiscal year 1967 over 1966 was 319,000, and, for fiscal year 1968, it is stated that in this fiscal year, it will rise over 400,000.

Despite these dramatic rises in the number of AFDC recipients, the program does not come close to reaching all those poor families who are categorically eligible—that is, children in families with a parent dead, absent from the home, disabled or, in some States, unemployed. For example, in 1965, 55 percent of those categorically eligible for AFDC did not receive assistance, and the number has risen since then.

What is perhaps even more significant is that these 8 million welfare recipients represent only approximately one-fourth of persons living in poverty, as it is currently defined. While the welfare population is a heavily dependent group—the aged, children and youth, the hand-icapped—the poor population at large has a different character. If we exclude the 5 million aged poor, the bulk of the 27 million nonaged poor live in families with a breadwinner who works at a job all or part of the year.

In 1965, 70 percent of nonaged poor families were headed by men of whom nearly 50 percent held full-time jobs and 86 percent worked at least part time. Thus, the typical poor family is not only headed by a man, but a family in which the man holds down a full-time job. The typical poor family, in other words, resembles the typical American family.

These able-bodied poor and their families have historically been excluded from public assistance programs. Thus, it should be clear that the present system is not broad enough to include a wide range of persons of great need. It should be equally clear that the present system also fails to meet adequately the needs of those who do participate.

Dissatisfaction with welfare, and especially with AFDC, is universal. For the people on welfare, it is demeaning, incentive destroying, and inadequate. The nonwelfare poor seem to have mixed feelings—both resentment and pride—because they do their best to make it and do not get any help from anyone. And many of the nonpoor seem to feel they are supporting the unworthy and undeserving in a shiftless way of life.

Society, on the other hand, is relatively generous in its financial aids to those it deems deserving, and proffers this aid without taint or stigma. Veterans' allowances, social security payments, income tax benefits, unemployment compensation and the like are regarded as rights to which beneficiaries are entitled, earned through the performance of service or through actual purchase, or because of some special status. There is no such legitimacy attaching to public welfare payments in the minds of most Americans.

Studies have shown that welfare recipients also tend to feel that receiving welfare is a privilege which requires them to relinquish some of their individual rights in order to obtain support from society. Welfare programs tend to place recipients in a different class both in their own eyes and the eyes of the larger community. Welfare seems to reinforce the alienation and the low self-esteem that is common among the poor. Even the services offered to recipients of welfare reinforce their isolation in the narrow restrictive manner in which they are offered.

While it is obvious that having the program as we now know it is much better for the millions on welfare than having no program, steps must be taken to eliminate some of the more offensive elements of public assistance programs and to broaden the program realistically to include the many more who need assistance.

There are several basic reforms in the existing programs which I believe to be essential. None of these are original with me.

First, we need a national standard for minimum payments. Payment levels in most States are very low, in most cases below the minimum subsistence levels States themselves define, and below the poverty level. For a woman on AFDC who has three children, for example, 14 States provide $1 per person per day or less to meet all needs. It is obvious that a level of payment must be set and payments made on the basis of a national standard.

As a second necessary reform, I believe that persons should be eligible for welfare on the basis of need and on no other basis. Arbitrary considerations about who should and should not be permitted to participate in the program should be banned. Eligibility would be established by a simple declaration of need for support. Use of declarations would imply that we trust poor people as much as we trust the nonpoor to declare annually accurate statements of income for tax purposes. The system could be monitored as the tax system is—by random sample checks. This would have the additional virtue of simplifying the legion of bureaucracy which constitutes the welfare system.

As another improvement I would like to propose that we separate welfare services from money assistance. Some persons need the services which the welfare program offers while others need only the money. We should get away from treating those who are on welfare as cases. The services provided by welfare should not be forced on those persons who neither desire nor need them.

But before any major income maintenance programs are enacted—or even seriously proposed—the American people will have to know a good deal more about them and the need for them. At the present time there is no more than a handful of people in this country who understand questions you will be discussing or who have given them any thought at all.

Statement of George A. Wiley, Executive Director, National Welfare Rights Organization

The National Welfare Rights Organization is an organization of welfare recipients and other poor people that has been developing over the last couple of years. It now has a membership which encompasses more than 30 States and 60 cities. Out national representatives appreciate the opportunity to bring the views that have been developed through this people's organization to the attention of this committee, and we appreciate the fact that the committee has been willing to hear from welfare recipients and from their organization.

Let me say simply that the basic issue for welfare recipients and the overriding issue for welfare recipients and poor people is for money, for income, and for income at an adequate level. There has been no significant demand or no significant interest in our organization, as the goals have developed from the recipients, for services. The interest in services is very, very secondary. The basic issue for welfare recipients is getting enough money to support their families. The present system simply does not allow enough money to support their families. Furthermore, it has investigative procedures and harassment, violation of constitutional rights, violation of their own laws and regulations which make it very difficult for recipients and other poor people to get the benefits that are afforded even by this system, which is inadequate.

We estimate, in support of the information presented by Professor Cloward, that there are probably at least as many people who are eligible for assistance and receive no assistance at all in the cities and in the North, South, East, West, everywhere we have looked into this problem, we have found the same pattern, that people are arbitrarily illegally denied even this meager benefit that welfare affords. The benefits that are afforded are totally inadequate. We find that people consistently do not get all of the things they are entitled to under the regulations. They cannot find out what they are entitled to. In most places, the practices and the policies that govern are arbitrary, are capricious. There is no fixed set of regulations that are easily accessible. In fact, no State, to my knowledge, has presented a simplified set of regulations that is widely distributed to recipients or potential recipients so that people can know what their rights are.

There can be no justice in a system that does not even tell people what they are entitled to or what avenues there are for redress of grievances. Fundamentally, unless the country comes to grips with the basic issue that they are prepared to give at least a minimum decent income to every citizen who is in need, we are always going to have a system that is plagued with these kinds of problems.

Again, as Professor Cloward has pointed out, there are different attitudes toward subsidies for the rich or for the middle class or for the farmers than there are when it comes to subsidizing the poor in any way. We want to see an income maintenance system that allows people enough money to live on at least a minimum level. We say that that minimum level should be at least at the low-income line. That would afford a family of four a federally guaranteed minimum of $4,400 a year.

Now, that $4,400 a year does not allow anybody luxuries, does not allow anybody any real opportunity for even some of the simple luxuries like a car, like a telephone, like many of the things that are even necessities. But that seems to be a minimum level that ought to be established by the Federal Government. We say it should be a sliding scale with an adjustment per child up and down for additional or fewer members of the family.

This is something that this country has never seemed to grasp; that in talking about minimum wage laws, in talking about social security, there has never been an adequate arrangement for people of varying family sizes to get enough money. So that basically, there should be a level that adjusts to family size and that provides a minimum adequate level of income.

The amount of money that that would cost, to bring everybody up above the so-called poverty line to this low-income level, would be about $20 billion to fill that income gap; $20 billion to bring everybody up to a level where we would not have starvation in this country, where we would not have hungry children in this country, where we would not have the kinds of conditions we have which I think are breeding the violence and the disorder that we have in the ghettos and the barrios of the country, because people are so dissatisfied when they see affluence all around them and when they know that the country has adequate resources to give them at least a minimally decent living.

We say in the National Welfare Rights Organization that we have four basic goals. Those basic goals are income, No. 1, adequate income; No. 2, dignity; No. 3, justice; and No. 4, democracy.

Now, dignity, justice, and democracy are dependent on there being a system, first, that provides an adequate level of support; second, a system that distributes that support in such a way as not to degrade, harass, intimidate, and deny people their basic rights as citizens. We think an income maintenance program should be a simple system, should be a system that is administered uniformly throughout the country and throughout the population, not a system based on a States rights principle that is as antiquated as the States rights notions have been in the civil rights area.

Finally, the most sensitive issue in income maintenance from our experience with it as far as the general public is concerned, is the so-called work incentive. Now, I have found no problem with work incentive among welfare recipients. The welfare recipients in our organization —and we are in contact with some of the hardest working people in this country, many of them work 18 hours a day for no pay to try to raise their children, to keep their households together. It may come as a great source of shock and information to many people that fully 15 percent of the welfare recipients, the AFDC recipients, work at the present time for wages, wages which are quantitatively and completely turned over to the welfare department. They work for nothing, in other words, because that money is immediately taken away by the welfare department.

Now, how can you accuse people in such a system when significant numbers of them work for nothing; how can you accuse such people of not having incentive to work? It seems to me this is the most ridiculous notion that has been foisted upon people, that the issue around welfare is that people do not want to work.

Now, I can think and the organization feels that it would be desirable to build in a modest work incentive program—if you got a job you could keep a portion of that income you got from the job. But it has to be borne in mind, and we should be very clear about this, that if you have a work incentive provision, more people become eligible for the program, simply because the level you are willing to support goes up, and you must support people for a long period of time. You are putting money in for the people who do not need it the most.

Statement of Henry Hazlitt, New York City, Formerly Contributing Editor, Newsweek

I wish to testify now on the proposals for various forms of a guaranteed annual income, including the proposal for a so-called "negative income tax."

The guaranteed income proposal in its most uncompromising form has been put forward by Mr. Robert Theobald. He "would guarantee to every citizens of the United States . . . the right to an income from the Federal Government to enable him to live with dignity." Everybody would be guaranteed this income, regardless of whether or not he worked, could work, or was willing to work. As Mr. Theobald has put it, having this income handed to him, would be an "absolute constitutional right," not to be withdrawn "under any circumstances."

The recipients, in other words, as I understand it, could continue to get this guaranteed income not only if they resolutely refused to seek or take a job, but if they gambled the money away at bingo or at the races, or spent it on prostitutes, pornography, whisky, gin, marihuana, heroin, or whatnot. They would be given "sufficient to live in dignity," and it would be apparently no business of the taxpayers if the recipient chose nonetheless to live without dignity, and to devote his guaranteed leisure to dissipation, drunkness, drug addiction, or even a life of crime.

Proposals for a guaranteed income have differed regarding what the exact amount should be. The general range suggested has been between $3,000 and $5,000 for a family of four. A social security board estimate has fixed the minimum "poverty line" figure at $3,335 a year for such a family. Several guaranteed-income proposals have adopted this figure as the standard.

The first thing to be said about this scheme economically is that if it were put into effect it would not only be enormously expensive to the taxpayers who are forced to support it, but that it would destroy the incentive to work and production on an unparalleled scale. As one commentator has put it: "Those who believe that men will want to work whether they have to or not seem to have lived sheltered lives."

Who, in fact, let us ask ourselves, would be willing to take the smelly jobs, or any low-paid job, once the guaranteed income program is in effect? The guaranteed-income sponsors propose to pay, say, $3,300 to a family without any income, but to families already earning some income they would pay only the supplementary sum necessary to bring the total up to $3,300.

Now, suppose, say, that you are a married man with two children, and your present income from some nasty and irregular work is $2,800 a year. The government would then send you a check for $500. But it would soon occur to you that though you now had $3,300, you could have got this $3,300 anyhow without doing a stroke of work. You would conclude that you would be very foolish to go on working at your nasty job or series of odd jobs for $2,800 when you could get $3,300 without doing any work at all.

So the 30 million population now judged to be below the poverty line would stop producing even most of the goods and services that it is producing now.

The money cost of the guarantee, of course, would be enormously greater than any of its sponsors calculate, because these sponsors all assume that those who are getting less than the guaranteed income of $3,000 or $4,000 would nonetheless continue to work for the smaller incomes that they are already earning.

Not only would the scheme destroy the central incentive to work, not only would it drastically undermine even the incentives of those earning more than the $3,300 guarantee—because of the heavy taxes imposed on them to pay the guarantee—but the scheme is indefensible on grounds of fairness and equity. If "everybody should receive a guaranteed income as a matter of right"—the words I have just quoted are Mr. Theobald's—who is to pay him that income? The advocates of the guaranteed income gloss over this problem. When they deal with it all, they tell us that the money will be paid by the "government."

The guaranteed income and negative income tax are proposed by some of their sponsors as a complete substitute for all existing forms of relief and welfare. But does anyone seriously believe the present beneficiaries of social security benefits, or unemployment benefits, or medicare, or veterans' benefits, or training programs, or educational grants, or farm subsidies, are going to give up what they have already gained? The new handouts would simply be piled on top of everything else.

The welfare bill is already staggering. Federal aid to the poor, under that official label, has risen from $9.5 billion in 1960 to $27.7 billion in the fiscal year 1969. But if we add up all the welfare payments in the 1969 budget—farm subsidies, housing and community development, health, labor, and welfare, education, and veterans' benefits, we get an annual total in excess of $68 billion. Even this is not all. We must add a social welfare burden on the States and localities of more than $41 billion, making a grand total of $110 billion. This load has already brought not only very burdensome taxation, but chronic deficits and inflation that are undermining the value and integrity of the dollar and bringing social insecurity for all of us.

I have talked here only of what should not be done, and have left myself no time to discuss what should be done. But if I may take the liberty of stating, as I see it, the problem that faces your distinguished committee—I should put it this way: How can the Government mitigate the penalties of failure and misfortune without undermining the incentives to effort and success? I do not wish to underrate the importance of the first half of this problem, but it seems to me that the second half deserves much more earnest attention than it has recently received.

31

Power to the Community: New York's Puerto Ricans demand change

The impatience and dissatisfaction of the poor themselves with their powerlessness have never been more acute than today. Almost for the first time, the poor are aggressively demanding their rights, insisting that welfare not be a handout. Impatient with professional social workers, whom they find unresponsive to their needs, and eager to press their views and regulate their own affairs, the poor today are more vocal and active than ever before. These perspectives have affected not only black groups (through such organizations as HARYOU) but also the newest immigrants to the United States, the Puerto Ricans. In 1967, New York's Mayor John Lindsay convened a community conference on the theme "Puerto Ricans confront problems of the complex urban society." The following comments by Manuel Diaz and Raymond F. Narral, two leaders in the Puerto Rican community, represent well the sentiments of the group.

Puerto Ricans Confront Problems of the Complex Urban Society: A Design for Change. Sponsored by Mayor John V. Lindsay, April 15-16, 1967, excerpts from pp. 165-176, 245-255.

Statement of Manuel Diaz

I am happy to see today such an impressive gathering of so many community people and public officials concerned with what is happening in the Puerto Rican community of New York City.

There is good reason for the widespread interest and response. Our community, in the course of the last two decades has gone through a process of growth and development which far exceeds the pace of all previously arriving newcomers to this metropolis.

The 1960 census states that the New York Puerto Rican population numbers 612,574 or 7.9 percent of the total city population. Today's estimates are closer to 750,000 or 9.5 percent of the total city population. No one doubts that by 1970 the figure will be over 800,000 and 10 percent of the total population.

To have seven hundred thousand Puerto Ricans in New York City, however, does not per se make a community. A community has to develop a self-awareness and a self-identification. It has to have a common heritage or interest. It needs the bond of language; but the real test of a complete community is the degree to which it develops a set of functioning social organisms through which it can express its cultural strengths, define its problems, and confront relevant social and economic issues. Institutions are the instruments through which a community speaks and sets its goals. It is through an interplay of these institutions that conflicts emerge, are defined, and get resolved. It is through these institutions that a minority community can address its grievances in a complex urban society as we know it in the United States. In other words, power, whether it be black, white or brown, is not power until or unless it is organized. Sociologists now agree that poverty, in the final analysis, is a matter of differences in power—or to put it differently— is a matter of deciding and controlling how the resources of a society get distributed. No effective change in the distribution of such resources can take place outside of an arena where a community's power can be manifest.

Politically speaking, the Puerto Rican is impotent and powerless outside New York City. In New York City, however, he is a highly political actor and becoming more so by the day.

Our power, however, by and large still lies dormant. Only the top of the iceberg can be seen. It will reach its full potential only when maximum voter registration is achieved, and the franchise is exercized. This was the real meaning for the Puerto Rican of the voter registration act of 1965. It created the opportunity for full citizenship and maturity.

East 100th Street, New York City. America's newest immigrants, the Puerto Ricans, face the problems of making a living on their own. Photograph by Bruce Davidson, Magnum Photos.

If we fail to utilize that opportunity, we will remain an indigent and powerless community.

The organizations which existed in the late 1940's and early 1950's were concerned more with life on the Island than life in New York City. There was little or no confrontation with the hard issues of life in New York City as there is today. In the sense that the early migrants tended to see New York as only a temporary experience, with the idea always on the surface of returning to the beloved Island, such desires not to confront New York City were only natural expressions of felt reality.

The last decade in the development of the Puerto Rican community in NY may be characterized as "the differential period." It has been mainly during the years from the mid-1950's that strong, articulate, independent and somewhat unconnected issue-oriented organizations have emerged.

The last decade has marked, for example, the strong emergence of the Puerto Rican Forum, concerned with broad social questions but concentrating on youth and educational issues; El Desfile (The Puerto Rican Parade), largely an expressivist federation but which very effectively demonstrates the political power of the community; the Congress of Home Town Clubs, bringing together these separate groups into a potentially powerful federation in order to respond to social and community issues; a variety of councils in the Bronx, Brooklyn, East Harlem and Lower Manhattan which have created social services, housing clinics, consumer programs, etc.; two civil rights-oriented associations, N.A.P.R.A. and NAPRCA; a merchants association of over 2000 small businessmen which attracted 200,000 visitors to its exposition at the Colosseum last November and, recently, anti-poverty corporations and agencies such as the Puerto Rican Family Institute, Aspira, the Puerto Rican Community Development Project, and the East Harlem Tenant Association.

The conference today, with the kind of broad representation it has brought together from all sectors of the community, with the kind of sharing of concerns taking place during the planning period and in today's activities, and with the kind of mutual trust it can generate, may very well prove to be a giant step towards reaching that goal as a community which would allow us to direct our energies to the issues of the day.

I do not speak here of sterile harmonious working together. Such thinking is utopian. Conflicts must exist, they are necessary. This is how we grow, they are birth pains. Differences spell commitment and struggle. We need, however, to learn how to bring to bear the total weight of our community on a given issue *even when we disagree as to tactics*. We need to learn how to develop alliances with other groups, ethnic or otherwise, which will enhance our political power, and, consequently, our ability to resolve our problems. Just as the Negro has learned, we need to learn how to resolve our conflicts behind closed doors and then close ranks as a community. We need to learn that progress comes through many roads; quiet negotiation as well as social protest, petitioning as well as picketing, education as well as legal redress. Yes, even an occasional retreat can mean an advance over a long pull. We need to differentiate between the self-serving public official and the well-meaning one who is hamstrung by bureaucracy. We even need to learn that public officials, just because they are Puerto Ricans, do not necessarily serve the community well unless held to their responsibilities.

A democratic society is built upon the notion that each individual has a right to dignity and self-respect. When individuals and groups participate in decisions which affect them, then change can be brought about more effectively. This means that Puerto Ricans and their institutions must be directed at issues and actions which will help decide the nature, design and implementation not just of welfare services, but of the nature and design of New York City as a commercial and industrial complex, not just what happens in health and hospital services, but what happens in transportation as well; not just in education, but in parks, in recreation, in sanitation, in air pollution, in museums and in cultural complexes. It means, in short, that we have a role to play in the *total* life of the city—*not just on the ethnic issues.*

The War Against Poverty. Despite the rapid progress of the Puerto Rican institutionally, poverty in all its ugliness still stalks the Puerto Rican day and night. Although proportionally not as conspicuous nationally as the Negro, the Puerto Rican nonetheless faces poverty as noxious and stripping of dignity, as debilitating to the families afflicted, as any ethnic group in America. Yet, for the Puerto Rican the anti-poverty program is failing to fulfill its promise. Too many of the programs are still directed toward traditional social welfare paternalism rather than a genuine war on poverty. Many programs have become a bread and butter circus for their staffs. CPC elections are decided by sophisticated overly manipulated regulations and procedures which have in effect eliminated real representation by autonomous and long-standing organizations and leaders in the Puerto Rican community. The elections generally result in victories by the middle-class non-poor over the poor, especially the Puerto Rican poor.

The heart of the anti-poverty program, as originally conceived, lies in its community action aspects. Programs must reach people directly and not through professional social brokers. Community action programs are in retreat, and safe programs like Headstart, the Job Corps, and cultural and recreational activities are being pushed. Communities must be offered *real* opportunities to help themselves with the strength of their own convictions and perceptions, else you add fuel to welfare dependency. When people become involved in their own community's problems, they usually begin to think and act as responsible citizens.

There is no educational substitute for this kind of involvement and experience.

There have been some successes in the Puerto Rican community with the anti-poverty program, but there is also too much bickering within the community agencies. Too much energy is devoted to internal struggles for power. There is too much preoccupation with Robert's rules of order and the minutiae of minute taking, too much concern over process and too little over substance. Strong effective staff leadership is lacking in many programs serving the community, but even where you get strong staff leadership, their boards of directors fail to support that leadership with the considerable and growing political influence and power they possess.

Community development is a method by which the creative energies of a community may be marshaled and directed *in a decisive way* to the resolution of its basic problems. In our case, the issue defines itself in terms of how the community can marshal its own resources in a collective way, how to achieve the third stage in our development, the stage when the full weight of the community can be brought to bear on the total problem of the city, not just our own.

We Puerto Ricans do not lay claim to the solution of the pervasive problems of the city, its tax base, its shrinking industry. We may not even know where to begin at the moment, but the intelligence, the strength, the desire and commitment of this community to grapple with these issues exists, and it feels it has a stake in how this is done.

Statement of Raymond F. Narral

Social Welfare Agencies and Legal Ramifications.   If our democratic society is to survive, social welfare agencies must play a role different than that being played by them today. These agencies were initially founded to serve noble causes. They are necessary in order to maintain a balance of power between the class structures that exist under our present-day democracy, and to attempt to provide those "things" which poor people lack as measured by the "haves" of our affluent society. It is the uneducated and deprived, the poor, the Puerto Ricans, who seek and need the assistance of these agencies.

I have found that social welfare agencies in our city have failed to accomplish the goals they were originally established to reach. It has become obvious that a change is desperately needed.

Some agencies have relegated themselves to providing no services, instead they have become recreational arenas. They have allowed other agencies to usurp their original purposes and are satisfied in providing basketball courts and handball walls. They have stagnated, tired and are on the verge of total collapse.

There are those agencies that work in a vacuum. They often reflect ideas and programs in total conflict with the community in which they are based. Conflicts arise on occasion when rapid shifts in ethnic population take place in the area surrounding the agency.

On a wider scope, there are those agencies that require a complete overhaul, if they are to continue to function. It is this type of agency, usually governmentally based, which today is providing the major source of social services to the Puerto Rican.

In attempting to deal with the problems of the poor Puerto Rican in New York City, I have found that social welfare agencies are enveloped in a sea of complex systems of law, regulations, statutes, and manuals of procedures that tend to block entirely the possibility of their being able to provide the services needed. Added to this complexity are case precedents, legal departments, court interpretations, decisions, and administrative rulings. In this penumbra, the Puerto Rican is asked to function in an attempt to meet his needs. This complexity, this overburdening potpourri of institutionalization is heaped upon those least able to carry this burden. The inability to cope with the system leads to denial of benefits, denial of services and finally total apathy on the part of the client. This complexity is increasing by leaps and bounds instead of decreasing as the Puerto Rican's needs increase.

The U.S. Department of Health, Education and Welfare, Social Security Administration, is an agency established to provide certain benefits to citizens meeting certain prerequisites. These benefits are not to be obtained by forceful advocacy but by simply making application and stating all the necessary prerequisites. However, as it applies to Puerto Ricans and other ghetto residents, forceful advocacy is the rule, not the exception.

A recent *New York Times* article stated that the United States Department of Labor has found that "one out of every three residents in the slum has a serious employment problem."

The poor Puerto Rican suffers from seasonal work, menial jobs, prejudice, bigotry, and needless to say is the first to be discharged at the whim of employers. As a necessity the Puerto Rican seeks unemployment insurance.

The Unemployment Insurance Law of New York is complex and its interpretation is based on reported case precedents. The unsophisticated

Puerto Rican who seeks benefits cannot possibly prepare or cope with the statutes and regulations which he does not understand, written in a language foreign to his own and administered by people who have lost the true meaning for its existence. Because of its complexity and the other reasons mentioned, an unemployed member of our community, with a wife and eleven children, is thrust upon the relief rolls when he fails to request a hearing before an impartial referee within the thirty-day limitation required by statute, after a discharge from his employment, indisputably through no fault of his own. This Puerto Rican dilemma leads to suspensions of greatly needed benefits because of willful misrepresentations, voluntary "quits" and poor or unrealistic job efforts. An explanatory pamphlet, how to seek benefits, written in Spanish, and sparsely distributed, is not sufficient to meet the mandate of the law.

A Puerto Rican mother was recently suspended from benefits because "her job efforts are unrealistic; her job searches must be restricted to factory work in which she has some experience and not to that of a salesgirl," even if her diligence was not subject to dispute. Suspensions are made for willful misrepresentations because the claimant, unable to make himself understood, allows a fellow claimant to insert in his booklets "N"s instead of "Y"s, or after summary of interviews taken by agency employees who speak no Spanish from claimants who speak no English and subsequently, use these interviews to prejudice the position of the claimant.

Again, obtaining benefits for Puerto Ricans has become a matter of luck, to be left to chance.

The Department of Welfare of the City of New York, is an agency which today services the greatest numbers of Puerto Ricans in the City of New York. It is the agency which is charged by law to assist the needy of this city. Hopefully, Commissioner Mitchell Ginsberg recognizes its failings and is attempting to make corrections. He is aware that in order to correct the failings, a total effort must be made. As he has stated in the past, steps must be taken if "public welfare is to leave the 1930's and come of age."

Welfare recipients are today suffering untold hardships and the Puerto Ricans take part in this suffering. It has been my experience to find a Puerto Rican woman and children sleeping in hallways for lack of shelter, hungry for lack of food, and out of school for lack of clothing. I recognize the Department is making valiant efforts to rectify the situation but more must be done and it must be done yesterday.

Puerto Ricans should not be told to return to Puerto Rico because "it is socially more valid to go back to Puerto Rico" or "your intent in coming to New York City was to get on welfare" and sent away without money for food or shelter. The law requires that a family in need of assistance be given emergency money immediately pending a final determination on any given case. Case precedent has made this clear and unequivocal. However, the non-residence welfare center continues to function and Puerto Ricans who have been denied emergency assistance keep coming to my office for help.

The State Social Welfare Law requires that a welfare family maintain a minimum subsistence level regarding household furniture and clothing. Recently, clients have been requesting that they be brought up to "minimum standards" by writing to the local welfare centers. Many clients have received funds to purchase these needed items but why is it that my office is able to document the fact that clients receive a greater amount of money when a lawyer writes a letter than when the client writes? Why is it that an investigator who, after having made an investigation regarding the items requested, and having sent the client a check to purchase all the items required, when challenged by the client with counsel, a second check is delivered? Why not the entire amount initially? Although the client is entitled to "minimum standards" of assistance, he must wait as long as 30 days after making the request, for a check to be issued. Some have waited for 3 or 4 months, others have never received an answer to their letters.

Puerto Ricans are plagued by unlawful searches of their homes, inhuman investigators, on-the-spot psychiatric examinations, commitments and a host of other illegalities. They have suffered this treatment because of the lack of assistance and will continue to do so until the scales are balanced between recipient and investigator. It was not until the *19th* day of January 1967 that Commissioner Ginsberg issued an informational to all his centers allowing clients to be accompanied by another person, in their dealings with welfare investigators. Finally, welfare recipients can be assisted with their own interpreters, social workers, and even lawyers. I am happy to say that this type of change was brought about by forceful advocacy of poverty lawyers. All of the welfare rules and regulations should be published in Spanish and English, distributed to the community at large, including the appeal procedure of the State Social Welfare Department.

Investigators should be instructed on all phases of the law and made aware of recent interpretations of same. Finally, welfare recipients should be trained and helped to obtain gainful employment.

Briefly, I have attempted to relate some of my experiences in dealing with agencies set up in the City of New York to deal with social welfare problems. In attempting to make recommendations, I would press for complete reevaluation of the principles and functions of these agencies, looking towards the complete eradication of the needs. In the meantime, advocates must be trained, paid and made available to recipients of the agencies' largess in an attempt to equalize the bargaining positions of the giver [and receiver] and bolster the individual dignity of the recipient. When the giver is under the impression that he is doling out charity he is blinded to the needs of the recipient.

Social welfare agencies must adopt a new framework of services. Services can no longer be looked upon as charity but must be seen as the giving of a legal right to be possessed by the recipient. Only then will the Puerto Rican be able to confront the problems of the complex urban society.

Suggestions for Further Reading

Students interested in the history of poverty in America will find the following volumes of particular interest.

David J. Rothman, *The Discovery of the Asylum: Social Order and Disorder in the New Republic* (Boston, 1971).

Robert Bremner, *From the Depths: The Discovery of Poverty in the United States* (New York, 1956).

Allen F. Davis, *Spearheads for Reform: The Social Settlements and the Progressive Movement* (New York, 1967).

Roy Lubove, *The Professional Altruist: The Emergence of Social Work as a Career, 1880–1930* (Cambridge, 1965).

Clarke Chambers, *Seedtime of Reform: American Social Service and Social Action* (Minneapolis, 1963).

Josephine C. Brown, *Public Relief, 1929–1939* (New York, 1940).

Edith Abbott, *Public Assistance* (Chicago, 1940).

Elliot Liebow, *Tally's Corner* (Boston, 1967).

Edward Banfield, *The Unheavenly City* (Boston, 1970).

Daniel P. Moynihan, ed., *On Understanding Poverty* (New York, 1969).

Francis Fox Piven and Richard A. Cloward, *Regulating the Poor: The Functions of Public Welfare* (New York, 1971).

ABCDEFGH798765432